Anchors for the Innocent

Inner Power for Today's Single Mothers and Fathers

by Gail C. Christopher

Printed in the United States of America.

Library of Congress CIP Data:

Anchors for the Innocent:
Inner Power for Today's Single Mothers and Fathers

Includes Index
1) Parenting   2) Divorce   3) Family Health and Wellness
4) Single Parenting   5) Self-Help, Stress and Loss

Library of Congress Card Catalog Number: 93-079063

ISBN: 1-883811-00-7

Published by: The Human Capacity Press
                  P.O. Box 81118
                  Chicago, IL 60601

Distributed by: Login Publishers Consortium
                  146 W. Randolph
                  Chicago, IL 60607

Portions of this book appeared in *The Body Owner's Workshop* published by Nutrassessment Centers, Inc., 1979. They are reprinted herein with permission.

Lyrics from   "God Bless the Child"—Billie Holliday, Arthur Herzog, Jr.
                © 1941 Edward B. Marks Music Company
                Copyright renewed.
                Used by permission. All rights reserved

For additional information on Anchors for the Innocent workshops, tapes and lectures, contact:

                  Gail C. Christopher, Ent. , Inc.
                  75 East Wacker Drive, #620
                  Chicago, IL 60601

Design & Cover by The Print Group, Chicago, IL

Dedication

This book is dedicated to my children:

To Ntianu, my first born. Her name means *Noble Spirit*. Although she is deceased, her spirit lives in my heart;

To Daniel, who understands more than a child needs to; and

To Charisse, whose growth teaches me about life's sweetness.

It is also dedicated to my parents who tried so hard to give me more than they had received.

Acknowledgements

I must first acknowledge the inspiration for the book which came through a lifetime of spiritual support and guidance. Secondly, I wish to acknowledge my administrative assistant, Rochelle Weber, for her tireless work on this manuscript, and my editors, Mark Harris, Elaine Zimmerman and Carole Skog for their support. Monica Paxson, Michael Pietrzak, Gloria Bannister and Patricia Deer are friends whose faith and belief in this project helped to bring it to fruition. Thank you all.

Contents

Part I: The Innocent

Part II: Anchors

Anchor One: Self-Esteem

Anchor Two: Support

Anchor Three: Solvency

Anchor Four: Strength

Part III: Conclusions

Foreword: A Fable

Once upon a time long ago, a soul, an individual of a very curious, almost impertinent nature, was informed by the High Council of Angels that it was time to sojourn to the Earth. The High Council of Angels had just given the particulars. The soul was visibly shaken.

"May I speak freely, your Holiness?" asked the Soul. The Guardian Angel seated to the right responded favorably, so the individual began to speak.

"Well now, I can handle most of this. I don't mind the gender part. I understand things are going to get better for women in the sixties and seventies. My sources tell me women will gain property rights, greater career mobility and some measure of sexual freedom. By the 1990s they will even begin to have a political presence.

"I can handle the ethnic part too. You say there will be a leader who emerges to spark a civil rights movement that dramatically changes the laws for African Americans. I'm also intrigued about being born into an African American family with a strong Native American heritage.

"1950 is a good year, too. I'll come of age in some exciting times. Look, I am not even complaining about the physical disability. My ancestors were healers, authentic medicine men and women. I'll have enough memories to help me handle this physical handicap.

"But really, don't you think sending me in as a single parent is taking this to the extreme? Now, I need to formally protest, for the record. I think that's just too much. Can I just be single and forget the parent part?"

The High Council responded almost in unison, "We don't understand."

"But you must! Surely you know the odds against succeeding as a single parent. And there's no movement on the horizon for this group..."

"Go on," they said. "Tell us about these odds."

"Well, first of all, I am five times as likely to be poor, and that means my children will probably be poor. There's a significant risk that we'll be homeless, too. Do you know what the toll is on a child to be poor in a country that has the wealth of the United States? I mean the spiritual toll?"

"Yes, go on," the Council replied.

"Secondly, I'll be disdained by the larger society, misunderstood, showered with guilt in multiple forms.

"Then there's the emotional stress. In order to become a single parent, I'll probably be abandoned or forced to leave an unhappy relationship. I'll have to face all the loss and grief.

"And what about the children? This really isn't fair to them. In addition to poverty, they'll face a greater risk for school problems, health problems, involvement in crime—maybe even violent crime. They may earn lower wages as adults and will most likely be destined to repeat the single parent dynamic in their own families.

"I've got to work my ass—excuse me—my behind off trying to help them beat these odds; and I'll feel responsible—yes guilty—if they don't.

"But the worst part, your Holinesses," the individual said, while rising from the chair, "I've got to carry the weight of the other biological parent who chooses to absent, in this case, himself from the parenting process. Excuse me, but he IS heavy—he ain't my brother!"

Realizing that things had gotten a little too heated, the individual responded to the Guardian Angel's gesture to sit down and be quiet.

The High Council of Angels conferred. Then one was appointed to speak directly to the about-to-be-born person.

"We are well aware of the challenges, odds and barriers that each soul faces on Earth. Single parents are not exceptions. We want you to think of your journey as an opportunity, however. You are being offered the chance to accomplish tremendous spiritual growth.

"Think about it—if you do succeed, you will learn how to value yourself and you will show your children how to value themselves in a world that doesn't. By playing dual or multiple roles as caretaker, nurturer and provider, you will overcome society's limitations and develop new capacities. You'll also learn how to care for your body and manage stress so that you have all the energy you need.

"You'll learn how to dissolve barriers to your happiness, because you'll know that you, alone, are creating the life that you want and deserve. You'll learn how to forgive.

"And, not to worry, dear one, you'll learn the most important lesson of all—that you are never alone. Divine guidance and your Angels are always here for you. You need only ask for help."

Introduction: Why This Book?

I am writing this book for and to other single parents for one purpose, really. I hope that by sharing lessons I have learned during my nineteen years of experience as the single head of my household and mother of three children, one now deceased, I will offer something of value to other single parents, female or male, who face similar challenges and conflicts.

This book is written to, not just about single parents. It grew out of a series of workshops by the same title that I conducted over a three-year period in Chicago, Illinois. Parts of the book are autobiographical. The information in the Anchors workshops and now in this book has been designed to respond to some of the real human needs of single parents, to inspire single parents like myself to take pride in their accomplishments and learn to better advocate for and support each other. It is also designed to help heal the wounds that divide us as men and women—wounds that serve as barriers to truly loving, committed relationships. Ongoing changes in family structure and roles, and escalating poverty rates among single-parented households compel us as a nation to find better ways of relating and establishing authentic caring bonds that assure the healthy development of all human-ity—of all our children.

Life's Work

Anchors for the Innocent is also based on my work over the last two decades as a holistic health-care practitioner and human re-source administrator.

What do I mean by holistic? The concept of "holistic" is based on the word whole. The underlying belief is that the "whole thing" is always greater than the sum of its parts. An apple is made up of several parts—a core, seeds, pulp and skin. If we took each part separately, we'd miss the pleasure of biting into the whole apple.

The human body is made up of many parts, but each part has a relationship to the whole. Isolated, or added together, each part would not a human body make. In my professional work, I always consider four parts of the whole individual. These four aspects include the physical, the emotional, the mental and the inspirational. Another way to say this is to remember that we are always living life through our senses, our thoughts, our emotions and our beliefs about our relationship to a transcendent source of life or creation.

1. Physical	2. Mental
Senses and Body Experiences	Thoughts and Images
3. Emotional	4. Inspirational
Feelings and Memories	Beliefs about the World and Your Place in It

When the term holistic is commonly used today, it is often defined as including body, mind and spirit. I depart from this three-sided approach by including "feelings" as a unique aspect. Feelings or emotions have a powerful impact on our bodies and our behaviors. Some psychologists even suggest that feelings ultimately dictate our behaviors—"I think...I feel...I act."

Why Inspirational?

The United States was founded by people escaping many forms of tyranny. Among other freedoms, they sought religious freedom. The freedom to believe and to exercise belief in a transcendent force has been a key factor in shaping American culture. It is a factor in our legal systems and institutions, as well. The First Amendment in the Bill of Rights guarantees this fundamental freedom: "Congress shall make no laws respecting the establishment of religion or prohibiting the free exercise thereof." According to the 1992 Statistical Abstract on the United States Population, 89 percent of the population claims some religious beliefs, and 80 percent report having a Christian affiliation.

Inspirational beliefs can have a powerful impact on shaping our world-view or approach to life. Therefore, when I say holistic, I include this inspirational or spiritual dimension. I don't suggest that it should be expressed in any one way. It is our individual constitutionally guaranteed and inalienable right to choose our own form of belief, or we may choose not to believe. The choice we make will have an impact on our general view of the world and our way of living.

Parenting is the essence of our world view, our way of living. As parents, we model for and impart to our children our attitudes, beliefs, expectations, fears and joys. To parent is to parent wholly. In this book, I am suggesting that as single parents, we must become more intentional. We must parent with greater awareness of our own selves: physically, emotionally, mentally and spiritually, and model whole-self affirming behaviors for our children.

Since 1974 I have provided direct health education and wellness services to thousands of parents and their children in my clinical practice. I've spent countless hours helping single parents to better cope with the stressful demands of their own and their children's lives. This has meant helping to improve their energy levels through dietary changes, exercise and body work, as well as exploring beliefs, feelings and expectations. I have created and directed several holistic programs to help single parents, including The Family Development Institute, The Body Owner's Workshop and The Families' Motivational Institute. I have also co-founded a program that assists women in becoming financially solvent through self-employment. As Executive Director of a national membership organization for families, I represented a network made up of thousands of community based family education and support programs across this country. My most recent project, a national multicultural education program, has broadened my own perceptions to include how our diverse cultural and family traditions affect us and our capacities to parent, to teach and to learn.

If someone had offered me a crystal ball through which I could have seen the future some twenty years ago, and given me a choice (conscious, anyway) about becoming a single parent, not only would I have refused, I would have thrown the crystal ball out of the window, attacked the person for exposing me to such trauma and run for my life in the opposite direction.

Yes, this is an exaggeration, but only a slight one. I, like so many other single parents, have felt victimized, deserted, abandoned and burdened for the larger part of my own and my children's lives. Yet, like other single-parent families, we have survived. Actually, we have done more than "survive." In many ways we have prospered, grown and learned how to cherish our special dynamic. I don't think my children or I would have it any other way now!

Our initial "we are victims" and "life is a great struggle" mind-set has not characterized the last seven years of our lives together. Quite the contrary. My children and I have developed a way of living and perceiving our place in the world that brings us profound peace, optimism, joy and comfort. This "way of living" is what I want to share in this book. It is my holistic philosophy of parenting—of life, really. I am determined to make it simple, because it is.

This book is also directed to people who care about single parents. This first section, "The Innocent," provides an overview of many of the key issues that single parents, and subsequently our society, must face. Myths need to be dispelled through a compassionate, insider's view of the landscape of the single-parent experience. Single-parent families must be placed within the context of this country's overall family realities and be embraced as part of America's diversity.

Who are we? More important, how are we? The answers to these questions help to establish the need for more support for, and insight about, the unique world of single parenting. The second half of this book, "Anchors," offers needed support, information, and motivation to single-parent families who are coping with day-to-day realities and succeeding in spite of the odds.

Part I

The Innocent

In many ways, what we
see as children determines
what we become as
adults. Family pictures,
images and experiences
create thoughts
and feelings which compel
us to shape our world as
we would or would not
like it to be. As adults
we may continue to
perceive reality as we
lived it as children—in a
state of love or in fear.

One

Family
Pictures

"If you ever leave me, I'll kill you! You won't get the baby, either! You'll leave with what you came with, B____. You'll take nothing else."

His words cut through her body like a knife, with the same force that his finger had when he jabbed it into her chest as he berated her day after day.

"Can't you cook, B____? Can't you do anything right? Didn't anyone ever teach you how to treat a man? You're hopeless!"

His personality change had caught her completely by surprise. Where was the charming, romantic, seductive man she had married? Where was the person who showed such gentleness and kindness, the person she had decided to trust? He was gone, it seemed. Lost somewhere between his rum and Coke and occasional cocaine, somewhere between his fear of failure and the weight of family responsibility.

They lived upstairs from his mother, who knew no boundaries. One day, she rushed into their bedroom without knocking, and upon realizing what she had interrupted, simply told him, "Get up, Bruce. Get up now and bring those groceries upstairs for me. Didn't you hear me calling you?" His wife, shocked, embarrassed and hurt, scurried into the nearby bathroom, avoiding eye contact with either her husband or his mother.

Later that day, in the marriage counseling session, she would describe the incident. The therapist responded by asking the husband to draw a picture of what had happened as he saw it. When the picture was finished, the therapist asked each of them to interpret what the husband had drawn. Each gave a different view—the husband and wife saw things differently.

But, the psychologist noted one key thing. He said, "Each of you are missing the main point in this drawing. Look at it again." They both looked again. There was silence. Then finally he said, "Well, I guess neither of you get it." He turned to me and said, "Gail, you're not even in the picture."

I, like so many women who exist in abusive relationships, had yet to realize my own "invisibility"—to myself and to my mate. We are usually the last to realize it when our mates cannot love us, or even see us, because we can't love and cherish ourselves. The abuse they project onto us is also an extension of their own self-hatred and emotional self-abuse. Undoubtedly they perceive that, in some passive way, we are failing them in return. The laws of life and love don't discriminate. We cannot give love to another in the absence of self-love. We cannot really see and respond to another's needs while we are blind to our own. In fact, it was only after I thought my son was suffering psychological damage that I had the courage, the determination, to leave.

People have asked me what the most courageous thing is that I have ever done. The answer is simple. My most courageous act was leaving and facing the world as a single divorced woman responsible for the care and protection of two children. We moved out on Mother's Day.

Action

Not only did the decision and the act require courage, it required strength. I had to exert the force of my identity—my self-worth—

for perhaps the first time in this relationship. I recall confronting him and saying "If you're going to kill me, then kill me now because I'm leaving and I'm taking the children."

To my surprise, he didn't try to hurt me again. As he saw me trembling, he broke down and cried. He said, "How will I tell people that my wife me left because I terrorized her?" He had asked me why. I told him about the threats, the violence, the rapes, the promises to kill me. I told him how he said he would cut up my body and burn it in the furnace in the basement of our building. He said he didn't remember those things. He blamed the alcohol and feebly apologized. Later, I came to know and understand the power of alcohol. It can lead to "black-outs"—to states of unconsciousness where the individual acts and does not consciously recall his or her actions.

Body Memories

But my body remembers. My self remembers his hands around my throat. My body remembers being taken in ways that left me torn and with no sense of control of me. These were not new memories. They found a place in my subconscious along with the early infancy and childhood perceptions of violation, intrusion, near-suffocation and abandonment. My body has been cut by surgeons' knives repeatedly. As an infant, I had been forced to stop breathing as I was held down by the anesthetists who forced an ether cup over my nose and mouth. As a child and as an abused wife, I learned to survive despite these traumas. I automatically tried to control everything, to build barriers around my "feeling self" to lock out—block out—new intruders. I did not realize that without professional help I probably would be compelled to first, repeat and relive the abusive relationship with someone else; and second, pass on these childhood memories to my children and compel them to draw comparable experiences into their lives.

Something had already compelled me to marry a man who could not demonstrate genuine tenderness and care for me; a man whose own childhood memories of emotional abandonment had left him locked inside a facade of manipulation and usury. He not only carried childhood patterns that were like my own father's, he drank in the same ways and, like my own father, was accustomed to being controlled and dominated by women. He twisted my meekness and apparent fear of his menacing behaviors into signs of victory and affirmation of his manhood. The more I trembled, the more he terrorized.

The Promise

But my Guardian Angels must have interceded. A new tenant moved into our building. Her stay was brief. She was only there for two months. But in that two months she visited me often. She reminded me of my spiritual beliefs, and of the promise that has been made to us all. She left me a little card one day and asked me to read it every morning and every night for inspiration. It read:

> "In each moment I am given the opportunity
> to choose anew, to begin fresh and truly live
> from the power of good, of God that abides
> in my heart and my mind. There is no per-
> son, personality, will or force that is greater
> than the divine presence that lives within my
> heart. I turn to it, within, to find the strength
> that brings peace, harmony and order to my
> world."

It was this daily reading and the kind outreach of a stranger, coupled with my five-year-old son's quiet cry (he started to regress, to wet his pants) that gave me the power to face my greatest fear and get a divorce.

It would be fully ten years later before I processed the traumatic memories and scars left as a result of this marriage. Fortunately, my former husband sought alcoholism counseling and support immediately. He began to heal and to live a more balanced life without the chaos caused by alcohol. I did not have time to heal. I, like millions of other single parents, had to "survive" and to care for my children, the Innocent ones who turned to me to Anchor them.

Two

Single Parents Today: Who are We?

Who are we? According to figures presented in the *Committee on Ways and Means of the United States House of Representatives 1992 Greenbook*, there are 34.7 million families with children in the United States. Of these, 9.7 million, or 28.1 percent, are single-parent families. Eighty six percent of these single-parent families are headed by women, 14 percent by men. These figures have increased significantly since 1980, when only 21.5 percent of United States families with children were parented by one parent.

Over 3.1 million, or 32 percent of all single-parent families in the United States are African American. Considering declining birth rates among African Americans, coupled with divorce rates and rates of children born to never-married parents, more than half (61 percent) of all African American families are single-parent families. In contrast, 22 percent, or less than one-fourth of all "white" families in the United States are headed by one parent. It is worth noting that this 22 percent figure was the percentage of single-parent families among African American families in the 1960s! If current trends continue, estimates are that 60 percent of all children born after 1990 will spend some portion of their lives in families headed by one parent.

Single Parents Today: How Are We?

We are usually coping with deep personal wounds from disappointment or loss, and often from abandonment or desertion. Typically, we are adults (or teens) who have ended relationships that caused us to feel more than we could bear, or relationships in which our needs were simply not met. In some areas, homicide, drug related violence and incarcerations cause single parent households. All too often the separation was so shocking, so complete and so hurtful that it constituted emotional trauma or abuse. Sometimes, physical abuse was also involved. Most of us did not "plan" to become single parents and simply are not prepared for the awesome responsibility.

Myths

It is time to dispel some of the myths that abound concerning the single-parenting experience. Myth number one concerns choice. Many people condemn single mothers because they "choose" to leave their husbands or mates. In truth, most single parents who choose to leave, do so to protect their children and help them survive, in spite of their negligent and/or abusive mates. Many others have learned that a happy, loving environment is better for a child than the chronic stress associated with marital discord and family violence. Most others have been abandoned.

Myth number two is that single parents are lazy and live on welfare, and that in fact they have babies to get more welfare benefits. In truth, most single mothers work, full- and/or part-time. Only half ever receive welfare. There is no factual correlation between numbers of children and AFDC benefits. Ninety percent of single mothers with school age children are in the labor force.

The third myth relates to the causes of poverty among single mothers and to the belief that single parents need to become more "self-sufficient." Policy makers seem to want to compare single parents to a mythical, self-sufficient American family image that can be traced back to early American history. In truth, so-called "self-sufficient American families," from pioneer families in the 1800s to suburban families in the 1950s, were not so self-sufficient. They had government help. Pioneers were given cheap or free land as homesteaders and various bills helped post-World War II families get the most basic family need—suitable housing. Many of this country's earliest families had the help provided by the unpaid labor—slave labor—of African Americans and Native Americans, that enabled these families, and in fact the nation, to prosper. Others had indentured servants who agreed to work for families in return for passage to this country.

Single mothers are poor for three reasons: 1) Single mothers have less earning power, earning half as much as fathers heading two parent families and only three quarters as much as single fathers; 2) Contributions from other family members are low, particularly from absent fathers. Less than half of all single mothers receive the full amount of child support awarded and one quarter receive nothing at all; and 3) Public assistance payments to women who head families (except widows) are meager compared to such payments to two other groups, the elderly and the disabled.

The fourth and final myth I want to dispel is the idea that single-parent families make up an "abnormal minority group" that has developed because of the "disintegration" of traditional "family values." If current trends continue, more than 60 percent of children born in this decade will spend part of their childhood in a home headed by a single parent. Sixty percent is not a numerical minority, it is the majority! This is due, primarily, to divorce rates. Historically, United States divorce rates have increased each decade. The only period in United States history when this was not the case was during the 1950s, which was the isolated period in American family life immortalized in the televised Nelsons', Cleavers' and *Father Knows Best* households.

This special period in our nation's history (referred to by some as the "golden age" of families) grew out of the post World War II marriage, birth, employment and housing increases and *did not* occur in any other period. It was also the era when average households obtained televisions, and for the first time, we began having perceptions and family values heavily influenced by this media form.

In 1989, the Mass Mutual Life Insurance Company commissioned a national public opinion survey to uncover what people believe to be the most important elements of family and how their families affect the way they conduct their lives. They asked respondents to define what is meant by the phrase "family values." There was a high degree of consensus about which values can properly be called family values. These are: 1) Love and emotional support; 2) Respect for others; and 3) Taking responsibility for one's actions.

According to this survey, "family values" address the nature and quality of relationships among people. And values Americans call "family values" are the most important values to Americans' personal lives.

Quality relationships are also important to single parents. Family values and the single-parent experience are not mutually exclusive. You can have one and still have the other. Single parents value love and emotional support, demonstrate respect for others, and take full (often too much) responsibility for their actions. The debate must be reframed. The issue is not family values, but *valuing families*. Families need not be defined or measured by structure, but rather by purpose and their capacity to fulfill that purpose as "people makers."

Obstacles

Since more than 85 percent of single parents are women, and day-to-day parenting responsibilities are generally assigned to women, the single-parenting issue in many ways can be viewed as a women's issue.

The obstacles single parents face are primarily women's issues. The greatest external stress factor for female-headed households is poverty or economic instability. This is caused by lower wages stemming from economic and social policies that do not place a high market-value on women, on women's work, or for that matter, on the care and development of children. Social policy to date, does not insist that non-custodial or absent fathers pay for the expenses that are involved in raising their own children. This policy threatens the very lives and hopes of the mothers, the children and ultimately the country as a whole.

Other related stress factors include lack of affordable housing, access to needed transportation, quality health care and adequate child care. Efforts to overcome these challenges can be all-consuming, and can detract from our capacity to meet our own needs and our children's critical emotional needs.

Income is the key factor that determines whether children from single-parent families will succeed or fail in school, work, etc. Income increases as the mother's education increases. Poverty is the greatest risk factor. When single parents can rise out of low income circumstances through education and employment, these single parents can and do Anchor their children and families well.

Loss

The incidence of stress-related illness is disproportionately high among single parents. The greatest internal or emotional stress factors confronting us today are fear and unresolved feelings about separation, rejection, abandonment and abuse. The pain of loss and seeming lack of control over our lives and choices can create tremendous anxiety, anger, resentment and, if not expressed, depression. These feelings often propel us into physiological and psychological stress reactions that may impact our own and our children's health.

The Good News

Family structure is not the determining factor for family values and successful "people making." Stress management, family function, quality parent/child relationships are. When, as parents, we can overcome emotional and personal stress factors, we can create family environments in which our children thrive. They receive appropriate care, nurturance and encouragement and they usually develop strong self-concepts and a clear sense of identity. Single-parent families can, and often do, create quality environments and relationships that lead to positive outcomes. At least one third of all single parents do break out of the cycles of poverty and acute stress. We overcome the countless barriers and successfully guide our children through to responsible adulthood. Successful single parents have learned some of life's most valuable lessons; and they've given, and continue to give, a great gift to society. As such, many single parents stand as examples—models—of high degrees of personal excellence and self-mastery. They have learned how to clarify priorities and to garner and direct personal energies toward achieving selected purposes and goals.

As successful single parents we learn how to define ourselves "wholly"—to exercise our competencies in multiple ways, and not to be limited by expectations or role assignments that could be imposed from without. We are adaptable, and have often found a deep value for ourselves that we impart to our children. We have learned how to build our own communities of support around our families. In most cases, we have become magicians with finance, and most importantly, we have accessed an unlimited reservoir of inner strength and of wholeness that enables us to carry on. In the words of the civil rights anthem, "We have overcome."

Our children mirror our growth. Children from successful single-parent families have unique skills and capacities. They are often independent, adaptable, self-reliant and determined. They become responsible adult citizens. They are not limited by constraints of roles and are often very self-defined. Yet the cycle of the single-parent experience does seem to be generational, and statistically, most children do not have such positive outcomes. The risks are higher for school failure, unemployability, adolescent pregnancies, violence, victimization and chronic health problems. Children from single-parent homes seem to repeat the pattern in their own families. Often this occurs despite conscious attempts to break or change the pattern.

These generational and statistical realities make it even more crucial that we as a nation find new and positive ways to view and experience single parenting. There are vital lessons here for us as individuals and for us as a society. These lessons are about relationships, families, parenting practices and beliefs. They are also about our human family, our potential for adaptation and growth.

Three

Who Values Families?

When people speak of "traditional family values," and picture a two-parent household dominated by a breadwinning father supported by a mother who works only at home, they are clinging nostalgically to a relic that applies to less than 10 percent of today's families—a relic which also ignores the historic diversity of American families. United States Census Bureau data reveal that fewer than half of all children born since 1940 have come into families that meet these criteria.

Ever since its origins, one of the most distinctive characteristics of the United States has been the diversity within its borders. Census data from colonial times reveal this diversity in language, ethnicity, religion and ancestry. It is only logical to assume related diversity in culture and customs—and yes, in family types, traditions and values. At that time, there were more than 240 distinct groups of Native Americans each with its own language, community, kinship and family structure. These often contrasted with European customs. Examples include communal houses that supported multiple families and, in some groups, shared labor for men and women. Mexican American and Asian American cultures were also part of the historical patterns of diversity in United States family life. They had distinct traditions and values that often embraced extended family care and diverse roles for men and women.

The laws did not recognize the marriages of enslaved African-Americans, and slaves could make no legal claim to the custody of the children born to them. They were the property of the slave owner, and were often sold away—even though they were frequently the slave owners' biological children. African Americans, who were actually the majority population in some Southern states, developed a unique system of family and kinship relationships in order to survive the brutalities of enslavement. These family relationships included remembrances of African cultural traditions, as well as adaptations to European rule. In many African cultures, traditional family values included a reverence for all children, and the community passed the lineage or family identity through the mother.

Why Families are Changing

Clinging to a rigid view of family life and roles also ignores the evolution of the roles of women, children, and men within American families. This evolution is an outgrowth of the traditional "democratic" and human values espoused by our society.

Women and children are no longer considered the "property" of the male head of household and today's marriage partnership is becoming more of an equal partnership between men and women. For example, the unequal partnership model upon which outdated family law was based, is being replaced by new approaches to families and to family transitions such as break-ups. Instead of shameful, guilt-laden lawsuits based on infidelity and cruelty there are now no-fault divorce laws in 49 of our 50 states. These changes are not a result of declining family values, but of many economic, social and educational realities. One key factor is the public exposure of domestic violence, and public policies begun in the 1970s which made it easier for women to "say no" to the abuse of themselves and their children, and to end relationships that didn't work. Another factor may be the increased mobility of families due to economic demands. One out of five Americans moves at least once a year.

Moving means leaving networks of kin that once supported and reinforced marital and family bonds.

We cannot ignore the 1960s and the impact of the women's movement. This era increased self-esteem and equal employment opportunities for women. The women's movement also challenged men and women to find new ways to relate to one another. Today we have more females in professional careers than in the past. We have fewer women who are willing to be confined exclusively to the traditional supportive roles in their families. This is not to disparage the choice of women and families who choose the breadwinner/homemaker model. This is a valid, important and meaningful choice.

The truth is that most families no longer choose or can't afford this model anymore. In most two-parent households, both parents work outside of the home. Most of the other families have one parent who lives in the home.

Money Matters

Perhaps the strongest influence on all families has been the declining economic stability of our nation, which has caused the traditional family's dollar value to decline dramatically. United States social and economic history tells us that marriages and families fall apart and are postponed during hard economic times. Marriages and births boom in eras of economic prosperity, like the 1950s. It is indeed ironic that the 1992 presidential election and the party that made "family values" a key campaign issue did so in a period when its own economic policies eroded the foundation of all families. Most family incomes have declined in the last two decades. Among the poorest, which includes most single-parent families, it declined by 14 percent. Among the middle class, income declined by at least 6-7 percent, while the wealthiest, the top 1 percent of families, saw their wealth increase by 49.8 percent.

If we are to have true family values, indeed if we are to truly value families, we cannot afford to judge, condemn and impoverish more than half of our nation's youth who, due to circumstances over which they have no control, will spend part of their childhood in single-parent households, most likely headed by women.

About Successful Families

Success for single parents means achieving the goal of having families that work, that meet our own, our children's, and ultimately society's needs. We can do this. We do need help, however. Every successful family—single or dual, step or even royally parented—needs and gets help of some form or another. As single parents, we can Anchor our children through their growing years by creating and sustaining families that successfully perform vital family functions. What a family does is as, or more important than how it looks. When families work well, they perform these seven basic functions:

1. They provide a sense of security for all members, enabling each family member to feel safe, supported and free from danger or harm.

2. They nurture and nourish—physically, emotionally, mentally and spiritually.

3. They socialize, teaching us about expectations and rules, roles and consequences, and in essence, right and wrong within our society. In so doing, families fulfill the fourth function.

4. They provide basic self-esteem, the sense of and value for each member's "self."

5. They educate, preparing us for, and reinforcing our school learning experiences. Education is still very much a family matter.

6. They validate each member. When the outside world confuses, frustrates or devalues, it is the family that can validate and value through unconditional love.

7. They support. Through life's different stages, different kinds of support are needed, but it is the family that must be there to provide ongoing support.

These seven primary family purposes or functions are sum-
marized here:

Support
Validation
Education
Self-Esteem
Socialization
Nurture
Security

Any healthy family, regardless of its structure, must perform
these functions and meet the emotional needs of its members,
both adults and children. However, the process of creating and
sustaining a well-functioning family as a single parent can seem
so complicated that it overwhelms us. At times the task can seem
"bigger than life." But I believe it can be mastered—and millions
of people, primarily women, are working hard to do so in the
United States and throughout the world. European industrialized countries like Britain, Austria, Germany, Finland, Italy,
Sweden, Denmark and Norway have also experienced a significant increase in the number of female-headed families in the last
twenty years.

Four

Prepared and Equipped

Our ability to deal with any challenge is directly related to how much we know about that challenge. When I started my journey as a single parent, I didn't know where I was going, how to get there, or how to tell I was there when I arrived. In fact, I was too scared, too confused and too shocked to even know that I didn't know.

We can master our roles as single parents if we have clear goals and become prepared and equipped for the challenge. This begins with our expectations, which influence our "mind-set," or attitude. My goal as a single parent has been to create and sustain an environment that meets the needs of my family while it supports my own and my children's growth and development.

As single parents, our goal cannot be to just "survive." It cannot be to just make it from one day to the next or from one check to the next. That kind of mind-set leads to stress, misery and exhaustion. It takes too much energy to live in fear and worry all the time. Unknowingly, many of us as single parents are mentally focused on survival and on the barriers or "lack" in our lives. This "mind-set" has caused us to have limited or unclear goals as single parents. Don't get me wrong—we want what's best for our families, but we're so busy surviving that we're unable to focus on our real desires—our true goals. As a result, we are not always free to succeed.

If we are to succeed as single parents, we have to learn as much as we can about the process, about the challenge. Let's begin with an overview of the challenge of single parenting.

The Challenge of Single Parenting

In order to create family environments that function as well as or better than other families, we must first learn about healthy families. Then, as individuals, we must have the mental, emotional, physical and spiritual capacity to perform as well as (or better than) individuals who co-manage two-parent families.

Single parents have to fulfill multiple (or at least dual) roles as both provider and primary care-taker. While we must be strong enough and organized enough to "bring home the bacon" and "fry it up," we must be tender, attentive and responsive enough to nurture ourselves and our children simultaneously.

- These roles and multiple performance responsibilities demand energy, fitness, wellness and resilience. This requires high levels of self-discipline and consistent self-care.

- Since (despite contrary expectations) we are single individuals in one body, we must be extremely resourceful and create ways to literally be in two places at once. This requires the ability to delegate responsibility to others.

- Good information is our number one ally; we must access it and use it effectively. We will have better outcomes if we know what to expect from our children. We should learn as much as we can about normal child and human development throughout all stages of life.

- We usually cannot rely on one source of income for the financial resources we need to successfully support and sustain our families. We must obtain adequate income from multiple sources. We must also manage that income extremely well.

- Excellent people skills are critically important to our success as single parents. We must be able to communicate well, to reach out to and garner ongoing support, feedback, validation and kindness from others. We cannot parent or even live effectively in isolation.

- Child care is a critically important resource for our families. We must be skilled at finding and monitoring quality care for our young children.

- Optimum health that comes from prevention and healthful lifestyle choices is a crucial factor. Our families depend on consistency and predictable performance from all members. Disruptions due to illness are costly. An ounce of prevention is worth more to us than a pound of cure.

- We live in a culture that is not designed to appreciate, honor or support the single-parent family. As such, our families are often misrepresented as "minorities" or "different." We are bombarded with biases and negative expectations that we cannot allow to become our truth. We need good self-images and high levels of self-esteem.

- The more love we have, the more we can give. While we have accepted the role and responsibility of being single parents, we cannot neglect our spiritual responsibility to continue to develop as individuals. We must take charge of our own ongoing healing, growth and development, as well as the growth of our children.

- Education is vital to ourselves and to our children. Quality learning and achievement is the key to success for children from single-parent families. We must learn to be advocates for quality educational opportunities and be committed to excellence in this area.

- As single parents, we must choose communities that are not hostile for us. We must creatively surround ourselves and our children with people and environments that offer safety, understanding, respect and love.

Positions Available

We are seeking individuals to fill a risk-laden position that offers no salary. If you want to work in an unpredictable setting for at least 18 years and meet the following qualifications, please apply. The successful candidates must be self-starters, able to work well without support or validation. They must be knowledgeable about the psychology of families, and have the capacity to function well under extreme stress. They must be strong and well organized, yet flexible and able to demonstrate care and nurturing capabilities as well as management and supervisory skills. They must be entrepreneurial and have excellent financial management skills as well as excellent networking and communication skills. They must demonstrate commitment to ongoing personal growth and show optimum self-esteem and self-regard. Some fundamental knowledge of child-care standards, early childhood and human development stages, literacy and education planning, an understanding of preventive health, fitness, nutrition and food service management are also needed.

This position has no possibility for career growth or promotion. There are no retirement benefits, sick days, paid vacation days or disability insurance. A 24-hour-a-day call schedule is required, plus an 80 hour week. Anyone may apply. A training camp is provided for inexperienced candidates, offering only grief, loss, separation and survival experiences. We are an equal opportunity employer.

Self-Affirmation

While we are doing all of this—functioning remarkably well; being organized, strong, and responsible; experiencing self-discipline; delegating and being creative and resourceful; winning friends and influencing people; accessing information; and advocating and developing—we also have to take time to praise and applaud *ourselves* and our children for succeeding against prophesies and odds that have been stacked against us.

Affirming our experience is the key to mastery as single parents. It is, indeed, progression from the complex to the simple. Each time we remember to affirm, to accept and embrace ourselves as single parents and our opportunity to guide the development of other human beings, we are moving closer to mastering our roles as single parents.

Five

The Other Single Parent

Most of the data on single-parent families relates to the parent who has "custody" of the children, or to the parent with whom the children live. Research and census information often describe single-parent families as female-headed households. These numbers do not embrace the millions of parents who are absent physically from the home, or who are not legal guardians. Millions of these non-custodial or "other parents" are still single parents who are dramatically affected by the issues of single parenting. These "other parents" often share the parenting responsibilities in multiple ways.

Non-custodial parents can also experience the complex psychological impact of separating from their own children. While this book is directed primarily to custodial single parents who have day-to-day parenting responsibilities, I would be remiss if I failed to address the needs, issues and concerns of the absent parent in a positive way. I say "positive" because most references to the absent parent are negative and too often tied to issues of child support, kidnapping or child neglect.

Out of Sight, Out of...?

It is often difficult for us to understand how the "other parent" can seem to behave as if they no longer really care about their own children. Frequently it seems as if they've cut off that part of themselves that once loved and embraced their own children. It's been replaced by indifference—coldness. As the parent who has custody, or who takes care of the children each day, we question our own judgement. How could we have been so wrong about the person we chose? How could we have selected a parent who would turn his or her back on the children they brought into the world? I've interviewed several non-custodial, or absent single parents and have gained a little more insight into their own process of grief and loss. One single parent described his reactions in this way:

> "No one—no father—ever loved his daughter more than I did. I held her and played with her every day. I watched her be born. But when I had to move to another city for my job, I couldn't handle the heart-break. It just hurt too much to think about her. I guess I did the only thing I could. I put her away in a place in my mind where it didn't hurt. When it hurts, you do what you have to do to stop the pain."

As I listened to him and saw the tears freeze up in his eyes, I was reminded of one of the gender differences in our society. Men are not taught how, nor do they get much practice in coping with emotional pain. For many, it's overwhelming.

Another non-custodial father described how the judge's ruling—the court's order of "custody" to his former wife, made him feel like he was not adequate to parent. He said:

> "I felt shut out—pushed out—and like less of a parent—in fact, less of a person than I'd been before. It seemed like this stranger was telling me that my opinion, my ideas, my input were no longer needed in the lives of my children. And the law said he had the right to do that."

24

I'm not suggesting that neglect of our own children is ever justified. I am suggesting that our feelings usually dictate our behaviors. When we feel a sense of low self-esteem or value as a parent, or when the pain and grief of separation is too great to bear, part of our coping process may include distance and denial.

Another non-custodial parent described her sense of shame and guilt because she initiated the divorce:

> "I just couldn't face my children. I didn't know what kinds of stories their father had told them. I didn't have money to give them gifts or presents. It just seemed better for everyone if I just disappeared. They seemed to be better off without me."

These scenarios are all too common. While they are understandable from an emotional perspective, they overlook the bottom line—the most important common denominator. Growing children need to know that they are loved unconditionally and cherished by their parents—both of their parents.

The "other" or absent parent has to work harder to communicate this "knowing," this awareness, to the children—no matter how much it hurts or costs. There are many creative ways to parent post-marriage. These are addressed further in Chapter Six, but if you are a non-custodial parent, try to remember to:

1. Get counseling or support to help cope with the loss, so your emotions and memories don't block your capacity to relate to your children.

2. Recognize that you are still a parent, and no court ruling can take that away from you. You can appear to give that status away, however, by choosing to absent yourself, psychologically as well as physically.

3. Find ways—phone calls, letters, cards, visits, etc.—to stay in the child's awareness and to keep the child in yours.

4. Try to create a lifestyle that acknowledges your role as a parent, even if it's only part-time. Maintain a physical space for your child to visit overnight—even a sleeper sofa.

5. Keep children's toys and books around.

6. Keep your children's pictures displayed in your home and in your wallet.

7. If the post-marriage or living together relationship with the former spouse or mate is strained, promise yourself to improve it for the sake of the children, even if it requires professional help.

8. Establish friendships with other single parents or families with children, so that when your children are with you, they can have other children to relate to. Pre-plan for child-care arrangements during vacations and holidays. Don't be caught by surprise.

9. Make sure your associates know you are a single parent and that your parenting role is important to you.

10. Brag about your children's growth and continue to read about and stay up-to-date on information about children's needs at different stages of development.

11. Communicate with your children's teachers, physicians, counselors, minister, etc., by mail, telephone or in person. Let them know that you are an active parent and want to be helpful, as well as to be kept informed.

12. Keep your own extended family aware of your children's growth. Make sure your family—parents, siblings, cousins—stay a part of your children's lives.

13. Ask your children for samples of their work—school projects, personal hobbies, etc. Display these in your home and work space. Keep a family album about you and your children.

14. Never let economic conditions override your emotional, spiritual and physical bond with your own children.

If, as the non-custodial parent, you are feeling less needed, or less important in the lives of your children, please re-think these reactions. You are still the most important person in the heart and mind of your child. You are needed and you are loved—unconditionally—by your child.

If, as the non-custodial parent, you are active, present and proud of your ongoing role in the lives of your children, take time to applaud yourself, for you are charting a new course for divorced parents. Whenever the opportunity arises, please be an advocate for the children, whose arms remain outstretched to their "absent" parent. Encourage other non-custodial parents to recognize and actively participate in the lives of their children.

Six

DKR

Have you ever noticed that when your children return from visits with their other parent they behave differently? There is an emotional distance, a seeming resentment or just sadness. In our family, particularly in my daughter's case, I learned to expect the "re-entry" process to take at least 48 hours. Visitations were scheduled every other weekend.

One time, however, I had just had surgery and was feeling a little weak, physically as well as emotionally. When I noticed my daughter's distance and resentment of me, the custodial parent, I said, "Now look. I can't take this right now. I need your support, and particularly, a hug. I've just had surgery..." etc., etc., etc. Well, my then nine year old looked at me with sympathy, hugged me and said, "Oh, Mom, you shouldn't take my mood seriously—it's just DKR."

I said, "DKR? What's that?"

She said, "You know, Divorced Kids' Response."

I asked her where she had heard that term. She said she made it up!

Divorced Kids' Response points out some relationship issues that are unique to us as single-parent families. How do we help our children deal with their confusion concerning the different roles of each parent? We must help them form realistic expectations, perceptions and impressions about themselves and both their custodial and non-custodial parent. First we have to decide how we relate to the non-custodial—or in some cases, absent—parent.

These attitudes affect our children, and the absent parent's attitude toward us affects the children. Working out these unique post-marriage or post-cohabitation relationship issues is at the heart of successful single parenting. Here are some guidelines:

1. Tell the child that they are the priority, and that no matter what happens in the parental relationship, you both are committed to assuring their protection, development and happiness.

2. Communication is vital. Just because children are young (even one or two years old), don't leave them out of the process. Talk with them. Try to explain the changes, assuring them of both parents' love. Try to reduce surprises and shocks. Keep routine and order in their lives. Help them to believe they can expect their parents to be there for them with some predictable regularity.

3. Make a social contract—an agreement—between both parents that each will consciously assure the child of the other parent's love for them. A child's heart breaks very quickly if it believes it is not loved by its parents.

4. Find ways to share some aspect of the child's life with the other parent. School or church events, for example. Divorced families can still share parenting, publicly and privately. Children feel validated when both parents "show up."

5. Avoid adult fighting or arguing in the presence of the children. Avoid denigrating or criticizing the other parent in the presence of the children. The child's self-esteem relates to their perception of their parents and how much their parents are valued by others. They especially feel this way about the parent of the same sex—little girls identify with their mother, little boys with their father. Remember, "If Dad or Mom is bad, what does that say about me?"

6. Don't suppress or deny your feelings. Get counseling or group support to help you express your feelings of abandonment, rage, anger, etc.

7. Create similar opportunities for the children. They often need to express their feelings to caring adults who are not their parents. Close relationships with extended family or friends can be useful here. But make sure the friend or relative understands your ground rules about valuing and not criticizing either parent as a person.

8. If possible, let children know that you are in communication with the other parent, particularly about them. Call to share news about school, health, plans, etc. Don't make the child feel that it is their job—or burden—to hold the parental relationship together. If you can communicate or relate positively around the children, do so.

9. Try to understand your child's innermost hope that Mommy and Daddy will make up or get back together again. Allow your child to express these feelings, but gently and lovingly encourage them to appreciate the relationship you now have as a divorced or separated family.

10. Keep family albums—pictures that show the history of your life as a family—pre- and post-divorce. Create opportunities for photographs that involve children and both parents, even after the break-up.

11. If it seems to be impossible to work with the other parent on meeting the child's needs fairly, then suggest counseling; and talk to the child about the challenges in ways that assure the child that they deserve the demonstrated love of both parents. And although there are reasons why they are not getting it, or why parents are having trouble relating to one-another, it doesn't change the child's deservedness.

Parenting: Post Marriage or Relationship

Most single-parent families today develop because marriages fail. Yet, after divorce, somehow the parenting work must continue. We can carve out a parenting relationship after the marriage or loving relationship is over. So many people have failed to realize that they can both still be good parents, even after they cease to be husband and wife, lovers or mates. The children still need security (love and protection), nurturance, self-esteem, education, socialization, validation and support from both parents. They still need a family that functions well. Our challenge as single parents is to find ways to share parenting responsibilities both in and out of marriage, or cohabiting relationships. The family still has the same critical role in our society, whether two parents are living together or not.

Conspiracies of Silence

My former husband and I never talked about the betrayal, violence, or the other reasons for ending the marriage. We suffered separately and we each found our own ways to heal. In retrospect, I believe this conspiracy of silence was an error. Although we were living separately, we were still bonded by our children. We should have tried to have counseling together to move beyond our individual pain to a point of truth from which we could better relate to our children. Honesty, humility and forgiveness are the building blocks of healthy lives. Distance, denial, repression and pain are the cornerstones of future psychological problems. Divorcing couples who have children need to get family counseling during and after the divorce process. We are still a family, just a separated or divorced family. Lies erode trust, our trust of ourselves as well as others. They also erode the child's capacity to trust—to trust us, themselves and the world. This erosion process must be halted if their and our capacity to love is to be regained—even the capacity to love ourselves.

Custody vs. Parenting

When marriages or relationships end, one parent is often awarded legal custody of the child or children. Sometimes joint custody is awarded to both parents, but principal physical custody is awarded to one parent, usually the mother, with whom the child lives. Courts may determine "custody." It literally means the right to guard, from the latin word custodia—to guard. But the right or responsibility to guard, supervise and/or control is a long way from parenting. Couples with children need to become clearer about this distinction and not consider them one and the same. All too often the court's custody ruling is interpreted as the family's parenting contract. The mother gets the child, the child gets the mother. The father is excluded or excludes himself, or vice versa. Many couples who have either joint or single custody rulings have found creative ways to keep each parent actively engaged in the parenting experience.

Parenting is About Doing

Time is the key factor. Find ways to structure routine involvement by both parents in the children's lives. Living within close proximity of one another is an important requirement. Sharing transportation responsibilities to and from child care and school is another strategy. Homework time, recreation and church activities can also be shared. Finding ways to stay engaged in the daily routine events is, I believe, better than periodic weekend or weeknight visits. First of all, parenting is about doing. Too often, non-custodial parents see their role as peripheral and as entertaining or "extra." To the degree that the children and the parents experience the joy and the responsibility of participating in the child's daily life, the mutual benefits of parenting will be shared and the stress may be reduced. This is an ideal reality, however. In most cases it simply doesn't work. The relationship break-up causes too much strain on each parent.

In some cases, it is impossible for both parents to live close to the children. However, it's still possible to take an active role in parenting long distance. Regular phone calls and letters are important. One non-custodial parent gave her children her telephone credit card number so that they could reach her anytime they needed to—at home or at work. Many single parents now use beepers. If it is impossible to participate in school events, etc., a phone call before the child leaves for the event helps them to know that you would be there if you could, and adds support and encouragement. Distance does not end parent-child relationships when children grow up and move away, and it certainly does not have to when the marriage or cohabiting relationship ends.

The strength to forgive and to work together as adult parents for the growth and healthy development of our children is the greatest challenge for single parents. We must remember our promise—to the Universe—to guide a new soul to adulthood, even when we've chosen to sever our bonds to one another. The degree to which we can solve this dilemma may help to break the repetitive cycles of single parenthood that pass from generation to generation.

Forgiving

When we hold on to hurt, resentment, anger and pain (consciously or by repression) our body, thoughts and feelings resonate that woundedness. We pass it on like a virulent plague. We are also unavailable emotionally to our children and loved ones. Life is without its sensational sweetness. It may be devoid of the touch of lovingness.

When our children are deprived of needed responses from us, it can have a negative impact on their self-esteem. My husband and I were civil in the immediate post-separation and divorce phase.

Visitation rights were established. My daughter saw her father twice a week as ordered. My son went to live with his own father, my first husband (who lived in another city), for awhile. Overwhelmed by feelings of guilt and failure, I thought that his father and his paternal grandparents could offer him a less stressful environment. I guess part of me knew I had little emotional currency left. I needed time to heal. I also believed he needed positive male role models that his father and grandfather could provide.

He only stayed with his father for a few months, however. But those months were important to him, and to me. There are times in our lives as single parents that we need to reach out to others like our extended families for support, particularly during separation crises. Extended families can include our in-laws or former in-laws. But remember to let your extended family members know about your "ground rules," in terms of talking about or relating to the "other parent." Minimize negatives. Try to keep children out of the middle of the conflict.

Overnight Visits

The demands of our lives during separation crises and shortly after may necessitate that our children spend time—overnight, a few days, or longer periods—at someone else's house. We must take time to prepare our children for this change. Begin by discussing it with them. Talk, listen, share feelings and stay in close touch with your children emotionally. It is critically important to let them know what to expect. How long will they be separated from us? Why is it necessary? If it is longer than one night or a few days, keep assuring them of your devotion, love and need for them as part of your life—your family—while you are apart.

Stay in close touch. Help them by letting them select special "transition" items (toys, photographs, blankets) to take with them. If at all possible, go with them to the new environment and help them explore it initially. The more they know that you know about their new circumstances, the more comfortable and secure they'll feel. Also make sure they know how to reach you—if possible, twenty-four hours a day. Assure them that you are still there for them. Try not to disappoint them during these separations. If you say that you're going to call them or visit them, do so on time. Our children are clinging emotionally to our promises as their anchors of security and assurance. Routine contact, predictable calls and visits can be critically important to them during these vulnerable times.

Seven

Compelled

The post separation and/or divorce phase hits us with one stark reality—survival! Get enough money. Find a safe place to live. Figure out transportation, child care, food, health insurance and education solutions. Sleep if you can and prove to yourself and the world that you can do it. Most of us also try to prove that we don't need anyone's help or pity. Underneath that determination is often the fear of being turned down or rejected if we asked for help. I'll always remember the gossip I overheard from persons I thought were my friends: "Well, he didn't beat her, did he? I don't understand why she left. She'll learn that half a man is better than no man."

Rather than listen to condemnation, we often become isolated, trying to make it on our own. This pattern of isolation is unhealthy. In doing so, we are misusing our strength. We are using our energy to suppress and deny our real needs. This denial will lead to distress and unhappiness. During times of crisis and loss we need to be gentle with ourselves, and to express our feelings. Friendships are vital!

Affirming Our Choice

Self-care is a fundamental lesson for single parents. You see, there's something in the decision to be a single parent (and it is always a decision) that defies the needs of the self. Most single parents that I've talked with swear by all that's holy that "I didn't choose this situation. I did not go out and select to become a single parent." While this is true, we did choose to raise our children.

There is an important opportunity for healing here. Each and every one of us could have abandoned, deserted or turned our children over to someone else. In most of our situations the other biological parent did! No, we chose to accept the responsibility. We chose to listen to our hearts and act upon our love for our children. Single parents decide to devote their lives to providing safety, comfort, nurturance, education, validation and care for them. We choose, every day, to put their needs before our own and to Anchor them.

What gives us permission to do this? What compels us? What distinguishes us from the parent who walks away? In most cases, it's our female socialization that plays a key role. I suspect that even in males who accept single parenting, there is also a highly developed sensitivity to their nurturing, more commonly thought of as female-gender aspect.

Perhaps the connection that develops in utero and hormonal influences create different bonds between mothers and children than between fathers and children.

Perhaps biology compels us to demonstrate care. Maybe it is just the social expectation. Society does not seem to have the same level of condemnation for fathers who abandon or desert their children as it does for mothers. "What mother would or could abandon her child?"

Self Sacrifice

I believe there is something even more unique about most single parents that predisposes us to the self-sacrifice and denial of our own needs that usually accompanies the single-parent experience. Many single parents have been victims of neglect or abuse in the physical, mental or emotional aspects of their childhoods or adult lives. Many single parents have personally experienced prolonged emotional deprivation as well as touch deprivation, and have learned to live without daily demonstrations of love and appreciation. Many have become numb and deafened by the silence of aloneness.

I've worked with countless single parents, many of whom escaped battery or abusive mates, or young teenage mothers who were date-raped or coerced by people they trusted. Most have been deserted by people they believed cared for them. At the very least, most single parents are suffering the emotional and mental abandonment—the "abuse" of being left with sole responsibility for raising their children.

Some Single-Parent Profiles

Several programs have emerged around the country that are designed to help families become more self-sufficient reducing their need for AFDC—welfare-benefits. Most of these program participants are single parents. One such program decided to collect data on, or "profile" 360 families who have participated since 1990. Ninety-six percent were females, 4 percent were males. The childhood background of the single parents in this program revealed that 60 percent were children of alcoholic parents, 49 percent were known or suspected victims of physical abuse and 54 percent were known or suspected victims of sexual abuse. Their domestic history revealed that 35 percent were never married, 55 percent were cohabiting with a mate, 83 percent were present or past victims of domestic violence, 45 percent were currently or had in the past, abused their own children, and 70 percent reported that their pregnancies were unplanned. Substance abuse (drugs and alcohol) was a factor in 57 percent of these families, incarceration 15 percent, and no employment success applied to 37 percent. The characteristics typify the profile or domestic background of many single parents and their families today who face poverty and its related social barriers.

Yes, there are growing numbers of financially secure single persons, women primarily, who choose to parent as single adults. They are not the majority within the single-parent experience, however. Most single parents, like myself, did not plan to be in this situation. *To be left to parent alone, without adequate emotional, financial, physical and mental support is one of the cruelest forms of abuse.* It is part of a series of events that seem to perpetuate patterns of psychological, emotional and physical neglect in the lives of single parents and, often unknowingly, in the lives of the children. We deserve better.

Victims No More

My primary advice to single parents who have been (and who may still feel like) victims—women or men who have been abandoned, deserted, and who experience the unjust, unfair daily insult of "being left" with the sole responsibility (burden) of raising children (a promise originally made by two) is: Turn your disadvantage into your advantage. Begin by viewing your life situation as your choice. Honor yourself for having had the courage to make this choice. Honor yourself for having the heart, the capacity for love and the will to take care of your own children.

Victims continue to be victims. Believe me, I know. Victims become repeated targets for the projected sick, ignorant, abusive needs of others. Breaking the cycle begins with a simple decision on our part—a choice to be victims no more! A choice to be in control, in charge and able. Choice is a first step, but it is one of many. This step is critical, because as victims, we really have a low value for ourselves.

If we don't value ourselves, we teach our children not to value themselves. It's automatic. My heartfelt belief is that children learn more from what we are than from what we do or say. I'm not saying we're not hurting. I'm not saying we're not angry. What I am saying is that those feelings don't have to be used to create an ongoing "victim state" or life.

Counseling, therapy and support groups are good ways of breaking the cycles of victimization while dealing with some of those energy consuming feelings that often occupy our minds as single parents.

Things to Consider When Selecting a Therapist

1. Begin by taking time to be quiet with yourself and ask yourself what you want to accomplish through the therapy. Once you have an answer that comes from your heart, start doing some homework, gathering information about therapists—types, fees, availability, etc.

2. Talk with friends who have had positive outcomes through therapy. Ask them how they found their therapist and why they feel the process has been or is successful. Talk with people in your support network—your minister, physician, lawyer or teachers.

3. Allow yourself time to interview at least two or three potential therapists. Call them and request an exploratory meeting to help you determine if it's a match or not.

4. When you first meet with your potential therapist, let them do most of the talking. Let them tell you about themselves, their philosophy, their background and their expectations. Briefly discuss the single-parent experience. Find out their level of understanding and insight.

5. See if your therapist understands a holistic approach and is open to supporting your efforts for focus on your physical, mental, emotional and inspirational healing and growth. This doesn't mean the therapist has to be holistic in order to address all areas, but rather that she or he is willing to consider the potential importance of each area.

6. Share your goals or purpose for seeking therapy with the potential therapist. Carefully consider his or her response to your statements.

If you feel that therapy is just for people with real mental problems, or if you don't think you can afford psychological help, remember that the mind is as fragile and as responsive as the body. It deserves the same quality care and attention. Community mental health centers, neighborhood organizations and sometimes employee assistance programs can be sources of low cost, but helpful psychological care. Remember to explore group therapy and support-group strategies.

Often, in addition to professional counseling and programs, we have to develop self-help strategies that sustain and energize us. These strategies should keep us fit, help us to feel good and think clearly, and keep us aware of our loving relationship with the ultimate power for good in the universe. Many of these strategies are suggested in Part II of this book in the chapters on Anchors.

Eight

Complex to Simple

A teacher of mine once said, "Gail, you know, mastery of anything is progress from the complex to the simple." Her voice often echoes in my head. When things get too complicated I remind myself that I'm still learning, and that I need to reflect—to just be still. When my life as a single parent starts to feel more comfortable and less complicated, I know that I'm closer to true understanding—to true insight.

The lessons are simple. First, in order to have the courage and capacity needed, I had to learn to take control of my physical body. This required understanding my body's miraculous ways and learning how to care for myself. I had to develop a loving relationship with me. By beginning with an intimate-felt sense of connection to and appreciation for my own body, I was able to develop and sustain a higher level of *Self-Esteem*.

Our emotional patterns and ways of relating to people are established in early childhood and infancy. Next, I had to break free of the emotional prison that held me captive. Traumatic early childhood memories had taught me that the world is not a kind or friendly place. I had to explore the feelings of fear and insecurity that (unbeknownst to me) were dictating my behaviors and choices. This meant finding and nurturing my own inner child—my vulnerable self. It was important to discover what these patterns were so I could become free to reach out and attract the resources and relationships that I needed to *Support* me in my role as a single head of household.

Then I had to discover the power of my own mind and thoughts. I had to gain control over my own creative processes and realize how my mental focus was impacting my own and my children's lives. This meant learning that my actions were ways to enjoy what my mind, my thoughts, had already created. Once I understood this source of true inner power, the value of concentration, visualization and mental discipline, I was able to set goals and take actions that helped to lift my family out of poverty and into a state of financial balance, or *Solvency*.

Finally, I had to be reminded that I am never alone. This required developing a spiritual oneness with my understanding of divine love, or God. This involved learning to relate in a personal way to the energy and intelligence that sustains us all. This knowledge is what I consider spiritual. It gave me the faith to triumph against seemingly insurmountable odds. When I realized that God is love, and therefore so am I, I realized that I am always connected to a source of inner power that gives me the courage to live without constant fear and stress. In so doing, I model and teach the same spiritual awareness to my children. This knowledge and the faith that it taught became my greatest *Strength*.

These four learnings about myself—my body, my emotions, my thoughts and my spiritual beliefs—introduced me to my whole self. Over twenty years I have built upon this base to create a holistic approach to parenting—to life, really—which has guided me as a single parent.

These four levels of awareness or learnings are presented as foundations that enable us to Anchor our families in a place of relative peace, comfort and joy. Once we become aware of, learn to appreciate and take actions that assure our *Self-Esteem*, *Support*, *Solvency* and *Strength*, I believe that we can, as single-parent families, triumph in spite of great societal odds.

This process of becoming aware, appreciating and taking appropriate actions begins with knowing who we are. We are but another generation, another family in a line of families that began hundreds of years ago. From the old ones, from our past we have been given a legacy—patterns, behaviors, strengths and yes, weaknesses—that help to determine and, indeed, to shape our way of living and relating to others. How we function as parents and as heads of our own households is, I believe, influenced by our own family history—our own cultural legacy.

Nine

The Legacy

After finishing her part in grinding the corn, she looked and decided that the task was completed. She slipped away from the other women of the tribe and rode her pony down to the river's edge to meet him. How would she explain that she could not marry him? How could she explain her shame?

He was waiting as she knew he would be, and his eyes said that her protests were meaningless. "I know your secret; it doesn't matter to me. You are to be my wife. We will be together always." Tears of joy overshadowed her confusion, but she really didn't understand. Everything came through the mothers. It was the mother's rank in the tribe that would give her honor. And her mother, now dead, had carried the shame of rape, rape by a white man. She was the child of that rape and although part of their community, she was not part.

He tried to calm her, to assure her. "Your mother was brave, she was strong. She brought honor to our people."

Brave, indeed. She had escaped from slavery, pregnant, carrying her daughter. She was a healer, a medicine woman and told stories of her own ancestors in Africa. She spoke about the horrors of the ship and the time in its belly. She remembered her people—her kind, yet not her kin—who died or killed themselves to end their suffering. Her mother was strong. She survived and became a favorite of the master, a house slave. It was because he favored her that she was able to escape—to run away to join the Native Americans, the Seminole.

Roots

This scene could have been taken from a page in my family's history book. Every family in America traces its roots back to legacies that began hundreds of years ago. Family roots include rules about parenting and ways of relating, surviving and adapting to society's demands. Descendants of most of the Europeans who came to this land have family legacies of homes that were ruled by a man who was lord of his household, supported by a lesser wife. Her primary purpose was to serve him. Children were commonly disciplined with physical force—Calvinist beliefs held that children were "born in sin." Wives often expected to be beaten if they failed to please their husbands. Wives had limited rights to divorce or to child custody. They had no property rights.

Descendants of enslaved and conquered African and Native American groups were exposed to and eventually embraced some of the family values of Europeans. Many African and Native Americans experienced emotional devastation from the brutality of enslavement and displacement. Yet, many also held onto their own legacies of greater equality between men and women and extended kinship or family communities. Care of the children was, by necessity, shared by relatives and persons within the community. Child rearing and discipline styles, like everything else, were an adaptation, a reaction to the dehumanizing experience of enslavement and its terrorizing aftermath. But they also reflected diverse beliefs. Most Native Americans, for example, did not believe in corporal or physical discipline for children.

Generations

It is against this backdrop, this diverse cultural legacy, that my single-parenting story is set. I and my children must remember that we are descendants of a strong and courageous people who have historically survived against great odds. Most of our forebears were once enslaved and conquered, and triumphed though raped and subjugated. My people had thousands of years of culture—ways of living and believing in our own God, ways of relating male to female, and ways of parenting—that were disrupted for over 400 years. My ancestors, whose family name was often passed on through the mother, were forced to take on the ways of a people whose family name was passed on through the father. Many of my ancestors believed in equally shared work and authority between men and women.

What happens when disparate cultures combine? When one conquers the other? A people whose religion and spirituality was sun- and life-centered, and grounded in elaborate ritual, was forced to take on the ways of a people whose religion was man-centered and abstract. Their views about life, death, work and family were different. One was subjugated and almost destroyed by the other.

I do not believe that thousands of years of belief and culture can be conquered in just a few hundred years. The way of being lives on for generations in the genes, minds and hearts of people. The ways of the old ones manifest in our family circumstances, along with memories of reactions to oppression and ongoing struggles for survival.

Every single parent, whether of African, European, Asian, Mexican, Puerto Rican or Native American descent is being influenced by our ancestors' attitudes, perceptions and by generations of "family values" and traditions.

Ways of Parenting

Whether negative or positive, our automatic frame of reference for how we parent is the way in which we, ourselves, were parented. This frame of reference probably came from the way our parents were parented. My father spent a good portion of his childhood years in the home of an uncle and aunt. He and his brother were sent there at ages two and three after their mother died. The uncle had been raised by a former slave overseer and he horsewhipped the children in much the same manner as he had been. So discipline and punishment for my father, beginning when he was four years old, and for his brother who was three, meant being flogged with a horsewhip until his aunt interceded. She screamed and cried for it to stop. This pattern continued until he was eleven years old and he had saved enough money (secretly earned by playing his harmonica and doing odd jobs) to escape to Virginia. He later went back for his younger brother.

Dad carried one primary rule about parenting into his relationship with us as children. He would not beat us. In fact, he would turn over the day-to-day parenting responsibility for discipline (and everything else) to our mother. In doing so, he psychologically "absented" himself from our growing experience. His work as a truck driver made this easy. He was on the road for days at a time. His actual physical presence in the home was very limited. Ironically, not only did he not beat us, he did not touch us either.

My mother, on the other hand, remembered being one of too many children, and competing or struggling for attention, food, clothes, etc. She described her father as stoic, rigid, powerful and strong. He was, indeed, the "Lord of his House." Even his wife, who dutifully bore him twelve children—consecutively, two years apart—did not address him informally. She always called him Mister. My mother, like my father, had been disciplined by being brutally beaten as a child and she, like my father, escaped at a young age to parent herself. I guess if she were to sum up her parenting philosophy, it would be to survive—to make sure her children had food, shelter, were educated and not harmed; that they would grow up without avoidable disease or injury. Like my father, she did very little touching.

Abuse and Deprivation

Child abuse means that the child has felt too much to bear. Child deprivation means that the child has been exposed to too little to meet his or her needs. My family's parenting heritage is blanketed with trappings of abuse and deprivation. As children, both of my parents felt too much to bear and were exposed to too little to meet their needs. They are like millions of Americans who learned to live inside frozen feelings armored by determined minds and rigid bodies.

Both extremes, abuse or deprivation, impact on the whole child, and eventually upon the whole adult. A child's body responds, as does the child's mind and feelings. Ultimately the child's spirit is affected. Sometimes the damage caused by childhood trauma, abuse or deprivation, leaves scars that can cripple for life. These scars can destroy their capacity to love, and create impulses to harm others or to self-destruct. Regardless of the outcome, the scars of abuse or deprivation always impair. They undermine the quality of the person's relationships and the level of joy and adult fulfillment the person achieves. Childhood experiences always shape adult patterns.

My parents' stories are typical of millions of brave people who survived abuse and deprivation as children, and who grew up to become parents themselves. Their story is an admirable one, for they not only survived, they overcame many racial, social and economic barriers and tried to give their children more than they had received. My own parenting styles had to be "unlearned," however, and then learned anew as an adult. I chose to unlearn the parenting styles I experienced in my own childhood. I, too, wanted to give my children more.

A Matter of Focus

We can succeed in life despite difficult childhoods. We are able to create a stable emotional and economic base for ourselves and our families. But the parenting legacy in these stories of survival against the odds is often a legacy of focusing on the struggle for survival—of defacto distance and frozen emotions. When we are living with deep fear and focusing on survival, we cannot always give our children the quality emotional attention they need. We do not establish the loving relationship upon which their optimal development depends.

This is particularly true when there is only one parent in the family who must of necessity fulfill multiple roles as provider, nurturer, socializer, care-taker, etc., in a society that is not designed to support one-parent families. In such circumstances, there is the risk that we may give our children a legacy of day-to-day living without meaningful and heartfelt communication, family ritual, sharing, healing touch or affirmation of their importance and value. This type of legacy begets confusion, mistrust, alienation and low self-esteem. This legacy can shape the parenting philosophy of the next generation, as well.

The fact that our adult relationships are severed does not alter the emotional needs of our children. The realities of not enough time and/or energy do not change our children's constant need for adult affection, guidance and support. Children do survive when their needs go unmet—but they may compensate in ways that cost much more in the long run. Street gangs, for example, provide affection, direction and support, as do prisons. Have these become substitute belated families, providing missed family/parenting relationships?

Creating Our Own Parenting Philosophy

As single parents, we must revisit our own family histories and experiences, and draw from them what was good, filter out what is not appropriate for today, and learn to create our own viable philosophy or approach to parenting. This requires work. It may require counseling, parenting classes and/or involvement in community-based family support programs. Several family resource organizations are listed in the resource section of this book.

Our new parenting philosophy should enable us to pay day-to-day attention to our children's physical, emotional, mental and inspirational needs. In this sense, it must be holistic. If we can remember three simple keys as we create our own parenting philosophy, we will probably not go too far wrong.

- First, we must attempt each day to promote our childrens' sense of self by communicating that they are loved unconditionally. We must respond to their needs and cues, from their earliest cries and gestures (by holding and caressing them), to their moods and behaviors as they grow older, by taking time to talk, to play and to simply be with them.

- Second, we should encourage them to believe that they are valued and honored by listening to them and giving feedback that appreciates their communication. Doing so promotes their self-esteem and helps them to create needed boundaries.

- Third, we can help them know that they are capable by making sure they experience appropriate successes each day, like dressing themselves and feeding themselves, achieving in school, or simply getting our attention. Daily, small successes lead to skills and self-confidence. This helps children believe they can master or control themselves and their lives.

If we are to help our children grow into responsible adults, capable of forming and sustaining loving relationships and living well, we must pay attention to their energy, vitality, ideas and feelings from day to day. We must also teach them to have hope, to expect goodness from life, from a transcendent source of good. When we parent holistically, we model a way of living and being for our children that fosters optimism and faith in their capacity to create the future they desire.

Ten

Parenting Begins with Pregnancy

When I was expecting my second child, my son Daniel, an elderly woman came into my office and stared at me with a puzzled look. I was just beginning to "show," and she wasn't sure about my condition. Finally, she blurted out, catching me by surprise, "Child, is you makin' foots?" I said, "Am I what?" "Is you makin' foots," she repeated. Somehow her meaning came through my Chicago-by-way-of-Cleveland background, all the way back to my family's Alabama roots. I recognized (although I'd never heard it before) that "makin' foots" is an African American expression for having a baby, or being pregnant. And an apt expression it is, too. During the pregnancy, or gestation period, we are literally "makin' foots"—feet—as well as arms, eyes, legs, ears, etc.

This is an awesome thought that as the parent, particularly the mother, I am literally creating, building and shaping the physical body—the vehicle—for my child. Every ounce of food—its quality, nutritional content, etc.—that I choose to take into my body, coupled with environmental and genetic factors, are helping to determine the condition of the physical body that I prepare for my child.

By the seventh day of the pregnancy, the physical vehicle has moved through our fallopian tubes to be implanted snugly within the wall of our uterus. During the eight weeks that follow, all of the organs and systems are essentially established. It is not until the last seven months of the pregnancy that most of the growth in the unborn's physical body occurs. During the last seven months the baby's body will elaborate and expand, further developing all the systems that were started during the first eight weeks. So the first two months of the pregnancy establish the foundation upon which the rest of our baby's body is built.

The Wedding

It was the day of my brother's wedding. A day of ritual, hats, flowers, tuxedos and promises—vows that would last a lifetime. It was also a day of disappointment.

I had been unable to sleep the night before his wedding. An unusual level of anxiety, or excitement, I thought. My husband shared my curiosity. Why not sleep before a three-hour drive to another town, and a long day for all of us, but especially for our new baby daughter? We would take her to the clinic for her routine six-week checkup, and rush down to Athens, Ohio, in time for the ceremony. We'd pack a lunch, and arrive with time to spare.

The doctor kept listening and re-listening to her heart. He used the stethoscope, then put his ear to her chest. He made her cry and listened again. Then, as he handed our six-week old baby girl back to us, he shook his head compassionately. "I'm sorry, but your daughter has a congenital disease of the heart. I can't promise anything, really. I only know she'll need surgery. I've made an appointment for you to go directly to a specialist at Children's Medical Center. He will see you immediately."

I held my little girl and prayed all the way to the next hospital. We reluctantly handed her over to this stranger, this new doctor, to examine her and tell us his findings. He took her. When he returned, he too, shook his head sadly and confirmed the diagnosis. More appointments were scheduled. "Little can be done," they said. "She will need surgery. We can't guarantee anything."

We arrived at my brother's wedding too late for the actual ceremony. When the family learned of our traumatic news, they forgave us. We drove home in silence, disbelieving the entire day.

Six weeks later, on a hot, ninety-six degree day, she was terribly fretful. The night-time feedings were my favorite. She nursed until we both fell asleep. On more than one occasion, I had awakened to find her staring quietly at me with a mature look, as if to say "Why don't you lay me down and go to bed, Mom?" Then she'd close her eyes and I'd place her in her crib. We had purchased her crib from a resale store, repainted it with lead-free paint, and hung a mobile over it. But this night, she didn't nurse comfortably and I didn't fall asleep. In fact, my inner voice compelled me to place her in her crib while she was still crying— something that I'd never done. That "inner voice" is one I've come to know and respect. For that voice spared me the unthinkable experience of having my baby die in my arms. A few hours later, my husband awoke and went to check on her. He found her lifeless body, and attempted to resuscitate her. We both heard the sound that I now know as the death rattle, as coagulating fluids move through hardening tubes. We wrapped her body and carried her to the nearest hospital emergency room and handed her, once again, to a doctor. That was the last time I saw her.

Crib Death?

The medical report and death certificate called it a crib death. Why not? It occurred in her crib. In truth, her badly formed heart had simply failed. But what I now know, and want to share with all the passion I can muster, is the simple fact that while genetics may have played a part in the birth defect, she was a low birth-weight infant, and I was a poorly nourished expectant mother. Had she survived, her development would have been severely delayed.

I don't blame myself anymore, but I do acknowledge my ignorance. As a young, low-income couple who knew nothing about pre-natal nutrition, we made inappropriate decisions. But our little girl, whose name was Ntianu (En-tee-ah-new)—a Native American name that means "Noble Spirit"—taught me to value life. The experience of touching and holding her stiff, lifeless body cemented my commitment to life, to health and to wholeness. To her, I am eternally grateful.

The pregnancy had been fraught with complications, persistent nausea, vomiting, minimal weight gain, spotting and a long, difficult labor. I had worried about money and everything else through the nine months.

If I could, I would have a law passed in every state and create a special police force to enforce this law assuring that every expectant mother will consume the nutrients and foods required for optimal growth and development of her baby. The same law would require that the expectant mother's stress and anxiety inducing circumstances be minimized during the pregnancy. If such a law existed and was enforced, it would save this country billions of dollars in needless medical and social costs—and spare parents immeasurable degrees of grief, pain and trauma.

But alas, I cannot enact or enforce such a law to prevent comparable loss and suffering by others. I can only write a book and urge, plead, beg all family members, significant others and would-be, wanna be, or maybe (by accident) parents to heed this simple message. The best way to support our parenting process is to start with a healthy baby. We can influence this by our choices during pregnancy. You may be pregnant now, or know of a single mother who is expecting a child. Share this critical concept with them and/or begin now to put your nutritional health first. It can influence the rest of your own and your child's life.

Diet During Pregnancy

The mother's diet and drug intake during pregnancy impacts the child's development more than any other factor over which we have control. We don't control heredity or genetic content. Once the egg and sperm unite, certain factors are inevitable. But our choices—the chemicals that we introduce into our children's developmental environment—our wombs—will support or interfere with nature's plan.

The baby who weighs under five and a half pounds at birth is more apt to be afflicted with such conditions as mental retardation, cerebral palsy, epilepsy, hyperactivity, learning disabilities, respiratory distress syndrome and/or premature death.

One scientific study in Guatemala revealed how adequate nutrient intake (including calories and protein) during pregnancy, substantially increases birth weight and decreases infant mortality. The study's participants lived in abject poverty. The typical prenatal diet before the study consisted of approximately 1,500 calories per day and 40 grams of protein. The normal weight gain during pregnancy on such a diet was about 15 pounds.

Through their pregnancies, these women were given additional calories and protein. The effect was dramatic. Of the sixty-nine women who had the optimal nutrition, not one gave birth to an underweight child. When there is optimal intake of nutrients, infant mortality (death) and morbidity (illness) can be significantly reduced. The relationship between prenatal nutrition and infant development, particularly birth weight, has been clearly established by numerous studies. Knowledge about this relationship is critically important to us as single parents.

Birth Defects?

You're wondering, "What about birth defects? Is the mother to blame herself?" No, there are several genetic aberrations and/or birth traumas that occur during pregnancy, and some unknowns over which we have no control, that lead to birth defects and abnormalities. But the largest percentage of babies delivered that are small for their age and/or that are vulnerable to respiratory problems, infections and infant mortality or morbidity, can be traced to a prenatal/gestational experience in which care—nutritional, familial and medical—was not adequate.

Parenting begins with the pregnancy. What does all this mean to the single parent? Many single women go through their pregnancies without needed support and with ambivalent feelings—low self-esteem—sometimes depression. This low energy state can lead to stress, and to a life-style and dietary choices that are not in the best interest of the mother or the baby.

Many cultures throughout history have recognized the significance of prenatal wellness. For example, some African cultures place betrothed couples on special diets at least a year before the wedding (in anticipation of conception) to assure healthy offspring.

Anchors for the Innocent

It is during pregnancy that the parent first becomes the true Anchor for the Innocent. It is during those nine months of formation that our daily, moment-to-moment, breath-by-breath affirmation can be a resounding yes to the universe. We are agreeing to shepherd and to guide another soul along life's journey and we are agreeing to allow that being entrance into the physical world through us—through our physical body. We are their portal—their entry point—and their protection and support.

In response to our willingness, the intelligence that governs all life is willing to surround us, to give us all that we need. However, we must be willing to receive it.

We should not live in a state of mind, body, feeling or expectation that pushes away support and draws negatives, such as condemnation and punishment, into our lives. Pregnancy is meant to be a happy, joyful time—one of the most precious moments in the parenting process. The beginnings of demonstrated self-esteem, self-value and self-worth are here, right in the first nine months. Honor yourself as the mother. And contemplate the unborn child, who's spirit at the moment of birth will enliven the physical body that is developing, growing, becoming, within you.

High Risks

Several studies have illustrated the higher rates of abuse and neglect suffered by premature and/or special needs infants. For single parents, 60 percent of whom live in poverty, the risk of malnourishment during pregnancy is very high. It is often a great psychological and environmental stress for parents and infants to connect emotionally when complications and impairments accompany the critical first few hours and days of life.

Since the birth and infant death of Ntianu more than twenty years ago, I've done a lot of work with families of children born with multiple handicapping conditions. As I've read countless case histories and prenatal medical records, I cry over the cases that could have been prevented with adequate prenatal nutrition and care. My partner, an obstetrician, and I are now co-authoring a book on the subject, entitled "Makin' Foots," which will be available in Spring of 1994.

Some general prenatal nutrition guidelines are listed here:

Nutrition Guidelines for Pregnancy

1. An expectant mother must consume enough calories. She needs at least 1,900 to 2,700 per day.

2. Daily calorie needs can be met by consuming five or more servings of fruits and vegetables, four or more (1 cup) servings of dairy products, three or more servings of meat (or meat substitutes), four servings of breads and cereals, six or more glasses of liquids (in addition to milk) and from 1–2 tablespoons of unsaturated fats or oils. After these requirements are met, then the expectant mother can add desserts as desired.

3. It is important to get lots of protein each day, at least 75 grams. This may mean at least three 3-ounce servings of meat, fish or poultry, plus one or two servings of cooked dried peas or beans, tofu, cheese or other milk products, eggs or nut butters.

4. Even if a mother consumes enough protein, but not enough calories, she will be undernourished. The body will burn protein as calories, leaving her protein deficient. Protein is needed to build the unborn baby's body tissue.

5. Iron intake needs go up during pregnancy. Most doctors recommend using prenatal vitamins that contain iron, plus eating liver once a week. Don't forget to take your prenatal vitamins!

6. Folic acid is a key nutrient during pregnancy. It comes in green leafy vegetables. Eat lots of these. Folic acid is also included in most prenatal vitamins.

7. Do not restrict your salt during pregnancy. Adequate sodium helps your body create the extra fluid volume required during pregnancy.

8. Stay well hydrated. Drink at least two quarts per day of non-carbonated, non-caffeinated beverages.

9. The use of any drugs or alcohol during pregnancy should be avoided. If medicines are prescribed, discuss the potential effects with your doctor carefully.

10. Avoid excess fat and refined sugars. Consume lots of complex carbohydrates—whole grains, like whole wheat products, brown rice and cereals.

An expectant mother must love herself enough to demonstrate self-care in all aspects of her life from the moment the decision is made to bring a child into the world. Pregnancy should always be a conscious willing choice.

In the physical, self-care means optimum diet and circulation, which excludes drugs and harmful chemicals, while it includes all needed calories, protein, vitamins, minerals and accessory food factors—lots of fresh vegetables, fruits, grains and lean meats. It is important to get the best comprehensive medical and dental care available. (Dental problems can impact both the mother and infant.) In the mental, it means entertaining only positive/generative thoughts and images about herself, her life and her baby. In the emotional, the expectant mother must turn away from negative feelings and people that cause unhappiness or sadness. In the spiritual, the mother must affirm her connection to a loving, caring God. There should be no guilt, no shame and no self-punishment or denial of deservedness during pregnancy.

Key Points to Remember About the Innocent

1. All children are born with an innocent expectation and need for unconditional love and protection from parents. Since we were all children once, we carry that innocence and a need for unconditional love deep within our hearts throughout life.

2. The family pictures—memories—of how our parents and/or care-givers related to us help to shape, that is to condition, our automatic responses to life, particularly to our own children. This is a law of parenting.

3. Single parents are vitally important to our society. If current trends continue, we will shape the responses of from fully a third to more than half of all children born today.

4. The idea of family values must come to mean valuing families and creating public policies (like child care, housing, employment) that support the efforts of parents who are responsible for caring for our nation's most important resource—our children.

5. Effective parenting—post-marriage or relationship—is a necessity for both parents, not an option. Our challenge is to put the needs of our children first—both during and after committed adult relationships.

6. Child abuse means that a child has felt too much to bear. Child deprivation means that the child has been exposed to too little to meet his or her needs. Both extremes impact upon the whole child, and eventually the whole adult.

7. As single parents today, we face tremendous obstacles. We require almost super-human capacities in order to succeed—to create families that work, that provide needed security, nurturance, socialization, esteem, education, validation and support.

8. Our parenting capacity is enhanced by healing the wounds of our own childhood. We must unlearn our inherited negative parenting practices, and develop new ways of caring for ourselves—physically, mentally, emotionally and spiritually. We cannot give the love that we do not have.

9. Once the decision to parent is made, it is our responsibility to value and honor ourselves and our decision by creating (through prenatal care and optimal nutrition) the best possible body or physical vehicle for our child to occupy upon birth and throughout its lifetime.

Eleven

Love

It was a hot night in August of 1950.

She awoke at 5:00 in the morning, shaking her husband still trembling herself. "We've got to take her to the hospital now", she cried. "Something is wrong—I know it, I know it."

He tried to calm his clearly hysterical wife and make sense of what she was saying. Finally, he understood that the images of her nightmare included hospital scenes with doctors in white coats, shaking their heads sadly, as they handed an infant back to its parents. She was obsessed with the idea that these images were a warning. She was compelled to take her baby to the emergency room immediately.

It was 2:00 Saturday afternoon. They had been at the hospital since 7:00 a.m. The doctor finally came out of the examining room with their baby in his arms. He handed the baby to her mother just like in the dream. The young round-faced man really seemed to care as he shook his head sadly and said, "Look, we can't be sure that your baby will be able to see. She may be totally blind.

The baby has a rare, very rare eye disease for infants. It's called congenital glaucoma. Older people tend to get it—children are rarely born with it. We can operate right away and attempt to save what sight there is, but the procedure—at six weeks of age—is very risky. We will have to put your baby to sleep during this procedure. We simply can offer no guarantees that anything positive will result. It's your choice. We believe, however, that without immediate surgical intervention your baby, most assuredly, will be totally blind."

Why had it come to her in this dream? She had never experienced any kind of psychic or prophetic dream before. What did it all mean? Should they risk the surgery? For this young mother the stress was overwhelming. The unplanned pregnancy had been accompanied by the constant fear of losing her husband and being abandoned again, this time with not one, but two children, and now that that fear was beginning to go away, she had to cope with the real trauma of caring for a less-than-perfect child—a child with special needs. Maybe even—probably even—a handicapped, blind child. There were times when she wanted to simply curl up in a ball and disappear. No such option, however. She had to stick it out. And moreso, she had to fight—to do something.

Prayer

Raised in the Southern Baptist tradition, she knew how and when to pray. So she did, and her prayers were answered by an actual meeting with a then world-renowned evangelical healer—Kathryn Kulman. This Christian spiritual healer happened to be in their town on the "weekend of decision" and somehow the young couple made their way through thousands of people and placed their tiny baby in the arms of this woman who had been a vehicle for miracles—documented, recorded miracles. Just getting to her had, in fact, been a miracle.

Kathryn Kulman prayed for their baby and then told the young couple to go forward with the surgery. Her parting words were, "She will see. Your baby will see!"

Patterns

Twenty five years and seven surgical eye procedures later, that baby had grown up to give birth to her own first-born and now second child. She, like her own mother, was harboring feelings of abandonment and "aloneness" in the post-partum period following the birth of her second child. These fears of abandonment predominated, even though she was married and living with her young husband.

Her husband, boy/man that he was, seemed to be unable to keep himself gainfully employed. His own unmet emotional needs, and accompanying feelings of shame, pulled him farther and farther from his wife.

Like her own mother had done before, the young woman found a way to bury her depression. In the face of her husband's apparent unemployability, she found work and was managing to nurse her baby, work full time, go to school part time, suppress her frustration and anger with her husband who was slipping away emotionally and keep the kitchen floor spotlessly clean.

All of this surviving had its price, however. The eye disease that had dominated her growing-up years now began to get out of control. Despite numerous surgeries and multiple medications, a then partially sighted, legally blind (in one eye) mother was being told that she would probably lose her remaining sight. The visual fields were getting narrower. Darkness was, indeed, closing in. At this moment, part of her didn't want to see. Like her mother twenty-five years before, part of her wanted to merely curl up into a ball and disappear.

Awareness

City winters can be frigid. If her family was going to stay warm—indeed, to eat—she simply could not be depressed. Survival and caring for her young child were her only options.

Again, having grown up in a Baptist tradition and having always believed in a transcendent power, or force for good, she, like her mother, knew how to pray. Ironically, the young woman realized that she had never prayed for her own eyes or for her sight, even though she had grown up going to and spending hours in eye clinics every week; putting drops in her eyes every four hours since the age of six weeks; and having repeated eye surgeries. She had tried self-help methods, along with medical treatments and alternative healing regimes, too.

Everything from diet to acupuncture, from deep relaxation to herbal therapy had been tried, but she had never prayed about her own eyes. Only this time, the pain, the physical pain, like a toothache in her head, and the realization that her world was becoming a collection of barely discernable shadows, was more than she could bear. I guess it's one thing to be blind, and yet another to go blind—gradually, insidiously, painfully—despite heroic medical efforts and self discipline to prevent it.

Winter seemed extremely hard that year. When her doctors recommended a repeat of the surgery they had performed a little over a year before, she said no. It seemed futile. The eye pressure, despite medications and surgery, was out of control. When she declined the eighth operation, the confused doctor asked "Why? What will you do?" She answered quietly, with absolute resolve, "I don't know what I am going to do. I just know in my heart that I cannot allow my eyes to be cut again. I know it is not the right thing for me to do now."

Weeks passed. It was yet another day of pain and angst. Something moved her to cry out audibly—to ask, in fact, to beseech God for help for healing her eyes. She reports that in that moment she heard a very clear voice. The voice said simply, "Love your eyes as I do."

The pain—the blinding pain—subsided. Subsequent visits to the doctor showed no increased pressure in the eyes and no need for medication or more surgery. Vision improved to near perfect with glasses. Kathryn Kulman, it seemed, had been right. The baby would see, forever.

What has all this to do with single parenting? This is my own story. I am that baby girl, that young woman. It is my health and sight that have been restored—my healing that I chose to share. I was given a degree of love that day that I did not yet know how to give to myself. And for me, that is the ultimate lesson of healing, and of single parenting—indeed, of all life. When I was told to "love my eyes" as they are loved, I was gently lifted beyond all the ravages of disease to the truth of my wholeness. I know that my thoughts, experiences and feelings about my own eyes had been negative for all of my life. In fact, I had grown up hating my eyes. They were funny-looking with poor muscle control—partially crossed, as they said in those days. And they prevented me from having a normal childhood and life. So I learned to disdain them and to ask, "why me?"

All my medical and alternative healing efforts were done with this mind set of dislike, distance and separation. These things were done to, not for, my eyes or for my body with love. I certainly had never looked at them with love. But that day I did. I obediently walked over to the mirror in our apartment and stared into my own eyes. And for the first time in my life, I accepted—in fact, embraced—my eyes with love. Divine Love looked back at me, and in that moment the excess pressure in my eyes subsided.

Appreciation

That was eighteen years ago. I have had no additional medications or surgery and, with the exception of fatigue when I use computers, no problems with my eyes. For this, and the greater gift of insight, I am extremely grateful.

This is a simple message. Yet, despite my healing, it took me another ten years to get it. It took me another ten years and a lot of "learning opportunities" that I once called problems to truly progress from the complex to the simple, as my teacher would have said, and to see how to love myself, wholly. Ultimately, this meant accepting, embracing and eventually "loving" my self in my role as a single parent, too! It meant turning what others called my disadvantage into my advantage. I know this is a stretch. First of all, you ask, am I promoting the single-parent experience? Am I advising young (or middle-aged) persons to create single-parent situations? The answer is NO—an unequivocal, straightforward, unhesitant NO. I believe in our society the parenting process is most easily facilitated by the combined energies, devotion and commitment of two loving parents together. But the fact is that something in our sensibilities, in our relationship skills (or that lack thereof) is eroding—working against the two-parent family model. Single-parent families are here, have been here, and will always be here.

My single parenting and my healing journeys have had a lot in common. My mission as a parent has been to support and optimize my children's lives by enabling them to value themselves, to give them the tools to create and sustain quality relationships, to show them that they are safe, supported and secure (financially and otherwise) and to give them the inner strength needed to be resilient and successful in life as they grow into adulthood. But I could not give them what I did not have. I had to learn to truly love and value myself—all aspects of myself—to feel and to be supported, financially and otherwise, I had to learn how to develop quality relationships, to understand my own capacity to bounce back from crises and how to sustain a quality life for myself and my family. This process of personal growth and development for me was foreshadowed in my healing experience, but it has been a long journey of homecoming, a long sojourn to a state of awareness, appreciation and to actions that cherish my self—my whole self.

The affirmation to "love my eyes" as they are loved, was important because in that instant, I accepted a thought, triggering a feeling state that caused a change in the physiological (nerve, hormone and chemical) balance of my body. I contacted a part of myself that is in constant touch with a divine knowing, the intelligence that is universal love. Some people might call it my "higher self." Others call it our non-physical self. Psychologist Carl Jung called it "the collective unconscious." In that sacred instant, I was guided by a part of my consciousness, my being, that knows no fear. It knows only love.

To succeed in life, particularly as single parents, I believe it is important that we learn how to honor and listen to that loving part of ourselves—physically, mentally, emotionally and spiritually. This capacity is the greatest gift we can give to our children. It is their Anchor and can sustain them through life's most turbulent waters.

There is a very popular song entitled "The Greatest Love of All." It has a line that says, "Learning to love yourself is an easy thing to do." While I think this particular song is wonderful, that particular line is misleading. Learning to love ourselves is life's greatest challenge. For most of us, it is an ongoing process of unlearning. For single parents, women, persons of color, persons with disabilities and in fact all people who constantly receive degrading messages from society about ourselves, this is a life-long learning.

But as single parents, we are particularly charged to get this one. If we are to succeed in raising children who do not become statistics—children who achieve in school, who become employed, who enter into and sustain healthy adult relationships, children who can say no to drugs and alcohol and who realize their full potential—we, as parents must learn this vital lesson. We must truly possess the greatest love of all.

Part II of this book, Anchors, are steps along the way to this vital knowledge. Each Anchor—*Self-Esteem, Support, Solvency* and finally *Strength*, is a required learning, a necessary tool for us as single parents.

Anchors

As children, we are never born in sin. Each new life has its own capacity, its own potential. In this truth rests our innocence and our opportunities to thrive through caring relationships. We learn to care within families and communities that model self-esteem and give us support; families that are solvent and have strength.

Twelve

The Contract

On that third Saturday in September of 1989, I should have suspected that something was amiss when by 11:00 in the morning, neither of my two children had asked me for any money. My son had been in the bathroom for what seemed an unusually long period of time. Then his younger sister announced, "Mom, Daniel's been in the bathroom for over an hour. I think he's cutting his hair—he took the clippers in there with him and I can hear them."

As if he heard her, Daniel appeared on the heels of her pronouncement. There he stood, defiant, looking like the loser in a John Wayne western. His head, or should I say his scalp, was an atrocity. While I was being hysterical about what he'd done to his head, I saw it! There, hanging from his left ear, was what I then considered to be the ultimate insult to me, to his heritage, his manhood and everything that I insisted he respect. There was a small gold earring!

In shock, as I held his ear between my two fingers, I asked quietly and very slowly, "Daniel, is this an earring?" Then, as only a younger sister can do, Charisse blurted out, "Oh, he's been wearing that for weeks. You just haven't noticed." Her comment gave me a reason to turn away from this thing in Daniel's ear to tell her to just be quiet! She was right. Daniel had been walking around showing me only one side of his head for at least two weeks, because he had joined most of the other boys his age and pierced one of his ears.

At this point, I knew it was time. I ran to the cedar chest and found the black box. I took out the documents. You see, the only way to make this single parent thing work is to have a contract—signed in blood with each of your offspring. So I unfolded the agreement and forced my son to read it aloud. He read:

"On this 19th day of January, in the year of our Lord, 1974, I, Daniel Joseph Christopher, being of sound mind on this day of my birth, do solemnly agree to the following terms with my mother:

"1. I will sleep through the night, all night, never waking to cry and fret, beginning tonight.

"2. I will become toilet trained in one day and never, but never, ruin any of her clothes.

"3. I will eat what is given to me and not be finicky or fussy about food.

"4. I will have no accident or injury—attract no bodily harm to myself.

"5. I will contract all childhood diseases, but only briefly and have no complications.

"6. I will make all A's and B's in school, never fail any course, and graduate, yes graduate on time, and finish college.

"7. If I become sexually active while this agreement is in effect, I will not get anyone pregnant, and I will always, always use a condom.

"8. I will do everything my mother tells me to do, never question her judgement, have only friends that she approves of and most importantly, I will not do anything weird like shave my head or wear an earring, ever! "

"And, in response to my son's promises, I, Gail C. Christopher, as a single mother, agree to the following:

"1. I will work my behind off for at least 21 years—maintaining six jobs simultaneously to provide a safe home and environment for him to grow and play in.

"2. I will try out at least two replacements for my son's father when he decides to totally absent himself. Each tryout period is not to exceed two years. If the second tryout fails, I promise not to try out anymore.

"3. I will give up any semblance of a personal, social or sexual life (as is the expectation of any son).

"4. I will never beat my son (except once or twice when I lose it totally).

"5. I will force my son to consume every essential nutrient required for growth and development in pill, powder, liquid or food form.

"6. I will say 'no' at least once every day.

"7. I will listen, even when my son is not talking to me. I will pry, eavesdrop and read his mail.

"8. I will demand absolute perfection from my son and brag to all my friends about his successes.

"9. And finally, most importantly, I will never believe that any girl that he dates, or considers marrying is good enough for my son."

There, in blood from the umbilical chord, was his little "X" and my signature. It was clear—crystal clear—that Daniel had broken his agreement. The weird hairdo and the unthinkable earring were frank violations of the law.

And sure enough, he was punished. I think he punished himself. Within a week he had come down with a serious case of mononucleosis. By the time I cared for him and brought him back to health, he had re-committed to his end of the agreement. His hair had begun to grow back, he decided to "lose" the earring, and get all future haircuts from the barber.

Although this story is true, there was no written contract. Just unrealistic expectations and demands of my children and myself. Like most single parents, I wanted my children to make it easier for me to do this "parenting" thing that I feared I simply could not do alone. Maybe there was an unwritten agreement. So far they have been wonderful children, and their "goodness" has helped to make my task do-able.

Yet, I have evolved an approach to parenting which is built on four anchors, or resources, that enable us to hold our ships, our families, in place. These Anchors are: *Self-Esteem, Support, Solvency* and *Strength*.

Anchors

Self-Esteem is placing a high value on ourselves. Support is seeking out and interacting with those who also value us and are willing to demonstrate that by helping us. Solvency translates that value into living conditions that guarantee our security and well-being. Strength enables us to maintain what we have achieved. With these four Anchors, our families—our precious families—can be held in place no matter how turbulent the waters.

My son's bout with mononucleosis provided an opportunity for us to rely heavily on our Anchors. By taking extra time to care for his physical body through diet, relaxation, nutrient supplements and various forms of therapy, we were reminded of the value and healing capacity within his own physical body. This reinforced his self-esteem and value for himself, particularly his appreciation for his body. As I took time off from work to be with him, we became more aware of the importance of emotional support in our family and of quality sharing. We realized how much support means to each family member.

I was thankful that our life was stable enough to get us through his illness. We were solvent. Extra expenses included his need for a tutor because of missed classes, and a few visits to the pediatrician. But, perhaps most important was our reminder of the strength that came with love, faith and knowing that we could handle this situation and get back to normal quickly, a little stronger, and a lot closer.

These Anchors don't make the crises and challenges disappear. They do, however, provide the resources that we need to better cope with the issues and, indeed, to prevent or minimize negative outcomes. Let's now explore each Anchor.

Self-Esteem

Self-esteem is our belief
in ourselves which grows
from our capacity to
trust. We must trust
our bodies, trust our
minds to make right
decisions, trust our
feelings and trust our
relationship with our
family, friends and the
world as a whole.

Thirteen

Frogs Into...
Frogs

On the occasion of my second divorce my attorney noticed that I, unlike many of her other clients, was clear, quick and to the point. Upon noting that each of my marriages had lasted less than two years, and that I was so "sure about ending this one," she asked me, "Gail, why did you marry these men, anyway?" I thought about it. A lot of possible answers rolled across my mental screen—because I loved them..., because I was young..., because I thought..., or because I wanted.... But the real truth, the undressed, stark-naked Judgment Day truth is that I married them because they asked me. That's it. My self-esteem was so low that I really didn't believe any man would ever ask me to marry him! I was so damn grateful that a man (a halfway decent-looking man, especially) wanted to be with me and to "marry" me. Well, of course I said yes! As women we are often programmed to allow ourselves to be (hope that we are) chosen or selected by men. Women in this state of mind end up kissing a lot of frogs, but never do get their "prince." We must improve our own sense of self-esteem, and also learn to choose, not merely wait to be selected.

Choices and Decisions

A high level of self-esteem or value for ourselves is reflected in choices and decisions that work in our own best interest. In times of low self-esteem or self-regard, we tend to make decisions and choices that are not in our best interest. We seem to be bent on compromising, punishing, even destroying ourselves. Low self-esteem has been associated with drug and alcohol abuse, suicide, depression and violent behavior.

Over the years, I have come to view self-esteem from a holistic perspective. When our value of ourselves is high, we have a trusting, loving relationship with ourselves. We know and trust our own bodies. We are aware of and trust our true feelings. We listen to and trust our minds for inner guidance; and we trust our personal, intimate relationship with God or the force for good in the world. We trust and anticipate joy and fulfillment from our relationship with life.

All of this trust and expectation of good creates an immutable sense of "we know we can." But high self-esteem is not a static condition. We cannot get a good dose of it, and simply have it forever. It is built on our relationships and through our everyday experiences. High self-esteem has to be more than a "saying," or a thought. We have to demonstrate it—make it our way of life.

Separation and Self-Esteem

How many of us have lived through the pain of heartbreak? During the depression or sadness that often follows separation and loss of a husband or mate, our self-esteem may plummet. We may not feel very capable, attractive, or even well physically. We may even be totally unaware of our true emotions—such as anger or outrage—because we hurt too deeply to feel. Suddenly it seems that even our own thoughts are not within our control. Memories and images that relate to our loss may intrude into our waking and sleeping hours. Our spiritual base may be eroded causing us to want to "give up." In such times of low self-esteem, we may focus on the negative and be less than hopeful about the present or the future. Our "whole" being or person seems depressed and experiences devastation.

I used to know I was in big trouble when a situation, like a failed romance caused such depression that I was forced to "take to my bed." Oh, I went through the minimum nine to five work day requirements, but upon returning to my home in the evenings, I would crash and burn right into my bed much like a plane with engine failure. The rejection or perceived loss would have an impact on my "whole" self—my physical energy, my feelings or emotions, my mental focus and thoughts, and on my spirit or sense of faith. During these times, my self-esteem would take a nose-dive.

Requirements for High Self-Esteem

There has been a lot of research and theory brought to light about self-esteem in the last few decades. One researcher, Stanley Coopersmith, proposed four conditions that are needed to develop and sustain high self-esteem. These are:

1. Caring and respectful treatment from others;

2. Opportunities for success;

3. Congruency or harmony between the success and our own values;

4. Skill at coping with situations that devalue us.

These pre-conditions not only build a state of high self-esteem, but help us to "repair" our value of ourselves when we are shocked by life's knock-out punches. Can you see how being honored and treated well, experiencing success that's important to you and learning to minimize the impact of negative situations would lead to higher degrees of trust, confidence and self-regard? Perhaps the best part of Coopersmith's points is that we can create these conditions ourselves.

We can learn how to demonstrate care and respect for ourselves. In trying times, I recommend starting with our physical selves. Self-care should take the form of movement or exercise, relaxation using baths, whirlpools, massage, yoga, meditation, etc., and an optimal strengthening, renewing diet. This kind of body self-care translates into success—the success of simply feeling and looking so much better immediately. The process of taking care of ourselves physically, changes our focus away from that which devalued us, to our own value. By taking concrete measures for self-care, we are creating the pre-conditions for healing and sustaining our own self-esteem. Research has also shown that exercise can be very effective as an anti-depressant.

Exercising Saved Her Life

Brenda had been a single parent for five years. One night during the workshop session on self-esteem, she asked if she could share her story about depression. She started by reminding us all that depression is a disease, and like most diseases, it progresses in stages. "The final stage of depression," she said, "is death through suicide." Brenda told us how she had reached that stage within six months of her divorce from her husband.

"I was desperate. I didn't know what to do. The problems started when I was pregnant. Mark didn't seem to want to touch me anymore. He made me feel unattractive—ugly, really. After little Mark, our son, was born, things only got worse. I stopped caring about Mark's rejection. I withdrew and concentrated on the baby. Then, an opportunity came for me to get a promotion at work if I returned within eight weeks after the baby's birth. We needed the money and I needed to get out of the house. So my neighbor kept Mark Jr. during the day and I went back to work. I felt guilty, though, about leaving my baby. I felt guilty about not desiring his father, and I felt guilty about earning more money than my husband. When I think about it, I felt guilty or sad most of the time for months. The only thing that made me smile was my coworker, Jim.

"Jim could tell something was wrong. We started having lunch together—some days, just to talk. For the first time in months, I started having sexual feelings. But not for Mark, my husband. No, I felt excited when I was around Jim. Now I was more guilty. Mark and I seemed to argue all the time. We decided to go to our pastor for help. He suggested we read the scriptures and to concentrate on the book of Matthew, specifically, the chapters that address marriage.

"By now, I was feeling horrible, ashamed, guilty, confused and a little angry. Finally I asked Mark for time apart. I just needed to be separated for awhile, to think. I couldn't tell what I felt for Jim as long as I was with Mark every day, and I couldn't feel anything for Mark anymore. We either argued all the time or just didn't talk.

"Mark shocked me. He said no to my request for a separation. In fact, he gave me an ultimatum—either we stay together or we get divorced now! Well, I had believed that he wanted out for a long time. This convinced me. I agreed, and suddenly, without knowing how or why, we were divorced and I had custody of our son. Mark immediately moved in with a woman in his law school. He shut us out—me and his son.

"It was as if we ceased to exist for him. I was so confused. I turned again to my church community and started reading the same part of the Bible—Matthew, Chapter 19, Verses 6-9: '6 What therefore God hath joined together, let no man put asunder...9 And I say unto you, whosoever shall put away his wife, except it be for fornication, and shall marry another, committeth adultery; and whoso marrieth her which is put away doth commit adultery.'

"In my youth and confusion I misinterpreted this Bible passage literally and it was a real blow to me psychologically. To me, it meant that I could never marry again, without condemning the man to sin. I saw myself as shameful and deserving of punishment. Although I never went forward with the relationship with my co-worker, Jim, I was ashamed of ever having desired him. Every time I looked at my baby I felt guilty for depriving him of his father. The pain was too much. Eventually, some part of me decided to just kill myself, or to try, anyway. I took a lot of pills the doctor had prescribed for sleeplessness. All I got was very sick, though. When I finished throwing up, something inside me said 'Go to the gym.'

"My son and I had moved to an apartment building that had a small gym. The next morning I found myself there. Jogging around the indoor track and lifting weights, I stopped being depressed, even sad, within two days. I didn't even think about being sad or guilty.

"Suddenly life was filled with possibilities for my son and I. I started thinking more clearly. I was angry with his father, but not guilty and ashamed anymore. I kept exercising for the next few months. I will always believe that exercising saved my life. It was a kind of miracle to me. You see, I had never been athletic or even physical before this. I never even participated in gym classes in school. Whatever gave me the motivation to exercise was a gift, and I'll always remember how it changed my life, almost instantly."

Over time, Brenda began to value herself again. My experience with many single parents and divorcing couples is that condemnation and associated guilt are often causes for stress, emotional pain and depression. These feelings can interfere with our capacity to respond to our children's immediate needs. It is important to break the negative cycle as quickly as possible and replace depression with energy, condemnation with support, and hopelessness with belief in one's deservedness of the good that life holds. Exercise is one excellent tool for breaking negative thought and feeling cycles. One reason that it works is the fact that it increases the oxygen supply to the brain and improves over-all body metabolism. This kind of change begins to impact our self-esteem—holistically speaking.

Fourteen

Self-Esteem is Shaped by Our Families

Our general, sustained sense of self and value for that perception is built up through our childhood years. It is shaped by our family of origin, particularly by our parents, upon whom we are initially, fully dependent. Their responses to us, from the moment of birth, (of conception, really) give us important messages about our inherent value or worth. Although we live in the mother's uterus or womb for nine months, we are not fully mature upon birth. Humans might have been better served by "pouches" like kangaroos have, that keep us warm and close to our mothers; because human babies are so helpless, unable to stand on "all fours" at birth or on our two legs like some other species.

For the first months, we require the warmth, continuous nurturance and environmental protection that we knew in our mother's womb. This quality of maternal contact and assurance is provided during the breast-feeding phase. Nature prepares us as mothers and prepares our babies to continue the "gestation" or growth process after birth in an ideally bonded way.

Breast feeding gives our babies needed physical contact—the touch—that is reassuring, comforting. It also gives them opportunities for movement that help them develop skills—sucking, breathing, digesting, sensing. Breast-fed babies have significantly fewer colds or digestive problems. They tend to thrive and grow in more healthy ways, and have greater resistance to disease throughout life. They are generally more contented, happier, and less stressed. Now, it is possible to meet our babies' needs for nurturance and nutrition by holding and caressing while bottle feeding, but breast feeding is best for both the baby and mother.

Security

Psychologists have studied human behaviors and concluded that we have some basic needs that instinctively motivate or drive us. When we perceive that these needs are not met, we are driven to have them met—consciously or unconsciously. Although opinions vary among experts, there is general agreement about our most basic or primary need. It is for a sense of security, safety and belonging. Humans are social beings. We derive our sense of self from being related. So, after our safety (freedom from physical harm) needs are met, we need the safety and security that comes from being connected, from contacting and relating with others.

Nature models this in the mother-infant relationship. Throughout all of nature, touching is a life-stimulating, motivating experience. Relatedness, connection, begins with body or physical contact. When we are held, caressed and nurtured as newborns, we begin to know or sense ourselves. This is the beginning of our self-esteem. When infants are deprived of adequate touch, their overall development can be severely delayed or impaired. Without any touch or human interaction for nurturance, the infant can die.

Self-Expression is Part of Self-Esteem

After our security needs have been met through care and appropriate cuddling or touch, we need to interact, to express ourselves. As infants, we use our body to explore the environment by crying, cooing, reaching, smiling and perceiving the world and the people around us. Often, the mother or caregiver begins to tell the crying infant to shhh, hush as soon as they start to cry. It is important to regard the cry as the child's language and to note early on how it varies. Our babies have ways of crying for food, or from discomfort, or for our attention. If we learn how to respond to particular cries, it gives our children the message that they are succeeding in their efforts to communicate with us. Their cries are just that—efforts to communicate using their most developed tools.

Another important form of self-expression is play. Play is the most important vehicle of self-expression for developing infants and children. Play is the "work" of children.

Self-Esteem and Play

Since we have defined self-esteem as our capacity to trust, it is important to emphasize the role of play in developing this capacity. In the best of situations, play is a child's way of life from birth to about eight years of age. Play activities give young children a sense of comfort and mastery of their physical body as they explore their environment. Play also generates feelings of strength as they practice appropriate skills like running, jumping, climbing and skipping. Play teaches children how to create through imagination and fantasy. It also models group dynamics and ways of relating to others. Normal personality development requires the freedom to play. Play can provide the first opportunities for our life-long motivational needs for security, self-expression and empowerment to be met.

As single parents, we are often too busy to play ourselves and may, accidentally, impose our own sense of urgency and task-orientation onto our children. Patience may be lacking. We should take time to read books on play (and on toys), and to provide ample opportunities and resources for our young children to spend most of their waking time at play. Play is the only way for childhood to work.

Empowerment

A third basic human need is to gain a sense of empowerment or control over aspects of our world—to be independent, rather than dependent, and to demonstrate our capability. Some see the initial phase of this basic need for independence/empowerment as "the terrible twos"—the phase in which young children become defiant—full of "no's." If you have an adolescent or teenager, you may see the terrible twos return. Like the return of other monsters, this phase can seem to be frightening. Both the toddler and adolescent phases are periods in which new skills and competencies are emerging. Our developing children are learning, testing, finding ways to organize and integrate their new abilities. It is our task to support them appropriately, encouraging them within safe limits, to develop higher-order thinking and planning skills. But as children struggle to assert a sense of independence and control over some aspects of their lives, they really do need our guidance and support.

I'm not suggesting that we let them have total control. But we will experience less anger and stress if we work with them to create opportunities in which they feel empowered and help them utilize their new capacities. Allow them to make some decisions. Create options. This goes a long way toward responding to their (and to our) basic need for a sense of empowerment and freedom.

When people are not empowered, they feel oppressed. Underneath the perception of oppression, there is always anger. When this anger is viewed as unjustified, and/or if we can't give ourselves permission to express it, we often turn it inward and become alienated or depressed. Empowerment is a basic human need. We will be driven to find ways to feel it—either positively or negatively. In the absence of control over some important aspects of their environment, our children may convince themselves that fighting, indiscriminate eating, acting out sexually or other risk-laden behaviors, are OK forms of assertion. If our attempts to be more empowered are frustrated during our developing years, we may form self-destructive patterns that can take a life-time of adult work to undo. It is wise to encourage our children's safe sense of responsibility and success.

Basic Human Needs and Self Esteem

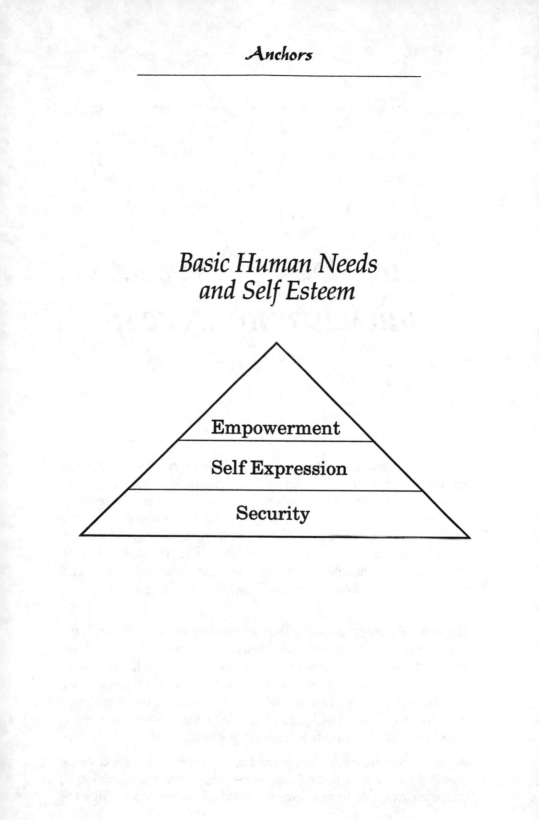

Fifteen

Low Self-Esteem and Chronic Stress

These same basic needs for security, self-expression and empow-erment drive and motivate us throughout life. Having these needs met is important to our self-esteem, and gives us a sense of competence. There are other "higher level" needs, but if these basic motivational needs go unmet, or if we think they are unmet, we will inevitably develop behaviors to address them. Young children will misbehave to get their parents' attention, and adolescents will defy rules and regulations to gain a sense of power.

These needs are so primary that when they're not met, we have some predictable feelings or "warning responses" that cause automatic body reactions in the form of stress. Feelings of fear, anxiety and insecurity arise when our security needs are unmet. Our bodies prepare to fight or flee—to protect us. If no such options exist, our bodies enable us to stand and just cope, provided the situation is not life-threatening.

When we are unable to express ourselves adequately we become bored and frustrated, and our body once again is signaled to move us away, or to energize us to take control—to change the situation. This, too, causes stress. The leading reason children give for dropping out of school is boredom.

And finally, we are naturally outraged and angry when we feel that we are denied our instinctual need to have control over ourselves, our right to be independent.

Our Feelings Help Us to Recognize Stress

The chart below relates our basic human needs to emotional or feeling messages—warnings that tell us that we're experiencing stress. The body stress reaction occurs whenever we perceive that we may lose what we value as a life's need or when our needs are not being met. As single parents, we must develop ways to reduce chronic stress states, particularly those associated with the negative emotions illustrated here. Chronic stress reduces our sense of self-confidence, trust and, ultimately, our self-esteem.

Feelings and Stress

	A	B
Need	**Feelings When Met**	**Feelings When Not Met**
Security	Joy, Comfort	Fear, Anxiety
	Happiness	Depression, Sadness
Self Expression	Fulfilled	Frustration
	Satisfied, Calm	Boredom
Empowerment	Motivated, Assured	Anger, Irritation
	In Control	Outrage, Out of Control
	High Self Esteem	Low Self-Esteem

The Stress Reaction:
A Total Body Response

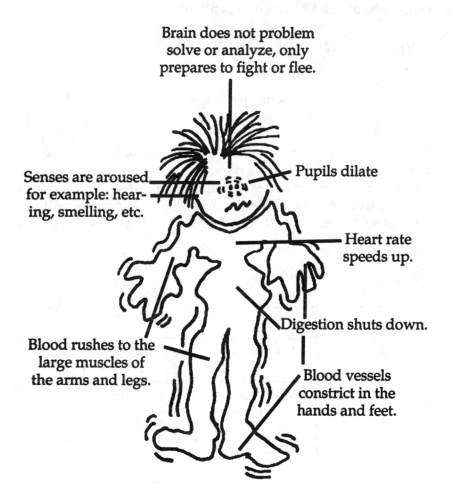

Brain does not problem solve or analyze, only prepares to fight or flee.

Senses are aroused, for example: hearing, smelling, etc.

Pupils dilate

Heart rate speeds up.

Digestion shuts down.

Blood rushes to the large muscles of the arms and legs.

Blood vessels constrict in the hands and feet.

Our body reacts to stress all over. When we're under stress, our heart rate speeds up and our body prepares to help us "fight or flee." This means that most of our blood supply leaves the digestive system and visceral organs, and travels through the extremities, to the large muscles of our arms and legs. The blood vessels in our hands and feet actually get smaller, constricting to help move blood back to our large muscles, thus preparing our arms and legs to run or fight. The body is responding physically to the perceived threat or loss.

We breathe more rapidly and more shallowly under stress. This reduces our capacity to feel or experience overwhelming sensations. This reaction is important because we actually store these feelings and perceptions at levels that lie beneath our conscious awareness. Our muscles remember our pain and trauma, even when we forget.

While our breathing is rapid and shallow, our brain shifts to a way of thinking or processing information that is almost instinct. We do not analyze and explore multiple options. No, when the house is on fire we simply react—run for the nearest door. This kind of "reactive thinking" is supported by greater sensory awareness. We hear, see, smell and experience touch or tactile sensations more in times of stress. At these times, we simply do not rely on our reasoning or higher-order thinking and problem solving.

Digestive functions literally shut down. The liver, the adrenal glands, and other organs and glands work overtime releasing needed chemicals and hormones. In fact, the stress reaction puts a lot of demands or strain on the body organs and systems. Our whole body works overtime when we're stressed!

This excess demand may well be the key to the stress/disease connection. Perhaps the most classic and well-known work in this field was done by researchers Holmes and Rahe. They created the Stress Index. It is a series of questions which relate to stressful life events. The higher your score, the more stress you've experienced within a year, the greater your risk for disease to develop. The index is included here for your own self-assessment. Also, I've included a list of stresses based on interviews with single parents, so that you can identify your own major stress factors not included on the Holmes and Rahe list.

Holmes and Rahe
The Stress of Adjusting to Change

Event	Scale of Impact	Event	Scale of Impact
Death of spouse	100	Spouse begins or stops work	26
Divorce	73	Begin or end school	26
Marital Separation	65	Change in living conditions	25
Jail Term	63	Revision of personal habits	24
Death of close family member	63	Trouble with boss	23
Personal injury or illness	53	Change in work hours or conditions	20
Marriage	50	Change in residence	20
Fired at work	47	Change in schools	20
Marital reconciliation	45	Change in recreation	19
Retirement	45	Change in church activities	19
Change in health of family member	44	Change in social activities	18
Pregnancy	40	Mortgage or loan less than $10,000	17
Sex difficulties	39	Change in sleeping habits	16
Gain of new family member	39	Change in number of family get-togethers	15
Business readjustment	39		
Change in financial state	38	Change in eating habits	15
Change to different line of work	37	Vacation	13
Change in number of arguments with spouse	35	Christmas	13
		Minor violations of the law	11
Mortgage over $10,000	31	**Total Stress Score: Col. 1**	____
Foreclosure of mortgage or loan	30	**Total Stress Score: Col. 2**	____
Change in responsibilities at work	29	**Total Stress Score:**	____
Son or daughter leaving home	29	150–Below	Normal
Trouble with in-laws	29	150–199	37% Risk
		200–299	50% Risk
Outstanding personal achievement	28	300–350	87% Risk
		350–400	90% Risk

Stresses Listed by Single Parents

___ Victim of rape or other violent crime

___ Death of child

___ Child separated from you

___ Departure of spouse or mate from city (i.e., joined service, job relocation, etc.)

___ Birth of an infant with special needs (i.e. premature, handicapped, intensive care)

___ Dual role: Sole financial support and homemaker for family

___ Spouse or mate has alcohol abuse or drug problem

___ Jail term

___ Alcohol or drug abuse problem

___ Stillbirth

___ Child arrested or prosecuted for criminal activities

___ Emotional illness or depression which requires therapy or drugs

___ Chronic use of medication

___ Hospitalization or surgery

___ Child develops behavior problems (hyperactive, poor achiever, gang participant)

___ Began or ended living with mate

___ Ended romantic relationship

___ Miscarriage

___ Accident involving personal injury

___ Victim of physical or mental abuse by husband or mate

___ Difficulty with baby-sitting child-care arrangements

___ Abortion

___ Fifteen pounds or more of excess body fat

___ Threatened or actual eviction

___ Unable to pay monthly bills

___ Change in use of alcohol, marijuana, cocaine or cigarettes

___ Installment (credit payment) over 30 to 90 days in arrears

___ Filed bankruptcy or Chapter 13

___ Use of birth control pills

___ Rent increase

___ Sued for non-payment of debts

___ Chronic allergies or skin problems

___ Chronic yeast infections

Negative Feelings Trigger the Stress Response

While we may not be able to control all of the stress factors in our lives, we can learn to control our reactions to them. Remember the emotional reactions we have when we believe that our basic needs are not met? When we are not feeling secure and loved, we react with sadness, loneliness, jealousy or hurt. These feelings will send our bodies into the stress reaction described above. The whole set of feelings listed in Column B (anger, sadness, frustration, etc.) in the chart on page 91 will trigger our body's stress reaction. If this goes on day in and day out, the body becomes exhausted. Our energy becomes depleted.

I suggest that you keep a feelings journal for one or two days. When you feel any of the emotions listed in Column B on page 91, you will see that you also feel stressed. If this was a "state" that dominated your entire day, you felt out of control. When we are out of control, we do not have a high state of self-confidence. If this becomes chronic, we begin to really doubt or distrust our capacity. Our self-esteem is lowered.

Self-Talk

Try using self-talk when you become aware of your own emotional states and the needs they are related to. For example, if you're feeling afraid, anxious, worried or sad, focus your self-talk on security. Say things that remind you of your well-being and protection. I have often used the 23rd Psalm or the Lord's Prayer from the Bible. I have also reflected back on miraculous moments when I have been helped or protected.

Or I may tell myself quietly, "Gail, you can handle this, you've come this far..." Self-talk is an old technique. Sometimes, if you're not alone and you're afraid people will think it's weird for you to converse with yourself, try writing a note to yourself or reading an inspirational passage. I suggest you always keep motivational, inspirational literature with you—Bible readings, quotes, The Daily Word, Unity poems, etc.

Sample Feeling Journal

	Feeling	Time	Situation	Need
Morning				
Afternoon				
Evening				
Example: Morning	Anxiety	8:00 a.m.	Car won't start	Security

If the emotion is frustration, or if you feel the need to just express things that need to be said, physical activity such as running, walking, or stretching is often helpful. You can also try writing letters that you don't intend to mail. (Don't forget to tear them up, however.) Or try placing the imaginary person in a chair and talking to them, honestly expressing yourself. All too often, we try to address boredom and/or frustration with compulsive behaviors like eating, spending, etc. Creating something—writing, dancing or singing—are better ways to self-express and reduce stress. True self-expression also enhances our value of ourselves—our self-esteem.

Finally, the emotions that are related to anger and irritation relate to the need to feel empowered, to take charge or to gain more of a sense of control in our lives. This can be achieved by changing a pattern of behavior—doing something different. Often just expressing feelings honestly and stating our needs or perceptions can give us more of a sense of control. As women, we often need to give ourselves permission to act on our anger, not to turn it inward and become depressed. Depression is anger turned inward.

There are so many ways to express anger that do not inflict violence upon ourselves or others. Screaming, crying, talking, writing, beating up pillows—all these methods can work. Expressing irritations and expectations, and establishing boundaries are good control techniques. For example, let people around you know that you find their behavior or actions unacceptable and will not tolerate that kind of treatment.

Prevention is also good. By recognizing our own as well as our children's intrinsic need for a sense of empowerment, we can learn to manage communications in ways that respond to that need. For example, if I tell my son to "shut up," he will feel angry, disrespected and unable to express himself. He will respond with anger. If, on the other hand, I allow him his self-expression and sense of dignity, I can reduce the potential for his stress reaction and mine to occur, while I model good communication styles for him. I can set limits for him without disrespecting him as a person.

The earring incident was a good example. He was expressing himself. I gave him choices—some measure of control. (He could either remove it by 5:00 that afternoon or by 10:00 the next morning.) But seriously, when I involve my children in planning and in decision-making, it helps their self-esteem. Caution: It hurts their self-confidence when we impose adult responsibilities and concerns on children. Children should not be facing life's security issues like housing, food, rent or violence. This exposes them to too much to bear. It is abusive.

Respecting and honoring family members' needs for a sense of security (safety, love and belonging), self-expression (activity, identity and communication), and empowerment (self-control and freedom) will go a long way toward reducing family stress reactions and improving our own and our children's sense of personal competence and self-esteem.

Stress Response Syndrome

Ironically, before actual stress-related diseases like high blood pressure, stroke or cancer develop, the body will show signs of the Stress Response Syndrome (SRS). Its symptoms will tell us that we are subjecting ourselves to too much stress.

The indicators are primarily behaviors. Symptoms like restlessness, fatigue, anxiety or confusion. Notice how many stress response syndrome symptoms are part of your life right now.

Symptoms of the Stress Response Syndrome

1. Restlessness
2. Irritability
3. Poor Concentration
4. Insomnia
5. Fatigue
6. Exaggerated Startle Response
7. Feelings of Tension
8. Anxiety
9. Depression
10. Personality Changes
11. Tremors
12. Confusion
13. Alcoholism (Drug Dependence)
14. Loss of Appetite
15. Nightmares
16. Preoccupation with Stressor
17. Digestive Complaints
18. Irrational Fears
19. Suspiciousness
20. Memory Loss

Now reflect. Did you score high or low on the Holmes & Rahe Stress Index on page 94? Did you list a lot of other personal stressors on the second list?

What about your usual emotions or feelings? Look at the Feelings and Stress chart on page 91 again. Could you say you operate from Column A or Column B most of the time? Now look again at the symptoms of the Stress Response Syndrome.

If you found a lot of symptoms on the SRS chart, you probably related to Column B, more than to Column A. You need support to help change the thoughts and reactions that are triggering negative feelings, all of which cause stress, thereby creating the stress response syndrome.

Some Ideas for Changing Thoughts and Attitudes

1. Increase your physical activity through walking or exercise.

2. Study inspirational material. Listen to motivational tapes, read books such as the Daily Word or your scripture or affirmations each day. Or read autobiographies of successful people.

3. Attend church or religious services of your choice if this makes you feel more loved and supported.

4. Join self-help support groups or form one.

5. Get massage or other body therapy like rolfing or reflexology. Take daily bubble baths or use whirlpools for relaxation.

6. Take a break—a day off for fun or play. Reach out to friends and let them love you.

7. Make a list of all the good things in your life—particularly your successes.

8. Imagine that you suddenly learned that you have seven days to stay on the planet. What would you focus on? What's really important?

9. Write affirmations concerning your desires, such as: "I now allow myself to have..."

10. Stop watching soap operas, movies or television shows that generate stress reactions. Don't listen to love songs on the radio if they make you think about your loss.

Begin by trying the ideas listed. You may also want to seek professional support through individual or group counseling. Don't let chronic feelings of worry, anxiety, resentment, boredom or frustration drain your energy and increase your risk for stress-related illness. You deserve better.

Sixteen

The Nutrition Connection

Our physical energy comes from the foods that we eat. We need to supply our bodies with energy to help them cope with these excessive demands for adaptation. Our bodies convert nature's foods into chemicals that we can use to create cellular energy for our body tissues, organs and systems that perform life-sustaining functions.

But converting food into chemicals for energy is a complex process. Ironically, it is a process that is impaired in times of stress. At the moment when we need more energy, our body turns its focus away from digestion. It relies on our energy reserves, which under ideal circumstances, have been stored within the liver. Perhaps this conflict of energy needs going up, while digestive function goes down, is the reason so many SRS symptoms are also symptoms of nutritional deficiencies.

A closer look at how our bodies actually produce energy within cells shows an even closer relationship. Certain key nutrients found in whole foods, are vital to our bodies' capacity to produce energy in the form used by cells—ATP. The next charts show this relationship.

Associated Nutrient Imbalance Chart

Stress Response Syndrome Symptom	Vitamin	Mineral
1. Restlessness	B₁₂	Magnesium
2. Irritability	B₁ (Thiamine)	Magnesium Calcium
3. Poor Concentration	B₁ (Thiamine) B₁₂	Iron Calcium Magnesium
4. Insomnia	B₃ (Niacinamide) Pantothenic Acid	Magnesium Calcium
5. Anxiety	B₁ (Thiamine) B₃ (Niacinamide) Ascorbic Acid (Vitamin C)	Magnesium Calcium

Associated Nutrient Imbalance Chart

Stress Response Syndrome Symptom	Vitamin	Mineral
6. Fatigue	Pantothenic Acid B_1 (Thiamine)	Magnesium Zinc Sulfur Iron Manganese
7. Startle Reactions	B_1 (Thiamine) B_3 (Niacinamide)	Magnesium Calcium
8. Tension	B_1 (Thiamine) B_{12}	Magnesium Calcium
9. Depression	B_1 (Thiamine) B_3 (Niacinamide) Pantothenic Acid B_6 (Pyridoxine)	Magnesium Calcium Iron
10. Personality Changes	B_1 (Thiamine) B_{12} Pantothenic Acid	Magnesium Calcium Lithium
11. Tremors	B_2 (Riboflavin)	Magnesium
12. Confusion	B_1 (Thiamine) B_{12}	Magnesium Calcium Iron

Associated Nutrient Imbalance Chart

Stress Response Syndrome Symptom	Vitamin	Mineral
13. Alcoholism	—	—
14. Preoccupation w/stressor event	—	—
15. Loss of Appetite	B_1 (Thiamine) Pantothenic Acid	Potassium Zinc
16. Nightmares	—	—
17. Digestive Complaints	B_1 (Thiamine) B_3 (Niacinamide) Panotothenic Acid Folic Acid B_{12}	Potassium Zinc
18. Phobias	B_1 (Thiamine) B_3 (Niacinamide)	
19. Suspiciousness	B_1 (Thiamine) B_3 (Niacinamide) B_{12}	
20. Memory Loss	B_{12} Folic Acid	

The bottom line is this. In times of stress, we need excellent nutrition, adequate calories and nutrients. We need to consume foods that are low in fat, low in salt, low in refined sugars and high in protein, vitamins and key minerals. A list of needed foods is included here. I have also included the nine dietary guidelines from the National Food and Nutrition Board. As we demonstrate greater self-care through better food choices, we are actually improving our energy levels and our self-esteem.

Magnesium Matters

Many of the indicators of chronic stress are also symptoms of poor or inadequate nutrition. Magnesium is one example of an essential mineral nutrient. It is used by our cells to produce energy in the form of ATP (Adenosine Triphosphate). If we do not consume foods that provide needed magnesium, we will exhibit symptoms like mild hand tremors, behavioral changes and in rare extreme cases, convulsions. The recommended daily allowance for magnesium is between 300-350 milligrams. Do you know what foods supply magnesium? Or what drugs interfere with its digestion, absorption and bio-availability?

Whole grains, particularly whole wheat products, are a source of dietary magnesium. White bread and white flour can also contain magnesium, however the refinement of wheat and other cereal products reduces their vitamin and mineral content dramatically. For instance, over 60 percent of the magnesium, phosphorous, iron and calcium are removed from wheat during the production of white flour.

The major source of magnesium in the daily diet is green, leafy vegetables, where magnesium is part of the chlorophyll molecule. Milk products are a reasonable source of magnesium, but for many adults few milk products are consumed regularly.

In addition to its vital role in cellular energy metabolism, magnesium deficiencies have been associated with elevated blood fats and increased risk of heart disease. A study published by Dr. Carl Johnson revealed that subjects who died suddenly from heart attack had significantly lower levels of heart tissue magnesium and potassium than did control subjects who died of other causes.

Choose from These Recommended Foods

Low Fat Protein Sources Meat and Meat Substitutes	Vegetables	Fruits	Grains and Breads	Fats and Oils	Liquids	Others
Fish	Greens (Kale, Turnips, Mustard)	Citrus Fruits (Orange, Grapefruit)	Brown Rice, Rice Cakes	Butter	Water	Low Sugar/Low Fat Desserts and Snacks
Poultry	Broccoli	Cantaloupe	Whole Grain Pasta	Vegetable Oil	Fruit and Vegetable Juices	Low Fat Ice Cream/Ices
Low Fat Cuts of Red Meat	Spinach	Strawberries	Dry, Unsweetened Cereals (Granola, Shredded Wheat, Total)	Salad Dressings	Other Caffeine-free Beverages	Whole Grain Cookies/Pastries
Yogurt	Carrots	Mango	Whole Grain Bread	Nuts		Whole Grain Cakes
Cheese	Squash	Papaya	Whole Grain Crackers	Avocados		Whole Grain Pies
Tofu	Corn	Guava	Whole Grain Muffins	Margarines		
Dried Beans, Peas	Potatoes (White or Sweet)	Kiwi	Bagels			
Nuts and Nut Butters	Cauliflower	Banana				
Milk (Low fat or skim)	Okra	Grapes				
	Tomatoes	Peaches				
		Apples				
		Apricots				
		Pears				

If your diet is low in green leafy vegetable and milk products, and high in pastries, breads and pastas made from refined white flour products, you are at a high risk for a dietary magnesium deficiency. So what? If your life is stress-free you may not need to be overly concerned. But if you have a moderate to high stress state, and are experiencing symptoms of chronic fatigue, depression, poor concentration and others listed as indicators of chronic stress, you may be making matters worse—exacerbating already energy draining circumstances by choosing to eat inappropriate foods. A simple commitment to consuming more green leafy vegetables and to replacing white flour products with whole-grain breads, pastas and cereals, could make you feel better—fast. It's just an added bonus that your risk for heart attack may be reduced at the same time.

These dietary guidelines are recommended by the scientists of the Committee on Diet and Health of the Food and Nutrition Board.

1. Reduce total fat to less than 30 percent of total calories, saturated fat to less than 10 percent and cholesterol intake to less than 300 milligrams.

2. Eat five or more servings of a combination of vegetables and fruits, especially green and yellow vegetables. Eat six or more servings of a combination of breads, cereals and legumes to increase complex carbohydrates and starches. (Although the Nutrition Board does not specify whole grains, I highly recommend whole grain products—whole wheat, brown rice, etc.)

3. Eat a reasonable amount of protein, maintaining protein intake at moderate levels.

4. Balance the amount of food you eat with the amount of exercise you get to maintain appropriate body weight.

5. It is not recommended that you drink alcohol. If you do drink, limit yourself to no more than two cans of beer, two small glasses of wine or two average cocktails. Pregnant women should not drink alcohol.

6. Limit your amount of sodium to slightly more than one teaspoon or less. Limit salt use in cooking. Avoid adding it at the table.

7. Maintain adequate calcium intake.

8. Avoid dietary supplements in excess of United States Recommended Dietary Allowances (U.S. RDAs).

9. Maintain an optimum level of fluoride in your diet, particularly in the diets of your children while baby and adult teeth are forming. (Drinking fluoridated water with meals meets this need. To find out whether your water is fluoridated, contact the water authority in your area.)

Some urban and suburban water supplies have unsafe lead levels. Parents may choose to use bottled water instead, particularly for children who are most vulnerable to lead burdens. Check with your pediatrician concerning fluoride needs and drinking water safety.

Since 1975, I have used computerized dietary assessments, physical examinations and related laboratory tests to evaluate the diets and nutritional health status of thousands of individuals. More than 80 percent of the clients in our database have had unbalanced diets that did not provide the Recommended Dietary Allowances for nutrients. Chronic illness, stress and any form of drug or alcohol use can also impact our need for nutrients. As single parents, we cannot just assume that our nutrient needs are being met through everyday diet choices. Care must be taken to select foods wisely and to select appropriate supplements that provide missing nutrients if they are indicated due to illness, stress or dietary abuses.

Seventeen

The Spell

My state of low self-esteem that led me into inappropriate relationships and marriages can be traced to many contributing factors, as can the bases of all of our self-esteem packages. But, let me describe a pretty basic source—the Spell.

You see, as a girl and as a young woman, I believed I was ugly. Plain old ugly. Oh, I could use a euphemism, and say something less offensive, like unattractive (that was true too—I didn't think I could attract anything, except mosquitos). But the real deal is that when I looked in the mirror, ugly looked back. I didn't have to look in the mirror for proof of my plight, I just needed to look down. My rusty, knocked knees were ugly; my skinny, chicken legs were ugly; my came-too-late breasts were ugly. My dark brown (darker-than-my-mother's) skin was ugly. My funny-looking crossed eyes were more than ugly, they were a horrible mistake. And the ultimate measure of a woman's beauty, my hair, now that was truly ugly. Or to use a Cleveland colloquialism of the time, I was U-gly (yoo-gly)—pure U-gly. My saving features were my hands, which were long and graceful, and my smile—I always had a pretty smile.

Persons of African American and Native American mixed with European American lineage often live under a spell that was cast about two hundred years ago. The spell condemned descendants of the survivors of the genocidal atrocities of enslavement and conquest to see distorted images of ourselves. We, our parents, and, until the spell is broken, our children, look in the mirrors of the world—television, magazines, books and other's eyes—but usually do not see flattering images of ourselves and our cultures. The images our brains receive, record and re-create are foreign to our own programmed sensibilities and may engender feelings of alienation. We often dislike ourselves. For instance, since 99 percent of hair products are marketed to persons with European textured, straight hair, the message is given to persons with African American curly hair is that it is not suitable, or that it should not exist. This type of devaluation may go on until we break the spell and learn to appreciate the beauty of our difference.

It is not only minorities that are imprisoned by the media beauty projections, however. Anyone who does not fit the media "models" image can develop deep feelings of self-doubt and low self-esteem.

Beliefs

Our physical packaging is not the key issue. What matters is what we believe about how we look, and whether we believe our looks make a difference in terms of our life's options. The feelings that our thoughts or beliefs create will determine our actions. The ugly image I had was reinforced by those around me. When I finally was rescued (like so many African American women) from the ugly hair syndrome by the "natural" or "Afro" hair styles of the sixties, one of my aunts reminded me that "hair alone does not a beauty make." I was visiting her during the spring break of my freshman year of college. She, like many older African American women, had spent her entire lifetime over-straightening (killing) her hair, trying to make it look more like the hair of European or "white" females. To her, the idea of letting the public see the natural texture, bounce, curl and form of African American hair was not only unthinkable, it was a sign of "moral depravity." So, she convinced me to let her straighten my hair.

As she stepped back and looked at my pressed-flat hair, she said in amazement, "Now that's so much better. Child, with some work and with your hair straight, you might just be 'almost pretty'." My mind registered the "might" and the "almost" and added this humiliation to the long list of reasons that I had for believing that when they passed the beauty plate around, I must not have been at the table.

My second husband's grandmother said it best. When he took me to meet her and told her we were getting married, she said, "But son, she's so different from the other girls you've dated. She's, well, she's so homely."

Halloween

When my daughter was born twelve years ago, I made her two promises. One, she would taste life's sweetness and two, she would have a high level of self-esteem. It's funny, but children can be some of our best teachers.

As a young girl, I carried out my ugly drama even at Halloween. Every year for five consecutive years, I dressed up as the ugliest witch possible. It seemed quite natural. Well, when my little girl was five years old, she came home from school and said, "Mommy, I don't know what to be for Halloween!" I said, "I have an idea! Why don't you dress up as a witch—a scary-looking witch?" She looked at me in a puzzled way and quickly responded, "Mommy, that's silly. Why would I want to make myself look ugly? I want to be something pretty, like a princess."

In my family of origin, our looks or physical packaging was one of the most important criteria for acceptance or rejection. We were a very visually oriented group as the United States is a very visually oriented society. Often, the first statement and the last statement to, or about a female centers around her "looks." We suffer from what one author calls "lookism." In our family, a woman either looked good or bad. Also, a woman's value was tied to how marry-able she was. My value, or self-worth depended on whether I was married or not, and that depended on how I looked. Feelings of rejection, sadness and alienation easily accompanied my perception of myself as unattractive and my status as a single woman.

Obesity and Low Self-Esteem

By the time I was twenty-one, these negative perceptions had generated feelings and images as well as eating and health (or "unhealth") habits that led to obesity. By age twenty-two, I weighed over 200 pounds. Somehow I had given my body instructions to protect me, to build a barrier—a wall—between my vulnerable self and the world. My body had responded to my heart-felt desires and fears and to my behaviors. It had insulated the real me inside layers of fat. I never exercised and I found my greatest comfort in butter pecan ice-cream.

The holistic journey away from that place of low self-esteem inside that oversized body was a long journey. It began with awareness—a deep understanding of the wonder and inherent perfection of my own body. This awareness led to a closer loving relationship with my body, which generated trust and finally expectations, actual images of the body I desired, wanted and would love. Those images eventually became my reality.

My journey from low, very low self-esteem to a point of higher self-regard took years. In fact, it is still in progress. It began with forming a new relationship with my physical self. As I became aware, truly knowledgeable about the wonder, beauty and genius of the cells within the human body, I was motivated from within to care for it and to value it. In so doing, I learned to truly value me. The requirements for high self-esteem (found on page 81) that Coopersmith's research revealed begin with care, respect and the right treatment of our bodies. Success begins with successful management of our energy levels, or state of health and physical well-being. The harmony begins with the comfort and exhilaration that comes with the success of vitality and high energy levels. Finally, our skill in coping with situations that devalue us begins with unlearning the wrong messages that our bodies internalize. The need to fear, to retreat, to armor and to protect ourselves causes excessive nerve and hormonal responses, which in turn cause a symphony of related bodily reactions. Indeed, self-esteem and its antecedents begin with our care and treatment of our own and our children's physical bodies. Our thoughts, feelings and spirit are mirrored in our bodies. Have you ever really felt terrible and looked wonderful?

We All Need to Know

In the last twenty years, I've spent a good part of my adult life sharing these insights and teaching about the miracle of our physical bodies to everyday people through a course I created called "The Body Owner's Workshop"™. Knowledge and a genuine understanding of our greatest resource, our bodies, should not continue to be confined to a few trained professionals.

Every person ought to know how their body works, and how to help it work in health. Cellular metabolism, body systems, immune response and adaptation processes must be understandable to everyone. Compare the body to a car or automobile. Cars are necessities—the vehicles that carry us where we want to go. Well, our bodies are necessities. They are the true vehicles that must carry us around this earth—our arms, legs, feet, knees, etc., are basic, needed equipment.

Our appreciation of cars compels us to invest money and time in their maintenance. We rust-proof them and tune them up in order to keep them looking good and running. Unlike cars, however, there is no trade-in option on our bodies. So their life-long care and maintenance becomes even more crucial.

Using this comparison, I've helped thousands of people learn the technology and disciplines of self-care. The course is outlined here.

The Body Owner's Workshop™

Parts & Service I Students learn exactly how and why the body works in health—its structure and function as it does what it does.

Parts & Service II What the body needs to function. Its specific lubrication and fuel (food) requirements.

Trouble Shooting How to recognize potential areas of trouble before they surface. Find out where diseases like hypertension, cancer, diabetes, impotency and arthritis begin.

Fat Proofing Excess fat to your body, like rust to your car, shortens its life span. Learn to correct and to prevent it.

Understanding Your Warranty Learn to recognize your God-given defenses against disease and degeneration. Learn how to optimize them.

Tune-up Each student learns to assess his or her own vehicle (body) and is instructed in a program for optimum self-care and health.

The Magic

When we focus on the amazing activities that are always taking place within our bodies, we have to acknowledge that there is an intelligence that orders and orchestrates the processes. In fact, it is upon the exit of this intelligence, this enlivening force or spirit, that death ensues and all movement, rhythm, and activity terminates. Most approaches to understanding our bodies begin with what the body is. The goal has been to identify body parts and their function. However, this analytical approach is inadequate. It causes us to miss the body's magic. It is far more awe inspiring, more exciting and humbling to focus on what our bodies do continuously.

The Body Owner's Workshop™ is designed to shift our focus away from parts and their associated pathologies to the whole with its unique harmonies and balance. In the Body Owner's Workshop, we focus on the living us. I've adapted parts of the course for this book because single parents need to know this. It is important to our own and our children's self-esteem.

Eighteen

Breathing: A Matter of Life and Death

Let's consider the basic function of breathing—inhaling and exhaling. It's a matter of life and death, you know. When we are feeling really good about ourselves, we are willing to take life in—to breathe deeply and fully. An important muscle involved in this process is called the diaphragm. The muscle provides the roof of our abdominal cavity and the floor of our chest cavity. The diaphragm's movement controls the flow of air when we breathe in and out. While most of us pay no attention to how we breathe, some of us have been taught to do "diaphragmatic breathing" by expanding our large stomach muscles, or pushing the stomach out as we inhale. This process reflects our general ignorance about how our body works as a whole. In truth, most of the surface of the diaphragm muscle is really in the back half of the body. True, healthful breathing that allows full expansion of the diaphragm, is related to expansion of the muscles in our sides and back. These muscles will effect circulation through the pelvis and down into our legs. In fact, the largest vein involved in blood return to the right side of our heart, the inferior vena cava, is lengthened and shortened with each breath or action of our diaphragm muscle. If our breath is shallow or the action of the diaphragm is restricted (due to poor posture, disease, habitual slouching, shallow breathing or weak muscles), our over-all circulation loses one of its most valuable aids. This contributes to the congestion of our abdominal and pelvic organs (stomach, pancreas, uterus, ovaries, etc.), as well as to back pressure in the legs as seen in varicose veins.

Congestion

This congestion increases the risk for disease to develop. Nature's most important protection and healing system is circulation, or constant movement—a literal bathing of our tissues with body fluids. A continuous blood supply delivers needed nutrients, and eliminates the waste products of cellular work. Congestion in our chest or abdominal area that develops due to inadequate diaphragm movement, habitual poor posture or misalignment slows down or impedes healthful circulation. Poor action of the diaphragm muscle can cause chronic irritation in both our abdominal and pelvic areas. This kind of chronic irritation may cause us to have digestive problems, constipation, gas, chronic inflammation or chronic pain that arises from inflammation, as in painful menstrual periods. The health of the organs in all body cavities is influenced by their position. Their position is influenced by muscle tone. This includes internal muscles, like the diaphragm, as well as external muscles. I have often recommended that clients begin to reverse their body sag, which comes from poor breathing and related poor posture, by lying head lowered and feet up on a slant board for five to ten minutes daily. If you don't have a slant board, simply prop your ironing board on a couch.

This is just one illustration of how we can learn to change our habits and focus, and as a result, change our perception about our bodies. Instead of continuing to take our posture and our breathing for granted, let's stop for a moment and visualize the diaphragm expanding to fill the rib-cage, and then let the muscles of our backs move as we inhale. Lets imagine the backs of our rib cages gently expanding, and the blood and energy flow passing down the muscles of our low backs, hips, thighs, calves, knees and ankles; all the way to the soles of our feet and into our toes.

Imagine the increase in venous blood return through our abdominal cavities to our hearts and then feel the subsequent improved circulation throughout our bodies. This kind of focus on the body's health and life-giving functions will go far to promote our well-being, and yes, to prevent disease.

Head to Toe Breathing

Most of us think of it as a local function involving only the mouth, nose, and chest. We fail to realize that breathing is a total body experience. In it we can observe the wholeness and splendor of our body. As parents, we need to understand how the body works in optimal health and wellness so we can make choices and decisions right from the start that enhance our children's probabilities for well-being. With a little education, we can learn to assist their movement and development patterns so as to enhance circulation and improve muscle tone, thereby assisting their natural motor development. Simply by using your fingernail to lightly, gently trace a series of precise straight lines on the infant's stomach, around the navel, you can stimulate a child to tighten and improve abdominal muscle tone. When changing the child's diaper, gently pressing the knees to the tummy encourages deeper breathing in and out. *The Baby Exercise Book* by Dr. Janine Levy is an excellent resource for instructions (with photographs) on exercises or movements for your young baby. Two important benefits in doing these activities with your baby are that first, you increase the quality and the level of interaction which is important for your children's healthy development; and secondly, you develop a deeper awareness and understanding about the uniqueness and subtleties of your children's bodies.

Life Begins with Breathing

By learning to appreciate the intelligence that governs the life-sustaining functions within our bodies, we can learn how to enhance the quality of health that we experience. We looked at the breathing process as a total body experience for the adult, but let's revisit its primary role in the earliest phase—in the birth process. The physical life of the body begins with respiration or breathing. It ends when respiration ceases. But what's fascinating is that the process of birth and separation from the mother's womb is a literal symphony of movements and sensations related to oxygen levels and breathing.

Our Newborn's Circulation

Let's imagine that we're in our mother's womb. When the rapid rate of our brain growth and size of our skull reach the maximum size that her birth canal can accommodate, it's time to be born and her labor begins. A message is sent to our mother's body that leads to lower oxygen levels within her womb around us. Without oxygen, we decide to split—to get out of there. This biochemical change causes the respiratory center in our brain to initiate independent breathing. Up to this point, there has been a little hole (or foramen ovale) in the wall (septum) between the two parts (atria) of our heart which permitted blood to pass directly from the right to left side. This hole or space now closes. Blood will now be carried by our pulmonary arteries to our lungs to be aerated and returned to our heart for general circulation. This move from dependence on our mother's respiration to independent breathing and blood circulation is the first indication of the intelligence that will, throughout our lifetime, orchestrate the processes by which we take in the basic raw materials—oxygen, water and life-giving, energy-yielding nutrients—utilize them, and then eliminate waste products. This is the beginning of our independent relationship with our environment.

Touch

The uterine contractions that propel us through the birth canal and into the world, provide gentle, rhythmic stimulation—a literal massage, or touching for our skin that plays a key role in stimulating and sustaining our impulse to breathe on our own. This impulse triggers several other responses involving the muscles of our chest, abdomen, heart, lungs and respiratory tract. The contraction of our mother's uterus also stimulates nerve messages that are carried to our central nervous system which then sends messages to the nerves in our other body organs. If, for some reason (cesarian section, premature delivery) our skin is not "touched," stimulated by our mother's uterine contractions during labor, then our related nervous systems are not adequately stimulated and our peripheral organs are not appropriately activated. It may be more difficult for us to breathe and respond to our new environment.

Both of these discussions of our bodies' breathing processes—as adults and newborns—point to the central function of breathing—transmitting energy (nerve impulses) and stimulating proper circulation to protect our body organs. Yet this fact, the importance of proper breathing, is one that is usually relegated to a low level of importance. How often do you listen to or observe your own breathing patterns? How many times has a doctor discussed breathing and posture with you? Do you usually relate breathing to self-esteem?

During childbirth, the natural labor and delivery experiences provide our first tactile or touch stimulation and impact subsequent respiration and development. Most adults pay little attention to breathing, unless they are athletes or vocal performers, or when disease develops. Few realize that a habitual posture that causes our shoulders and subsequently our rib cages to droop, can inhibit diaphragm muscle activity, which affects all muscles involved in optimal breathing and circulation. Remember, it was the rise in CO_2 levels that stimulated the labor process. Throughout our lives, changes in the body oxygen and carbon dioxide levels will activate or depress the muscular movement of the heart and intestines, as well as pulsations of the brain. While the natural rate of breathing is automatic, we can engage in conscious activities to affect our rate of respiration, such as deep breathing activities or aerobic exercise. When cellular oxygen levels increase, the body sensation level goes up. When CO_2 levels increase due to rapid, shallow breathing, sensation is inhibited.

Feelings and Breathing

Emotion has a strong impact on respiration, too. In times of terror, fear, alarm or rage, the brain sends messages to the muscles involved in breathing to slow down or suppress their movements. This inhibits sensations that may seem overwhelming. States of chronic stress create shallow breathing patterns and poor circulation to body tissues—hands, feet, etc. We may, as part of our denial and suppression of painful feelings, develop patterns of controlling ourselves, our muscles (internal and external) that will suppress breathing and sensation. This response pattern can over-activate the sympathetic nervous system causing stress, and reducing our energy and immune functions in ways that generate chronic fatigue and increased susceptibility to illness.

In many ways, self control is control of breathing. Oxygenation, through appropriate intake of air and release of CO_2 is the key to healthy life in our bodies. But this process involves the brain (and thought), the heart and feelings, as well as the body and spirit. It involves our whole selves.

A clear sign of chronic stress and even low self-esteem is poor posture, accompanied by shallow breathing. Given the ongoing stress of single parenting and the issues we face, correct breathing is a key factor in sustaining our vitality. This will help move us toward a deeper presence in our bodies and sense of mastery and comfort with our world. As parents we need to model good breathing and posture patterns and become sensitive to these basic indicators about our children's stress levels. Some forms of yoga can be used to improve posture and breathing patterns. Even in times of sadness, loss, depression and low self-esteem, activities that improve breathing will improve our energy levels and our capacities to think and to respond to life. Walking, running and swimming are examples.

Relaxation

Because stress, or the demand for adaptation and energy are so central in the lives of single parents, it is important to learn how to cope or respond to it effectively. One such coping strategy was introduced by Dr. Herbert Benson in his book, *The Relaxation Response*. Benson reminds us that western society is oriented toward stress or the fight or flight response. It is an automatic response, brought forth repeatedly in reaction to daily situations. The opposite response—also a bodily reaction—can only be brought forth if time is set aside and a conscious effort is made to do so. When we are in the state known as the relaxation versus the stress response, our breathing improves, our heart rate decreases, brain activity changes, blood pressure (if elevated) decreases, and muscular tension usually decreases. In short, the body is not working as hard or as fast to fight or protect us from perceived harm or threat. It is free to do other things—repair, heal, regenerate, digest, eliminate or create.

This state of relaxation can be achieved "at will" through various self-help methods or techniques. Progressive relaxation, autogenic training, self-hypnosis, transcendental meditation and some forms of visualization can all be used by individuals as self-help methods to move the body out of the stress and into the relaxation response. Check with your local hospitals, health maintenance organizations, wellness and/or stress management centers for information on learning these techniques.

Nineteen

Winners

We are the only Anchor our children have. Their lives depend on the quality of our lives. Our fitness and wellness levels determine that quality to a great degree. We have to overcome the odds that as a single-parent family we will be poor, that our children will not succeed in school, that our mental health will be compromised and that our susceptibility to illness will be greater. To succeed against such odds, we have to become highly developed, well-integrated individuals.

Along with self-esteem, we have to develop high levels of self-discipline, energy and stamina. I believe this requires that we understand and approach life with the competence of a winner—like an athlete or competing professional. We need to take charge of our bodies, energy and stress levels. We also need to be able to focus our thoughts and mental images, so as not to waste a lot of emotional energy on worry, anger or on suppressing negative feelings. We also need to develop an expectation from life that is based on positive outcomes. It is important to believe that we can have what we want—that our desires will be fulfilled. This all translates into learning to live holistically, and into creating and producing strategies that help us care for ourselves physically, mentally, emotionally and spiritually. This often means unlearning many things we learned about ourselves, about health and wellness from our families and the world while growing up.

How we are is, I believe, how we parent. Our young children view our behavior as their model for living. A holistic, wellness-centered approach to parenting grows out of a parallel approach to living.

Listen to Our Bodies

We have to learn to listen to the subtle messages that our bodies give us, which tell us that we need to give them more attention. When I say subtle messages, I'm talking about things like swelling in our hands and feet, headaches, frequent colds and/or dry skin. Now these are not serious diseases. They're simple discomforts and signs, often of our unmet nutritional needs. But if we simply take water pills or pain pills when we get these messages, it's like turning off a fire alarm.

The body tries to get our attention and tell us when things are out of balance. The first step in working toward optimum fitness and wellness is to set a standard for ourselves that says, "I accept feeling good. I accept feeling good all the time." Now, that means not being chronically fatigued, or waking up tired. It means having good digestion. For a while, my kids took turns on what they called "the bean patrol." They simply wouldn't allow me to eat beans. It was for their own comfort, not mine. Seriously, taking care of ourselves—demonstrating high levels of self-esteem—may mean not accepting something as simple as chronic poor digestion that manifests in the form of gas and bloat.

Digestion

Digestive disturbances are the leading cause of hospitalization in America today. They are not due to an antacid deficiency, however. Like breathing, normal, healthy digestive function is another illustration of our bodies' miraculous capacity to do amazing things. The process of converting food to usable chemicals is a complex, enzyme dependent process. Specific enzymes are responsible for converting specific types of foods. Protein, sugars, starches, each have their own enzymes. Milk products, for example, require a specific enzyme—lactase—to break down milk sugar, lactose. Many adults, particularly African Americans, do not have this enzyme in their digestive juices. So consuming milk or dairy products causes them problems. Many African American infants cannot tolerate infant formulas made from cow's milk. They, too, develop digestive problems. We sometimes call it colic. They may also develop allergies, diarrhea, constipation or chronic upper respiratory congestion, leading to colds and ear infections. There are many alternative formulas for infants that are made from noncow's milk sources, like soy products.

Adult symptoms of milk intolerance include gas bloat, loose stools, stomach pain or heartburn. Sometimes, people with milk intolerance also have a low tolerance to wheat products as well. Eating high-fat fried foods, or eating in a hurry, and of course eating when stressed, can all lead to impaired digestion and chronic discomfort.

The chronic stress reaction has a negative impact on digestive health. Enzyme secretion and production are altered during the body's stress reaction. Digestion is not considered to be an essential or life-saving function during the fight or flight response. As a result, the normal wisdom of the body diverts blood supply and physiological activity away from the stomach to other body parts.

If your body is showing signs of impaired digestive function, signs like chronic gas, bloat or heartburn, pay attention. Change your eating habits—both diet and style. When you are paying quality attention to your body's messages, you will not respond to digestive problems by simply suppressing your symptoms with over-the-counter medications. You should make sure your diet is providing quality foods and/or supplemental enzymes if needed. Lactase aids can be added to help pre-digest dairy products. Other digestion aids are also available. A diet that provides a variety of vegetables, fruits, grains and low-fat proteins, eaten slowly and in a relaxed manner will usually lead to healthy digestion, unless there is some real disease present. If poor digestion persists despite a moderate diet and low-stress meal times, consult your physician.

Sodium/Potassium/Fluid Retention

We spent time earlier discussing the effects of stress in a behavioral sense, and we also looked at nutrition. But I want to just remind us here of some key things to consider. Water-retention, or the bloat issue can be an important matter for women particularly in times of stress. It's also associated with pre-menstrual syndrome (PMS) and depression. Because the issue of fluid balance at the cellular level is so very important, we need to pay special attention to this.

Sodium and potassium are two key cellular nutrients. In combination, sodium, potassium and chloride are necessary for the balance of fluids, acids and bases inside and outside of all of our bodies' cells and the normal functioning of all of our muscles. These substances, when dissolved in water, separate into positively and negatively charged particles, called ions. Ions conduct the minute electrical current necessary for the work of the body systems. Because of this important function, these three minerals are called electrolytes. It is easy to get them. They are abundant in our foods. If we are unwise in our choices, however, we can (and most of us do) get excessive amounts of one electrolyte at the cost or expense of the others. We usually consume too much sodium and not enough potassium.

Unprocessed foods, especially fruits, vegetables and fresh meats provide the best food sources of potassium. Highly processed meats, cereals, and breads usually have increased sodium and decreased potassium. Adding salt to foods at the table, also increases sodium and chloride, and is not advised.

Water

Our bodies are more than half water. Babies are at least 85 percent water. We lose and use water daily for normal body functions like respiration, perspiration and urination. We must replace water by consuming, on the average, two-and-a-half to three quarts per day. That means eight to ten cups per day. We can get a running start on meeting our water needs by consuming foods that have a high water content—fruits and vegetables contain 80 to 95 percent water; meats, poultry and fish, from 50 to 75 percent. Baked foods like breads contain only 36 percent water. Liquid beverages like milk, of course, are high—87 percent water. Many so-called sports drinks that are sold to help replace electrolytes and water, are too high in their sugar content to be highly recommended. Their sugar content causes them to remain in the stomach for longer periods than plain water. If they must be used, the benefits will be experienced more rapidly if they are diluted with water. When we (or our children) are exercising, we should consume at least two to three cups of fluid before exercising to reduce risk of dehydration. We should also stop every 20 minutes to consume at least six ounces to a cup of fluids, especially in hot or dry conditions.

Remember, adequate hydration or water consumption helps the body's immune system, reduces our fluid retention tendencies and helps us utilize key nutrients. Avoid excessive use of carbonated and caffeinated beverages to meet your fluid requirements.

Transit Time

Transit time refers to how long it takes the food you eat to get from point A to point B, or through your digestive tract to the toilet. The longer it takes, the more likely you are to be, to use a popular phrase, "full of it." Seriously, though, our risk for chronic diseases like cancer, obesity, heart disease and diabetes are reduced if our elimination is optimal. Consuming diets that provide adequate fiber in the form of grains, or fresh fruits and vegetables, is a simple factor here. All too often, my clients have suffered with chronic poor transit time or constipation and been told that "it was normal" or OK to go for a few days without a bowel movement. I strongly disagree.

We eat every day, we should eliminate on a daily basis—both liquids and solids. Problems with varicose veins, hemorrhoids, menstrual discomfort, headaches and digestion are often relieved when elimination improves. The National Academy of Sciences recommends that we consume adequate amounts of dietary fiber. We can get this by eating five servings of vegetables and fruits and six servings of whole grains and breads per day. We also need to consume enough liquids—water, juices and non-caffeinated beverages. Yes, self-esteem is related to transit time. Care of our bodies is self-care, which is self-value at its best!

In my work with infants and preschool-age children, I have found the issue of transit time to be particularly important. Young children have a very low tolerance for constipation. Due to small body mass, their little bodies are thrown out of balance easily. Keeping our children well hydrated with lots of liquids, and feeding children (at the appropriate age) daily diets high in natural fiber—fresh fruits and vegetables and whole grains like cereals and brown rice—can help their resistance to illness. Good transit time makes it easier for them to handle and to eliminate excess sugars, fats or environmental toxins such as lead, chlorides and heavy metals. Good transit time for children is as (or more) important as it is for adults.

We Are Important

We are our most important asset and we are the most important person in the world to our children. So high levels of wellness and fitness are important. I've worked with many single parents who just don't have enough energy for self-care all the time. One young mom said that she motivated herself by asking "If this were my child, would I give her better foods, take her to the doctor or see to it that she exercised or rested more?" The answer was usually unquestionably yes! So, she decided that care for herself was at least as important as taking care of her child.

Sugar and Spice and Everything Nice?

Perhaps the best gift nature could give single parents would be perfectly behaved children, the kind described in the nursery rhyme that says what little girls are made of is, "Sugar and spice and everything nice...." Except there's an irony here. Sugar and spice, as we know them today, don't go along with everything nice—or at least, not everything that's good for our children.

While there is still a lot of controversy and debate about sugar, after twenty years of discussion, we are finally getting some leadership from the scientific community on this matter. In the dietary guidelines, complex carbohydrates are recommended. This means we are urged to consume more sugars found naturally in whole grains, vegetables and fruits as opposed to those concentrated, refined sugars found in candies and table sugar (brown sugar, raw sugar, syrups or honey). Remember that many commercially processed baked goods and pre-sweetened foods have been sweetened with concentrated refined sugars.

I have noted that children fed large or excessive amounts of sweetened foods, particularly beverages, are more active and poorly behaved. This is, perhaps, most noticeable around Halloween, when children are over-indulged in concentrated sweets.

In our house, we don't buy white (or any other kind of) table sugar. We also try to limit our intake of refined carbohydrates. Whole grain cereals, granola bars and breads are eaten instead of concentrated sweets. The disadvantages of consuming or feeding our children excess refined (white or brown), concentrated sugar are:

1. Refined sugar contains little (if any) other needed nutrients, but does provide calories.

2. Refined sugar provides no needed fiber.

3. Refined sugar contributes to tooth decay and may be related to other diseases of degeneration, like diabetes.

4. Refined sugar is somewhat habit-forming, and is often consumed in excess which encourages obesity and generally poor nutritional health.

Remember, children can be offered wholesome snacks that are naturally sweetened, such as fruits, nuts, dried fruits, granola, etc. Honey is not recommended for babies less than one year old.

As single parents, I think we need to take extra care to give our own and our children's bodies sources of carbohydrates that promote health, and not burden our systems with excessive refined carbohydrates that are low in nutrients, but high in calories. Remember that having children who "do well," succeed in school, are energetic and who behave appropriately is a key source of self-esteem in our lives as single parents. When our children are fine, so are we. When our children are in trouble, our own self-esteem and self-confidence may be negatively affected.

Minimize Intake of Foods High in Refined Carbohydrates and Sugar

Beverages sweetened with sugar
Breakfast squares
Cakes and icings
Candy, including:
    Candy bars
    Cough drops
    Hard candy
Chocolate
Coffee cakes
Cookies
Custards
Donuts and toaster pastries
Flour tortillas
Fruit, canned or frozen in syrup
Graham crackers
Hard liquor
Ice cream
Ice milk
Jams and jellies
Milkshake
Pies
Puddings
Sandwich buns and muffins
Sherbet
Sweet rolls
Sweetened applesauce
Sweetened gelatin dessert
Sweetened and sugar coated cereals
Syrups and sweet sauces
White and instant rice
White bread

Move It To Lose It— Move It To Use It

We're so busy as single parents, how can we find the time to exercise? How can we find the time to make sure that our muscles are in tone? I'd like to suggest a couple of simple things that we can put into our lives that won't cost a lot of money. One is to purchase a small 36" mini-trampoline. One company calls them "Rebounders." Just running in place on these to the count of 100, 200 or 300, is the equivalent of good walking or running activity, and you don't have to worry about damaging your joints, or going out and buying special shoes. Nor do you have to leave the kids while you go out and exercise. It can also be done year round. The largest muscles in our bodies are those in our hips and thighs, and this trampoline can be particularly useful here if we not only run in place, but we "high step" while running. That helps to exercise the buttocks muscles and the muscles of the thighs and abdomen. Good tone in our large muscles goes a long way toward controlling body weight. When these muscles are toned and lean, we burn more calories and fat even while we're sleeping!

The Thighs Have It

Let me talk a little about the issue of body weight. In order to be well and to be fit, we want to make sure that we keep our body weight in a desirable range. Some people believe that we automatically get fatter as we get older. But that is not automatic. We can actually get fitter as we get older, depending on how committed we are to our physical wellness. The quality of our muscular tone affects our metabolism. The reason that we tend to get fatter as we get older is because our metabolic rate, or our burning rate, seems to slow down and that's usually due to the fact that we've allowed our muscles to become flaccid (particularly thighs and abdominal muscles), like prime beef, marbled with fat. The cosmetic industry talks a lot about reducing cellulite. Well, cellulite happens to be fat. One of the best ways to avoid this is by stretching our large muscles and keeping them long and lean as a result of exercise and use. The other way is to avoid eating large amounts of fat or calories that turn to fat. Excess sugar is stored by the body as fat, and excess fat (found in fatty meats, donuts, crackers, cookies and dairy products, etc.) gets stored as —guess what?—fat!

Helpmates for the Heart

I cannot stress enough the importance of high levels of fitness for us as single parents. A five minute trampoline workout in the home every day and/or a walk every day for at least a half-hour to 45 minutes are highly recommended. This helps the heart, too. The heart is a muscle, and its job is to pump the blood through the system. But it was never intended to do that job without help. The helpmates for our heart are the muscles, the skeletal muscles of our legs and our thighs and our hips. If these muscles have good tone and are effectively used, they actually help to pump the blood through the system so the heart doesn't have to work as hard.

The phrase "heart attack" is ironic, really. We picture someone clutching their chest in pain as though the heart had literally "attacked" them. When in truth, this miraculous organ has worked tirelessly for us, non-stop all of our lives. Most of us have failed to appreciate it, or to support it by engaging our muscles as helpmates for our hearts. In truth, when our hearts become diseased, it is because we've attacked them.

So, in essence, by having muscular fitness, particularly fit hip and thigh muscles, we are reducing our risk for heart attack and high blood pressure. In the last 25 years there has really been only one known, reported cure for high blood pressure, and that has to do with the aerobic fitness levels that come from sustained exercise activity. Correct use of the heart and lungs and the right use of the large muscles of the body will cause our pulse rate to go up. When sustained at the optimum level for our age, this strengthens our heart and makes it more efficient. Aerobic fitness activities can help to cure as well as to prevent high blood pressure (do not, however, stop taking your medication unless advised to by your physician).

Taking care of ourselves physically is of paramount importance to our self-esteem as single parents. In so doing, we are modeling for our children a high level of self-value and self-regard. Being a single parent without a high level of wellness and fitness is a lot like riding a motorcycle without a helmet. It's a big risk—for everyone.

Touch

Another important aspect for us to consider in terms of maintaining our health, is our need for touch. We've already talked about the importance of touch in stimulating the skin of the infant as it comes through the birth canal. But touch is a basic adult human need, too. As single parents, we may not be involved in intimate, loving relationships, and yet we still have to make sure that our basic need for touch is addressed. I strongly recommend doing that through massage. Now many of you may think, "I can't afford massage." Here's where we can help one another as single parents, especially within families. Families and friends can learn the art of massage by looking at video tapes or reading books. We can actually become very skilled at applying gentle, loving touch—not a sexual touch, but a touch that helps to improve circulation and promote relaxation as it responds to one of our basic human needs. Massage is an important stress reducer. Learn how to enhance your ability to offer healthful massage to loved ones and teach them to give you the same. It's also very helpful within families to teach the children, to massage them, and show them the importance of massage. Massage and caressing are ways of showing caring and affection non-verbally. It can be a very bonding experience and it helps to reduce their focus on pre-mature sexual activity.

Our children need to learn directly from us about expressing care, caressing, tenderness, and other healthy forms of bodily contact. They need to learn about affection and communication that are not as risk laden as sexual activity. I recommend that the massage experience be a part of every single-parent family's life on a weekly or at least twice-a-month basis. At the very least, include regular back-rubs or foot massages for and from family members.

Twenty

Sex and Self-Esteem

Adult sexual activity can enhance self-esteem. Think about it. Sex provides one of life's most natural opportunities to receive care and respectful treatment. Through the sexual experience we can know the joy of successfully giving and receiving pleasure. Sex can be an opportunity for fulfilling the most deeply held, almost universal human value—that of loving and bonding. And finally, sexual experiences can provide the intimacy, touch, assurance and support that are needed for healing experiences that devalue us as individuals. Yes, under the best of circumstances, sexual intimacy meets the conditions that foster high self-esteem.

Yet, for many single parents—and for most women—some sexual experiences have meant the opposite. They have been sources of pain and shame that erode self-worth and self-regard. How many teenage pregnancies came about through coerced or unplanned sexual encounters that were at best confusing and at worst forced? Date rape and sexual coercion are more a norm than an exception. The media (MTV, music videos and cinema) eroticize aggressive, violent and sado-masochistic sexual fantasies, giving young people mixed-up messages about their bodies, their worth and expected or accepted sexual behaviors. We are bombarded with images and myths about violence, pleasure and gender roles.

One in four women in our country has experienced some sort of sexual abuse in childhood. Some estimates suggest that one in ten male children are sexually abused, as well. Most women who are raped, report that they are raped by an acquaintance—someone they knew and no doubt trusted. In one Ms. Magazine study 41 percent of the raped young women were virgins and 58 percent were between the ages of fourteen and seventeen at the time of the attack. Many studies also indicate that a large percentage of women who are in actuality raped by someone they know don't even identify their experiences as rape.

But the consequences of violation of personal boundaries, of our physical bodies are devastating emotionally, mentally, physically and spiritually. Rape and sexual violence leave us depressed, filled with shame, guilt, often suicidal and always less able to relate lovingly to ourselves and to others. The post-traumatic stress disorder is a common aftermath of rape or forced sex.

Not all destructive sexual encounters are a result of rape or coercion. There is a popular myth embodied in some of the sexual jargon that associates normal sexual acts with intrusive violence and force by men that is welcomed or submitted to and allegedly "enjoyed" by women. Such words as "banging" and "knocking-up" illustrate this idea. The literature on sex and violence could fill another book, but for us as single parents the issues of sex and self-esteem require taking a fresh look at sexual attitudes and behaviors, and establishing clear boundaries. We need skills in maintaining these boundaries as well as skills in healing memories from past traumas or less than loving sexual encounters. The AIDS reality adds to the urgency of these issues. Sex can be a matter of life and death in the lives of the parents as well as in the lives of children.

The adult human drive for intimate connection to another adult human being is a powerful biological motivator. It can be suppressed, but not easily and not without consequences. This urge for connection creates our natural sexual desires. These needs and desires do not diminish because we are single parents. The need to be touched intimately compels us to continue to seek out relationships that may or may not be good for us or our families. It is vital that we clarify our attitudes about our own bodies and our sexual expectations, so that we can create a psychological foundation for creating positive sexual relationships.

Let's begin by considering the natural, wholesome and healthy nature of the biological compulsion to experience intimacy, touch and sexual pleasure. Sexual arousal is a part of the body's natural rhythm. Nature equipped us to desire to perpetuate the human species, as well as to experience the pleasure of human connection. Sharing the rhythms and fluids of our bodies creates sensations—sensory memories—that can foster deep and meaningful bonding. Bonding through sexual fulfillment can be more powerful than any drug. It is the power of this bonding, along with its associated risks that make sexual decisions and choices so critical. Sex cannot be taken lightly, nor can it be allowed to be a tool for control, humiliation or violation.

Trust

Self-esteem is a state of being that is characterized by a high degree of trust. This trusting state encompasses our relationship with our bodies, our feelings, our thoughts, and our perceptions of life itself. It must also encompass our intimate relationships with others. Trust grows out of self-care based on understanding, exploring our experiences and honest communication. Trust enables us to make decisions and take actions that cause us to grow, to experience more health, energy, freedom and joy. From this trusting state, we can truly value ourselves. As single parents, we must know in our hearts that we value ourselves, and model this attitude for our children.

Always a Decision

A decision to share our bodies, our precious bodies, sexually with another person must always be a conscious choice. This choice should develop from trust, communication, demonstrated caring and some measure of, yes, commitment. Sex is never really casual. Oh, it may appear to be, but the depths of the being are always opened and touched to some degree during the sexual act.

Expectations

As women and men we need to seize the opportunity that sexual activities can give us to assert our true value for ourselves. When we take time to establish a relationship of trust and caring before agreeing to share our bodies, we are asserting our self-esteem to ourselves and to others. This means spending time to know the person intimately through conversation, play and non-sexual touch before moving to sexual intimacy. Non-sexual touch can include massage, dance, sports and play.

Diverse religious, cultural and family values generate different attitudes and expectations regarding sexual relationships. Gender attitudes also differ. However, women generally associate more intense relationship expectations with sexual encounters than do men. This difference can lead to disappointments that impact self-esteem. "Why didn't he call or treat me the same after we made love? Was that all he wanted?"

As women, and particularly as single parents, we need to face some of the gender realities that exist in our culture. Men are usually not encouraged to develop their emotional capacities. It is easy for them to associate the natural bonding need and attraction with sex, primarily. When the tension that is associated with sexual desire has been released through sex, they often experience a let-down or release of the "desire" for the relationship as well. This change in attitude is not anticipated or even always understood. Men are often as confused as women.

Yet, the result is disappointment, hurt and feelings of rejection. One way to break this cycle of "failed" or missed relationships is to delay the sexual involvement stage until after strong emotional bonds have been established. This takes time, sharing and opportunities for gaining real knowledge and insights about each other through companionship. Friends make the best lovers.

Boundaries and Barriers

Condoms protect against AIDS; condoms in combination with spermicides offer even more protection. These barrier methods of protection can also prevent the spread of many other sexually transmitted diseases like chlamydia and gonorrhea, as well as preventing unplanned pregnancies. When there has been no commitment to one partner or promise of monogamy, there is always an increased risk for sexually transmitted diseases. I would advise the use of condoms and spermicides at all times, unless both partners have tested negatively for AIDS and have made a commitment to confining their sexual activity to each other, solely and, of course, unless a pregnancy is planned and desired by both partners. You have to believe that the promise of monogamy is being kept and that the commitment to parent is lifelong. Condoms must be used correctly. I recommend the following book from the Women's Health Network on this subject: *Advice for Life: A Woman's Guide to AIDS Risks and Prevention.*

Empowerment

The decision to reserve sexual experiences for trusting relationships and the use of appropriate barriers—condoms—leads to a greater sense of control and empowerment. This sense of empowerment is a foundation that needs to be in place to create ongoing pleasure, joy and esteem-enhancing sexual experiences.

The quality of the experience must also be addressed. Does it promote general body arousal and fulfillment or does in involve primarily penetration and release? It is important to take time to understand our bodies' needs for gentle, nurturing touch internally and externally and find ways to meet these needs during sexual experiences. The old concepts of banging, knocking and rough treatment must be replaced with real information about men's and women's anatomy and the tenderness that is needed for pleasurable experiences that build self-esteem.

Self-Esteem Anchors for Single Parents

1. Honor your choice, your decision to parent your children.

2. Know that you are doing one of the most important jobs in this democratic society, and value yourself for doing so. See yourself as strong, capable, not as a victim.

3. Release stress by listening to your feelings and relating them to your innermost motivational needs for security, self-expression and empowerment.

4. Learn how to breathe deeply, to relax fully. Practice this often. Engage in daily activities that stimulate deep breathing, like aerobic activities or yoga.

5. Focus on the times in your life when you have been treated with care and respect by others. Accept no less from anyone.

6. Focus on your daily successes. Include the success in your own life and the lives of your children. Write them down in a journal or diary.

7. Identify the things that are important to you and make a list of the positive aspects in your life that relate to those things.

8. Find a picture of yourself as a child and begin to re-establish a loving relationship with that part of yourself. Think about how you deserved to be treated, and remind your inner child that loving-kindness and support are your birthright.

9. Identify symptoms of the stress response syndrome (SRS). Monitor your risk for distress. Work consciously on reducing the negative impact of stress through diet, exercise, relaxation and breathing.

10. Give yourself opportunities for support through counseling, peer support groups, and friendships. Seek help to heal experiences of loss, rejection, neglect or abuse. You deserve support, not aloneness.

11. Focus on your body. Start with relaxation and breathing. Increase aerobic activities, like walking. Increase relaxing activities like hot baths, whirlpools, massage and meditation. Learn about your nutritional health and eat wisely, particularly when under stress. Make sure your diet is rich in vegetables, fruits, whole grains and low-fat proteins such as fish, poultry, nuts and peas. Limit refined, concentrated sugars.

12. Set aside resources—time and money—for you. Do something you want to do because it feels good on a regular basis.

13. Keep a written journal of your positive parenting experiences—memories that brought you the greatest joy.

14. Develop a loving relationship with your body muscles. Improve tone, flexibility, strength in the large muscles of the hips, thighs and buttocks. This will enhance your circulation and general metabolism. You may also notice positive personality changes that relate to confidence and assertiveness.

15. Affirm your right and capacity to be successful in your role as a parent and learn to treat negative judgements and projections as an outgrowth of intolerance based on ignorance.

16. Affirm your children's rights and potential for success in all areas of life. Say no to less.

Self-Esteem Anchors For Those Who Care About A Single Parent

1. Tell the single parent that you respect and value them for their decision to parent their children.

2. Demonstrate care and love for their children—remember birthdays, holidays, weekends, etc.

3. Do not judge their actions or criticize or condemn them for what appears to you to be mistakes or errors. Let them know you believe in them.

4. Remind them of their successes and accomplishments in spite of challenges and barriers.

5. Identify simple ways to demonstrate that you care for and respect them—gestures like cards, calls, gifts, listening, sharing resources, social invitations, hugs, back rubs, etc.

6. Encourage them to take time for self-care, and to take a break or respite regularly. Offer to facilitate that break by caring for the children or helping to arrange for child care.

7. Learn how to help the single parent to explore their own childhood and family patterns. Listen empathetically and respond with care. Encourage them to seek counseling or group therapy if it seems appropriate.

8. Ask them if you may help them with transportation needs, if you can.

9. Remind their children that their mother or father is a wonderful person who has chosen to take on a special, challenging role in our society that requires great strength, skill and resourcefulness.

10. Support their healthful diet and wellness choices by only offering the children foods that are consistent with recommended dietary guidelines.

Support

Support is needed help and
encouragement that keeps us
from falling, sinking or slipping.
Support comes in many forms—
physical in terms of our body's
muscular strength, or
environmental including life's
necessities. Emotional support
includes love, understanding and
tenderness. Mental support
comes through education,
positive thoughts and ideas.
Spiritual support can come from
spiritual or religious beliefs, or
from a world view that creates
a state of optimism and
expectations of good.

Twenty-One

We Deserve Help

Years ago, I supported myself and my family financially by maintaining a clinical practice. All of our income came from this private practice. I worked six days a week, twelve hours a day for approximately five years.

One of my clients was an elderly woman named Mary Ellis, whose profession was domestic work. She had provided house-cleaning services for twenty-five years, but was now unable to work because of rheumatoid arthritis and the severe joint pain that accompanies it. When she came to me, she had no money to pay for the help she needed. I told her to just concentrate on getting better and on the time when she could work again. I suggested that she postpone paying me until then. About six weeks passed, and Mrs. Ellis made me a counter offer. She proposed that she would only continue as my patient if I let her do housework for me in exchange. Mary was not easy to say no to, so I agreed.

I'll always remember the feeling I had when I walked into my apartment and found it shined, polished, cleaned and organized by someone else! Now, don't get me wrong—I'm no slob. My mother raised us to know how to clean a house. But there is a big difference in enjoying a house that you've exhausted yourself cleaning, and simply enjoying a house that has been cleaned for you—with love!

This was my introduction to support. As I ran from room to room in amazement and experienced the care and detail with which Mary had cleaned my house, I was moved to tears. This was the first time in my adult life, particularly my life as a single parent, that someone had shared some of my day-to-day responsibilities (other than for child care), and had done so lovingly. I sat on the couch and cried. I called Mary to thank her. She said simply, "no thanks are needed—you deserve at least this much help, and I could never pay you for what you've done for me."

As single parents we deserve support—loving, caring assistance in many aspects of our lives.

Now, I know that most of you are immediately thinking about the monetary or financial support, commonly called child support. And I'm going to save that discussion for later in the section, "Solvency." The support that I'm referring to here, is not just for the children, it's primarily the support for us as the single parents. As the single parent who has accepted the custody and the responsibility for the child, we deserve to be helped in this process. That help will take many forms, but as we have chosen to create a family that meets the many functions of providing security, nurturance, socialization, education, validation, self-esteem and support, we simply have to get the help that enables us to do this.

Tip of the Iceberg

The truth is most of us, as single parents, have faced difficulties in accessing the support that we need on a continuous basis. Now, we may say it's due to a lack of money, but I believe that the lack of money and our inability to access appropriate support is just the tip of the iceberg. It's just the symptom. I believe that the real cause, or the real barrier to accessing the support that we need as single parents goes back to those issues that we discussed in the first half of the book—issues about our awareness of our deservedness that began in our own families of origin during our own childhood. In our struggles to make it and in coping with the stress of single parenting, we are often not aware of our own unmet needs, particularly our emotional needs.

The fact that we are in the unintended situation of being a single parent suggests that we have had a lot of experiences in which we ignored or negated our own feelings as human beings. We used to accept total responsibility for everything. I'm suggesting that once again, there is some personal development work that needs to be done. It will change our expectations about life and our role in it. This is necessary before we can go forward and create our needed support systems.

When Mary cleaned my house, I was overwhelmed with joy that she had helped to assume some of my responsibility for just one day. I didn't have an inkling about my other real needs as a human being. I had suppressed (or didn't even understand) my needs for day-to-day attention, affection, affirmation, joy and meaningful self-expression. Those things weren't even in my thoughts. I was so busy surviving and appreciating the fact that someone had given me a little help in "doing," I failed to realize that I also deserved support and help that related to my "being." You see, I believe that we have the power to create for ourselves the quality of life that we want, and that creation has to do with our focus—but not always our conscious focus. Sometimes it involves our subconscious focus. Our subconscious thoughts and energies are always focused on something. When we are overwhelmed with the responsibility of raising children, our focus is on just that—the awesome responsibility and the fact that we have to do it all. So that's what we subconsciously continue to create in our lives—more responsibility.

Having to "DO IT ALL!"

One of the major growth experiences that single parents must come to is getting past the state of being overwhelmed by the responsibility. We must step aside and experience our deservedness. Once again, this means unlearning patterns that we learned in childhood. It means going back and re-visiting how we first began to believe that we had to do it all. That's really what we're manifesting in our lives as single parents when we aren't getting needed support. We're manifesting the belief—the heartfelt, body remembered belief—that we have to do it all. Somebody, or some set of circumstances taught us to believe that. But it's not a good belief, it's a false belief. It's a belief that will kill us, lead us into an early grave, or to diseases that debilitate and take away from the quality of our lives. We don't have to do it all, and quite frankly, we cannot do it all well.

Awareness

How do we identify and change those beliefs, attitudes and patterns? The first step is the awareness phase. Begin by letting yourself imagine the kind of life that you would like to have. Imagine the kind of help that you want and need. Just think about it. Sit down one day and imagine the kind of help you'd like to have as a single parent. Would you like someone to prepare the meals? Would you like someone to do the laundry? Would you like someone to come in and clean the house? How about someone to care for your children just as you would care for them? Would you like a higher income that frees you to spend more time with your children? The list goes on and on and on. What about making sure that the house is winterized, or that the apartment is warm enough, or cool enough? What about the lawn, if you have one? What about transportation? Imagine all the things that you would like to see in your life, just as you would like them to be. And imagine someone else having the responsibility of taking care of some of those things.

If you are feeling isolated and frustrated with your life, it may be difficult to imagine things being any different. I often recommend going (with or without your children) to visit with another friend or family for a day or two. Select someone who lives far enough away to give you a change of scene or environment. It really helps if you pick a friend or relative that you admire or hold in high esteem. Sometimes seeing different pictures and being in new spaces helps us to create new images in our minds and new hopes.

Hold On...

I'm not suggesting that you start imagining yourself married here, or with your former spouse or mate. I'm suggesting that you stick to the current marital status reality and imagine that all these things are working well, and you are the single parent—the boss—that is making them all work well. Imagine it until you can actually experience how you think you would feel. Put yourself in a feeling state and almost laugh because you feel the joy, the satisfaction. Then remember that vision. You've taken the first step—Mind, Feeling, Awareness. This is the process of imaging or visualization.

The Fix-It Syndrome

Let's go back and revisit some of the unlearning that needs to be done before you are free to bring your vision into reality. Did you as a child take on the role of the responsible one in your family? It's very natural for children to believe that when bad things happen in the family, it's their responsibility to fix it. Young children are essentially self-focused and self-centered.

Children usually believe that they're responsible for the divorces that occur. Because of their innocence, tremendous love and their desire to be loved as well as needed, they can take on an immense sense of responsibility. Out of ignorance, that sense of responsibility, that vulnerability that children have, sometimes gets exploited by adults who are dealing with their own problems. We can find children assuming excess emotional and at times even actual practical day-to-day responsibilities. These include care for sisters and brothers, concern for parents' wellness, etc. When children take on adult responsibilities, or at least believe in their hearts that if things are going to be fixed, they have to do it, then they take these patterns into adulthood and may become obsessive "people helpers," workaholics, or other kinds of "–aholics,".

As single parents, many of us come from this mold. Part of our real happiness depends on changing this "excessively responsible" role or behavior pattern. One way to do that is through counseling and support groups. There is a movement in this country about co-dependency. It is for children who grew up in families where one or both parents were alcoholics. Alcoholism is just one kind of basic dysfunction that has plagued many American families—dysfunction that comes from and that fosters parents' inability to respond to the needs, the whole needs, of children. Families are often dysfunctional when chronic stresses (financial, social or emotional) preoccupy or distract the adults.

Many of us grew up in families that were similarly dysfunctional. As single parents, we are often re-living and re-playing those old patterns of existence. We are accepting a life that doesn't respond to our emotional needs and taking on responsibility for everything. Our innocent inner child and our surviving adult selves are making the best of unfair circumstances. We deserve better. We deserve the joy and fulfillment that comes from knowing we are loved, appreciated, accepted and valued. Change starts by recognizing that we need and deserve better treatment. And then we must take immediate steps to relate to, and to treat ourselves better. Many of the ideas for self-care mentioned in the self-esteem section are first steps along the road to better treatment of ourselves.

Twenty-Two

Hitting the Wall

Chicago was a frightening place. It seemed to me that one way to protect myself and my child was to move into a high-rise building that had a security guard. Of course, I paid the security guard's salary as part of my excessive rent. This meant working extra jobs, extra hours and extra hard. It also meant finding someone to "live in" or come to my home every day to care for my child since I was "away" working so much of the time.

But, because of my attitudes left over from childhood, and sense of responsibility for everything, I hired a child-care provider who was an absolute disaster! Oh, I checked references. But within three weeks, she was as much of a responsibility as my five year old. She had cramps, she had headaches, she had 100 reasons for not doing her job. Of course, firing and rehiring a child-care worker would have disrupted my work, which, since I was self-employed, disrupted the family income.

Eventually, she made it easy for me. I was investing almost all of my income in the rent and in her salary. So, we had little, if any, furniture. Oh, I had beautiful green plants, pillows and carpeting! The sunlight was awesome! My child's room was furnished. But this was a transition period, and furniture was not at the top of my list of necessities. I came home from a 13-hour day at the office one Saturday to find that my house, my apartment, was suddenly furnished! It was filled with the child-care worker's junk! She mumbled something about having had to take these things out of storage...and, only temporary...and, hoping I wouldn't mind...and,...etc. The van came to remove her and her stuff within 24 hours!

I asked my favorite aunt to keep my son for a few weeks while I regrouped. She agreed. I told the security guard to not allow anyone to disturb me for at least two weeks, to tell them I was not home, and I literally collapsed.

This story illustrates the reaction. In addition to the symptoms discussed in the last section, stress has three stages—alarm, resistance and exhaustion. The outrage and fight that I had to garner to remove that child care provider pushed my stress state over the edge. I moved directly to exhaustion, not passing "Go," not collecting $200.00. I hit the wall. At this point, I simply wanted to give up. In fact, my body did. I remember telling my body to get up and get dressed for work. But my body acted as if it hadn't heard a word I thought or uttered. It refused to respond. I literally seemed to have no control, will or energy left. I could only cry. And I did, for a long time. This state of severe exhaustion—burn-out—lasted for a few days. I recovered in about a week. A week's vacation, months before, might have helped to prevent my stress-related collapse. Or some professional or peer counseling or constructive, self-help support immediately after or during my separation could have helped to prevent this kind of crash.

When We Hit The Wall...

Instead of collapsing or drowning the pain of unmet needs in tears, drinks or chocolate cake, moments of crisis can be used constructively to break through and discover hidden feelings that may be dictating our lives.

You're absolutely furious, hurt, livid and "done" because someone has disappointed you, let you down. They didn't do what they promised, or are taking unfair advantage. Once again, it's up to you to make things all right. You're at the point of tears. Let your tears flow. But now, try to stop and think, to reflect, turn your focus, your thoughts, to your deepest feelings and sensations. What are you experiencing, feeling, in your body? Is your stomach upset or your head pounding? Is your heart racing or your lower back aching?

It's not an accident that feelings of anger, fear, sadness and joy are accompanied by particular body sensations. If we learn how to listen to and decode such information, it can help us to better understand ourselves. In some parts of the world, healing systems and medical practices are based on listening to the responses, rhythms and sensations of the individual's body. When we feel anger, it is often experienced in the center or upper abdominal area. Fear and insecurity sensations tend to be concentrated in the lower abdominal area, and particularly in the lower back area. Feelings of joy and happiness are often accompanied by increased sensation or excitement in the upper chest area and head. Expressions like "weak in the knees" or "he hasn't the stomach for it" have their basis in the simple fact that our bodies sense our emotions and react to our thoughts and feelings. So when we're in emotional crisis moments, we should learn to tap into our bodies' wisdom to help us figure out our needs at that point—our feeling needs. Once we're focused on the body sensations, we can ask ourselves about our thoughts, our heartfelt desires.

What would make it all right? What do you want to happen now? The answer will come from deep within. You will, at this moment of great emotional pain, be acutely aware of your demand, your urgent need for someone else to do what you want (demand) them to do. Often, the cry is "I just want him to help me, to do his part," or "I just want some help!" At that moment of release most of us will start to cry—a real, deep, total body cry.

So often, we learn as young children not to cry. But crying and tears are natural forms of self-expression. They are gifts to us and part of our self-healing process. If the tears or cry swells up from within you, breathe with it. Breathe deeply and let the tears begin to wash away the misconceptions and misperceptions that you have been holding onto about yourself.

You can help yourself consciously at this moment by reminding yourself consciously, maybe audibly. Say to yourself, "I am loved," "I am capable"—whatever is the opposite of your demand. If you desperately need help, then use your adult self-awareness to remind the vulnerable part—the inner child—that you have help, that you can access help, even if _____ doesn't help you. Change the words to fit the circumstances. The point is that things are never as absolute or desperate as they appear to be when we're upset or triggered.

In times of acute stress, our brains function in a survival mode. Our problem solving, rational/creative capacities are limited. We may not even see the help or the options that are available to us. If we stay in a chronic state of stress, we begin to develop constant attitudes, feelings and beliefs that come from this limited way of thinking or being. Our feelings and related beliefs are keys to the quality of our life's experience. So as single parents, we must learn to use the crises as doorways to discover what our deeply held feelings and attitudes are, as well as opportunities to release tension and pent up body (feelings) memories through necessary, often tearful, self-expression.

After you've cried, talk to yourself. Remember to breathe deeply and affirm a more encouraging attitude or truth about yourself and your capacity. You may notice how related thoughts or memories come to mind.

Then, as if a moving picture were being projected from your subconscious, you will probably remember related experiences from your own childhood, times when you felt the same way. Often, you may remember being angry with a sibling, parent or cousin. Were you often angry because a brother or sister didn't do his or her part? Or did you watch your mother complain and cry about "having to do it all?" Your mind may fill with pictures, images, of being burdened with excess responsibility.

Continue this process of using today's moment of crisis to access related old memories and images. Continue to say to yourself: "I am still OK, capable, even though he or she didn't help me. I am resourceful and am supported even though he or she didn't help me." Let the mature adult part of you reassure your vulnerable self (your inner child) that you are going to be alright, despite the experiences of your present and past. Learn a phrase that will reassure your vulnerable self. Repeat this phrase loudly and clearly to yourself about each painful memory. The names and situations may change, but the unmet need, the demand, is always there. We want to be honored, valued and treated fairly, not used. We want and deserve help.

After this emotional work is over for now, you can do mental work to help reinforce your new attitude and feeling about yourself. Eventually, I learned how to write affirmations and to do visualizations of myself receiving help and being supported. The affirmations went like this:

> "I now allow myself to be helped and supported in the ways I need. Gail, you now allow yourself to be helped and supported in the ways you need. Gail is now allowing herself to be helped and supported in the ways that she needs."

I wrote this kind of affirmation no less than 100 times over a three day period. Writing affirmations helps us to change beliefs about ourselves and our lives, after we've done some work to address the deeply held body and feeling memories.

I urge you to look at your life right now. If you're feeling unsupported, without help, there is a set of related memories— body sensations and feelings—somewhere within you that says you don't deserve help, or you can't have it. Begin by exploring these attitudes and their roots.

Self-Help Steps to Identify and Change a Feeling or Attitude About Yourself

1. When a crisis arises, explore the feelings. Listen to your body. Don't hold back the emotion. Let a friend assist you to process the experience, and be willing to do the same for them.

2. Identify your most heart-felt need or demand. Find out what you really want.

3. Use self-talk. Remind yourself that you are OK. You are safe and secure, even if the demand/need is presently not being met. Children see things in the extreme only, and can invest extreme emotion in their fears and perceptions. They don't have the adult capacity to understand and rationally explore subtle meanings. When we are in emotional crisis, we often revert momentarily to our own childlike state and need to remind ourselves of the whole truth, the bigger picture. We are never without some resources—some help.

4. Explore related memories that arise, using the same process.

5. Allow yourself to visualize. Imagine a different set of circumstances in your life—one in which your specific need is met.

6. Write an affirmation to reinforce the new image or feeling about yourself.

Next, let's do a support inventory by completing the following chart. Simply place a check mark in the "Have Help" or "Need Help" column for each item listed.

Support Inventory

ME	Have Help	Need Help	MY CHILDREN	Have Help	Need Help
Accounting/ Record Keeping	—	—	After School Care	—	—
Cleaning/ Maintenance	—	—	Child Care	—	—
Companionship	—	—	Clothing (Care/Supply)	—	—
Cooking	—	—	Crisis Care	—	—
Health Care	—	—	Discipline	—	—
Housing	—	—	Education	—	—
Income/Savings	—	—	Food & Feeding	—	—
Insurance (All Types)	—	—	Grooming	—	—
Intimacy	—	—	Health Care	—	—
Laundry/ Dry Cleaning	—	—	Homework/ Tutoring	—	—
Pleasure	—	—	Insurance	—	—
Recreation/Fun	—	—	Parenting Advice	—	—
Respite	—	—	Recreation/Fun	—	—
Relationship Advice	—	—	Role Models	—	—
Spiritual Nurture	—	—	Savings/ Spending Money	—	—
Transportation	—	—	Spiritual Education	—	—
Touch	—	—	Transportation	—	—
Validation	—	—	Travel	—	—

Make a list for yourself and a list for your children, of all the areas you checked "Need Help." Now, let's explore possible sources or avenues for specific kinds of help. Take child care, for example:

	Area of Help	Possible Sources
1.	Child care	Family, neighbors, church...
2.		
3.		
4.		
5.		

The concept of "self-sufficiency" for families, particularly single-parent families needs to be replaced with a more realistic view of the fact that, to some degree, we all depend on others for help and support. The truth is that we are inter-dependent, not self-sufficient. We don't come into the world independently or survive without help.

The help and support process is a two-way reciprocal process. Communities of people work together for the common good. This is what family means. As single parents, we must learn how to expect, accept, assess and give help and support. I have moved over the years from a very isolated, alone experience to one in which I have support in many areas of my life. Today, I can identify some form of support in almost all areas in the inventory. I am working on the others, too. You may want to create your own inventory, or add things to this one.

Twenty-Three

Selecting Child Care or Infant Care

One of the most important forms of help or support that single parents need is appropriate care for their children while they do the work that provides their needed income. Two-parent families need this, too. But survival of the single-parent family often depends on being successful in attaining and maintaining quality care for the children.

I'm so glad that it's no longer fashionable to refer to child-care centers as day-care centers. By changing the name, at least we emphasize the important thing—that is, the children that have to be cared for. In general, society underestimates the power of that word "care" and the natural need and desire that we have to care for our children.

When necessity demands that we access support and help in the form of child care, we as single parents, are deeply affected by the weight of that decision since we can't share it with a spouse or a mate. Yet, it's part of the reality of single parenting and should be planned for in advance. It shouldn't be a hasty, reactive decision. Amy Dombro and Patty Byron have written an excellent book on this subject, entitled *Sharing the Caring*. Some of their key points relate specifically to the needs of single parents.

Lucky?

I've been pretty lucky in my life in terms of accessing care for my children, because I've been an entrepreneur. Therefore, I was able to keep my children with me during my workday for their first few months. In the case of my daughter, I was very lucky in that I was able to place her in an excellent infant care center when she was only four months old. Maybe it wasn't luck. Maybe it was once again, the function of the growth and the belief system that I am sharing in this little book. By that, I mean our ability to use our mental energies and our personal resources to get the things that we truly want.

I think the first step in accessing quality care for our children is to create a mind picture of the desired setting. We should spend time focusing on exactly what we want in terms of the conditions, the environment, and the people who will care for our children. Many of us spend our mental energy focusing on all the things that could go wrong, because we're so filled with mixed emotions about placing our children in the care of someone else. Consider and examine what could go right.

All the Right Things

Picture the specifics and even write them down. Seek the perfect setting. Do we want a care provider who has the same attitudes and beliefs that we do about child rearing? Some people feel insecure about their own abilities to raise their children and they're actually seeking another person who would be older and more experienced, someone who they feel knows more about caring for children. Do we want someone who has the same discipline practices that we might have? Do we want them to be in a bright, well-lit, well-organized environment? What kind of toys and games and activities do we want our children to play with? What kind of children, or how many other children, do we want our children to interact with on a daily basis? And what about language issues? If English is not the primary language in our home, do we want a bi-lingual child care provider or setting?

What about food and diet? Temperature control? How about the energy level of the provider? Do we want an energetic, lively person or is it alright if they're more quiet and settled, less energetic? All these are things that we need to give thought to before we even start looking for the child-care center.

Once those questions and issues have been considered, then it's time to actually begin to shop. Actually visit different centers, or different settings and decide what you're going to do. Now generally, we'll probably have one of three choices. We may choose an individual to provide care—either a relative, neighbor, friend or individual that we take our child to or that comes into our home. Or, we may choose to work with a family care-provider who cares for a few children in her home. These arrangements are still often referred to as licensed day-care homes. Finally, we may want our child to be in a larger child-care center. A few employers now actually provide such centers at the work place.

While there are basically these three kinds of options, there is a great deal of variety within these choices. Licensed day-care homes vary dramatically in the quality of care offered. Factors like number and needs of children cared for, location, play equipment, meal menus and facilities will vary. Look for what you really want. Check references of other parents who use or have used the child-care home. The same guidelines are suggested for individuals and structured licensed centers. Be sure to ask about the child to care-worker ratio. Is there enough staff to give each child focused attention, or is one worker responsible for five or more children? Spend a day observing the child-care center activities. Pay attention to whether the child-care provider responds warmly to your child. Is the staff trained in the stages of child development so they will be able to note the special signs of your child's growth? Note their safety and sanitation practices. Also try to observe how they handle crises.

A Match?

Choosing which general type or place of care will work for us has a lot to do with what we perceive to be the needs of our child. How would they best function? If the child is very young and has had a very difficult early phase or infancy, we may not want to subject them to the stress of being in a large child-care center. We may feel that one-on-one care, someone coming to our home, or else our taking our child to them is the best possible arrangement. If we have a very outgoing, excitable child who enjoys people, then the interaction with other children in a child-care center, may be the perfect arrangement. We, as single parents, have to consider these questions and make a decision about the general place or arrangement. Based on that decision, we have to find out what our options are within our communities.

There are not enough resources available for quality care for children from single-parent homes. That's one of those areas in which we need to become more active in holding our elected officials accountable. But in the meantime, we have to work with what we have. I suggest that we can find out what our options are by working through our networks, be they relatives, friends, churches, places of work, public-aid offices, schools that we may be attending, or even grocery stores. Finding out what resources are available in the community may mean going beyond looking in the phone book. It may mean doing some underground networking. Talk to friends, community people or church members. You'll learn about people who are providing child-care who may not necessarily be advertising.

Getting There

An important consideration when selecting child care, particularly for single parents, is the issue of transportation and access. My advice to single parents is to reduce the stress as much as possible and make an arrangement that limits your transportation issues. I've heard so many stories from single parents who have trouble getting to work on time because of having to get back and forth to and from the child-care center within certain hours. If you can arrange the most convenient transportation around child care, it reduces stress dramatically and makes it easier on both the parent and the child. You may have a child-care arrangement that is not flexible in terms of pick-up times, yet your work requires flexibility. This can create some real challenges. It can create tension with the center itself, as well as confusion and feelings of uncertainty in your child when you don't arrive when you're expected. This can also create feelings of rejection in your child. Transportation issues around child care are something that we need to give a lot of thought to, and minimize the distance and the stress involved in that process whenever possible.

Key Person

Now that you have selected the location and the type of childcare your child needs, make sure that you know as much as you can about the care provider. We need to know as much as we can about the primary person who will actually interact with and provide guidance for our child on a daily basis. This person will see to it that our child's needs for a sense of security are met. This person must provide age-appropriate opportunities for self-expression to help our child develop a natural sense of empowerment, so they gain more and more control, comfort and confidence in their environment. This care taker must see to it that in our absence our child does not suffer from abuse or deprivation physically, mentally, emotionally or spiritually.

These are big responsibilities for someone to take on, and money is never their only reason. Most people in the child-care field make so little money, we know that they must be there for deeper reasons. Child-care workers usually have a basic capacity to love and to nurture. This is the first quality that we want to look for in the person. We want to look into their eyes and see if anybody's home in there. This is a real clear indication about their capacity to nurture. Their smile, the warmth, the connection that they make with us and with our children is a base-line indication about how they are going to respond to our child's basic, intrinsic needs for security, self-expression and empowerment.

Next, it's a good idea to observe how they interact with the children who are already in their care. Now this may not be as easy in a one-on-one situation as it is when you're going to a center or to another home setting. But even if they are coming to you or your child is going to be the only child they care for, allow enough time during that first interview or meeting to see them interact with your child. Note how the child relates to them and how they "wow" or attempt to make your child comfortable. Note how they encourage the child's activity and exploration.

Have them participate with you in a feeding situation, for example. Do they interact with the child? Are they aware of their normal developmental needs: For instance, do they know when the child needs to self-feed, or use finger-foods?

The process of meeting and interacting with the child-care provider is critical. We as single parents, should take more time to do it from a position of empowerment and not from a position of just being thankful and grateful that there's a place where we can put our child, which is all too often the case.

Right Questions

The really qualified child-care provider is going to want to ask us questions about our child and about us. Ideally, they're going to want to know about our children's preferences—eating preferences, allergies, etc. Minimally, they should want to know our children's health history. But they should also want to know about their normal routine in terms of times for naps, times for play, etc. These are the kinds of questions that an appropriate child-care worker would ask us. They should also want to know about our family—whether our child has brothers and sisters, and if so, what their level of interaction is with their brothers and sisters.

Separation

Once we get past the questions and answers, past the observations, and reach an agreement that this is the right place, how does our child separate from us? How does our child move into this new setting and do so with ease and minimal stress? This will have a lot to do with the age, habits and needs of the child.

Whatever the age is, the process of separation is made easier if we're able to create or build some rituals into the experience so that it becomes routine. Remember, the child's primary need is for a sense of security. Rituals, things that get repeated every day, are things that we can count on, and they seem to help to establish a sense of security. Departure to the care center or the time just before the child-care worker arrives in the home need not be so stressful. When the process is routinized or ritualized with certain activities that always take place, it makes the child feel more secure. For instance, breakfast can be made into a pleasurable ritual where the child participates in the process, or games are played, songs are sung, or something is done that makes it a fun time—and the child expects it. While our child knows that after this ritual occurs, the next step is going to be entry of the child-care worker or going off to the child-care center, etc., it becomes less of a threat. Make sure that they can count on a certain activity taking place every day. This may be a time when you choose to read a story just before you go, and the child begins to look forward to it and sees this as part of the routine. I found that creating a routine that's pleasurable, fun and predictable can ease this separation process.

A Matter of Trust

By the time you get to the moment of departure, though—either at the center or in the home, there is that "goodbye" experience, and the "hello" for the child-care provider. And that's going to be difficult. It's better not to minimize it. Don't try to sneak away to avoid the pain of the emotion, because once again, that sets up the belief that "I can't trust my parent." If we put ourselves in the place of the child, how would we feel when we have one set of trusting expectations and then we're surprised by another, particularly when it involves someone that we love or that we thought we could count on. A simple thing like sneaking away while the child is playing may be done with the best of intentions, but in reality, the effect is that it erodes the little child's sense of trust and faith in the world, and in us as the Anchor of their world. I think it's better to let the child cry and say goodbye and say, "I'm coming back at a certain time and you're going to be taken care of by so-and-so," and hug and love and help them to integrate this new reality into their experience. Also, let the child express what it means to them as you're departing. This can sometimes be an important indication for them that they're not out of control—that you will take a moment to listen to their feelings. Respond to their feelings and offer something in response to what they say. Gradually the process becomes a little easier.

Determining who will care for our children and in what setting they will receive this care is probably the most important element of support that we have that enables us to be effective single parents. I believe it's important to think of good child care as a support system for us as the parents, and to realize that even though we've found what seems like a good child-care relationship, we still have to monitor that relationship. We still have to make sure that it remains consistent. Circumstances in people's lives may change. What started out as a good child-care arrangement can change—personnel changes, other children enter the environment. We have to observe closely and listen carefully throughout the child-care experience.

Nuts

I'll never forget this incident. My daughter had been in the child-care center all day. When I picked her up, she looked a little strange. Her face didn't seem to have the right symmetry, the right balance. She looked a little swollen. Immediately, I went into denial and told myself, "No, no, no, no, she's fine. There's nothing wrong," because of course, the last thing in the world I wanted to see was that there could be anything wrong with my child. So, we were driving along in the car with Charisse in the back in the child-safety seat, and she said, "Mommy, I got a nut in my nose." And I said, "What?" And she said, "I have a nut in my nose." We got home and she kept telling me the same thing. I said "What do you mean you have a nut in your nose, Charisse?" And she said, "I have a nut in my nose," again. So, I thought "Does she mean she put something in her nose?" Now, children love to put things in the spaces in their bodies. This is part of their exploration. So, I looked carefully and realized that her nose really did seem to be swollen. I asked her to show me what she meant and she pointed to her left nostril. Apparently, she had put something up her nose.

I immediately called back to the child-care center to find out if anything abnormal had gone on there with her that day. Could they tell me about what happened in the course of the day? I wished now that I had acted on my initial impulse, and looked at her when I first thought that she looked a little strange. I wished I had taken a moment before we left the child-care center to inquire right then. But by the time I called, the person who had been responsible for Charisse's class of toddlers had left, so they really couldn't answer my questions. My daughter's word and my own observations had to be my primary sources of information, now. I looked carefully up her nostril and I didn't see anything and then I touched around her face and it was obviously painful. She said, "It hurts, Mommy." I called my pediatrician and said "My daughter tells me she has a nut in her nose." He said, "Run some pepper across under her nose and if there's something small in there, she'll sneeze it out."

So we tried that and she sneezed, but nothing came out. She was starting to swell a little more, and the pepper routine wasn't working. I tried to get her to blow her nose and that didn't work, so I began to panic a bit. I called the pediatrician again and said, "Look, something's really wrong here. She is swelling and getting red." So, he said, "Alright, meet me at my office right away and we'll see what's going on."

It's very important to have a doctor that you feel will respond to you in times of crisis. That's usually when you need them with young children. Knowing you can call and reach your pediatrician in a crisis is an important criterion for selecting your doctor. Many single parents today rely on emergency rooms and/or community centers for medical care. This makes it hard to have one person who knows and has a relationship with your family that you can call in a crisis. My advice is to try to locate and establish a relationship with a primary family doctor—either through your HMO, clinic, neighborhood health center or other community resources. Use churches, talk with friends. If you have to rely on clinics, try to get to know your doctors by name and get numbers for reaching them in a crisis.

At any rate, we got to his office. After it was all said and done, this little one-year-old child had stuffed an almond up her nostril. This nut was about to create some very serious problems for her because it was moving further and further up the nasal passage. That's probably the most serious child-care incident that I've had with my children, so I was really very, very lucky.

But this story illustrates the importance of monitoring the activities and listening each day to your child's verbal and nonverbal messages when you pick them up from the center or care provider. Take time to communicate with the child-care provider at the end of each day. Ask about events, progress, etc. Remember, as our children grow, their needs for care change. Monitor to be sure your provider has the capacity to respond to your child's changing needs for care. But no matter how well-managed or careful center workers are, there may always be accidents—unnoticed moments or incidents. This can happen in your home, too.

Back-Up Plans

Another important consideration for us as single parents is having what we call contingency or back-up plans. These are best when they're pre-arranged. It's important to have a relative, friend, church member or neighbor with whom we have a relationship that allows us to say to them, "If I get into a real crisis, is it possible that you might be able to help me out with my child for a day in case of an emergency?" We must pre-arrange back-up plans so that when an emergency strikes, we've already reached out and established a network of people that we can call. This is not a situation we'll want to abuse or take advantage of. It's just there so that we don't have to experience the trauma of suddenly having no one to care for our child which would mean having to miss work, and if we miss work, it would be catastrophic. Pre-arranging, reaching out and having a written list of people who are there as back-up plans in case of emergency, is an important part of being able to manage our lives.

Pre-planning also helps to heighten the awareness within your circle of friends—your relatives, the community, etc.—that you are a single parent and that single parenting is a 24-hour-per-day, 365-day-a-year job. Most people are desensitized to the responsibilities involved with single parenting. As a society we are becoming desensitized to basic human needs in general. By pre-planning and setting up back-ups and contingencies, you add one more point of awareness, not just for you but for your community of friends. They realize that this is a serious matter and that we all have to make a commitment to assure the healthy development and care of the children within our communities.

Home Alone

There are ten million children today who return home after school to empty homes because their parent or parents are working. Most of these children are left to care for themselves. Many of these young children are the responsibility of older siblings. "Play is the work of children." Learning and developing are their second and third jobs. Child care is not a job for children. Not extended care for themselves or for other children. Research has shown that lack of adult supervision increases risks for school problems, substance abuse and teen pregnancy.

Yet, as our children get older and become school-age (six and above) we may be more tempted to leave them at home alone for brief periods of time. For single parents, brief periods of child care are an ongoing challenge. We may need to simply run an errand or work later hours than usual. The cost of child care and the absence of other people to help out often means that children in single-parent families, of necessity, spend more hours at home alone. There are some general guidelines that should be considered, however. It is possible to protect and Anchor our children even when we are away from them. We need to remember their basic needs for security, self-expression and empowerment and try to create environments in the home that respond to these needs, even while we, the parents, are away.

We should simply never leave children under age seven alone for any reason, for any length of time, and it is not advisable to leave children under 18 alone overnight for any reason. If children must be alone for a few minutes or hours at a time, take these measures to assure their safety and comfort:

1. Let a friendly neighbor or someone who lives nearby know that your child is alone for a brief time and ask if your child can contact them should an emergency develop.

2. Give your child instructions, telephone number, address, etc., for reaching the neighbor in an emergency. Identify to your child situations that are "emergencies."

3. Establish and write down "rules" about answering the door, answering the phone, having company, cooking, bathing, going outside, etc. I suggest that you establish rules that minimize the possibility of accidents or unknowns. For example, some parents tell their children not to open the door for anyone who is not a "close relative." Some tell their children never to tell a stranger on the phone that they are home alone. I did not allow my children under age 14 to use the stove, light candles or use a major appliance unless an adult was present to supervise. Certain regions of the country face unique environmental challenges—earthquakes, tornados, blizzards. Safety procedures for these conditions should also be discussed, practiced and written down. Fire drills are also wise.

4. Once safety or security factors have been addressed, there is the issue of "what to do." Children are happiest and "safest" when they have structured activities—things to do. I recommend establishing a schedule of activities for children to keep them focused and engaged while you are away. If they are to be at home from three to six after school, then work out a schedule for specific activities that are to fit into specific time slots. Time the activities realistically. Here is a sample afternoon schedule:

   3:30 - 3:45   Change school clothes. Wash hands for snack.

   3:45 - 4:00   Eat snack (in refrigerator on second shelf—apple, granola bar, yogurt, lemonade).

4:00 - 4:30	Ride bicycle with friend. Do not go beyond Turner Avenue, South; Main Street, North; Washington, West; and Brown Street, East. If you park your bicycle, remember to lock it.
4:30 - 5:30	Ann can visit. Play games in your room.
5:30 - 6:00	Watch 1/2 hour television—Channel 32.
6:00 - 6:30	Begin homework. Do Math first.

Most parents arrange for periodic telephone check-ins to make sure children are on schedule. Sometimes, schedules should be posted and children asked to mark off activities as they are completed.

Afterschool hours should include nutritional snacks, recreation (play) and human contact before homework begins. Specific chores or responsibilities for other siblings can be included in the schedule, too. Adding structure and specific activities to children's time at "home alone" helps to respond to their basic need to feel connected, valued and parented. It is very frightening for young children to feel the weight or pressure of adult responsibility. When they have to figure out "what to do with themselves" for long hours of time, it can be overwhelming. Escape in television or "groups of other kids" is often the natural way out of this uncomfortable situation. By pre-planning these times, we assure our children that we are still responsible for them and responsive to their needs, despite our absence or focus on a different aspect of parenting at the time.

It may be helpful to plan the week's schedule in advance and to do so along with another single parent who has a child that plays with your child. Weekly planning enables you to fit in special afterschool events and to consider related transportation needs ahead of time.

By the way, it is a good idea to meet and greet the school bus driver. If your child takes the public bus, take an afternoon to meet that driver, too. Some of the most frightening encounters children have occur on public or school transportation. Knowing the drivers and letting the drivers know you can help to reduce risk factors.

A Wise Investment

Remember, in order to be free to earn the incomes that we need to sustain our families, we need the mental peace of mind of knowing that our children are OK. As long as they're OK, we're OK. I don't think there is any greater source of pain or distraction for me as a single parent, than the thought that there is something "wrong" with either of my children. I realized early on that the energy I consciously invested in addressing their needs for focused adult attention was ultimately an investment in my capacity to continue to be productive, to work and to produce adequate family income, the key to succeeding against the odds as single parents.

Child Care Advocacy

We also need to hold our elected and appointed officials responsible for seeing to it that appropriate child-care resources are accessible within our communities. Arrange a task force of single parents and work with local community agencies. Use the phone book to survey your community for available child care for infants, preschool- and school-age children. What are the options for children? Compare this to the number of children that need it. Then make this an issue in your community. Talk to school boards, newspapers, radio, television, church groups and political groups. As single parents, we must begin to make our issues public issues and, through the use of the democratic process, educate our elected and appointed officials in these critical matters. Children must be cared for while single parents produce the income required for raising them.

Twenty-Four

Your "Parenting Coalition"

I attribute my sanity at one point, to the kindness of a friend, years ago, when my son was about three. Without my asking her, Juriene offered to keep my son every Wednesday night. She had no children and said, "Gail, you need a break. Let me pick him up from day care on Wednesdays. We'll have dinner, play games, and you can pick him up on Thursday mornings." At first, I hesitated. Then my brighter self said yes. This arrangement lasted for a couple of years. It meant the world to me. It also meant a lot to her. She established a caring relationship with Daniel and contributed to his development. She was part of my parenting coalition. Thank you, Juriene, for offering me respite—a break!

Respite

As single parents we have many jobs. Every job requires a vacation. Time away from parenting responsibility is, I believe, as or more important than time away from income-producing responsibility.

Burn-out is a condition that is characterized by withdrawal from a role or responsibility. When top-level business executives burn out, they make costly mistakes and are sent on "retreats," transferred or fired. When doctors burn out, they may start writing the prescription almost immediately, and that means your appointment is over soon after they walk into your examining room. When a teacher burns out, he or she may begin to be absent, to focus on grades—"things"—more than on the students.

What happens when single parents burn out? The loss of role interest may translate into child neglect, or even abuse. It always becomes self-neglect and abuse. I believe the best way to prevent this is to build in or structure routine respite or breaks.

Perhaps, most importantly, Juriene helped me to learn to trust. Single parents need to learn to trust again—to expect and accept help from others. Respite can take the form of an overnight break, or simply a few hours in the afternoon. What is key is that these breaks are regular, predictable and agreed to by everyone, including the children. (Sometimes this takes time.) Many of the parents that I've worked with have found the "respite" role to be appropriate for the "other parent," or for extended family members.

Support From Family Members

I was born and raised in Cleveland, Ohio. But like many young people, I chose to stay in the city where I finished college. I never really planned to spend my life in Chicago, but the longer I stayed, the longer I stayed. The problem here is that the rest of my family—brothers, sisters, aunts, uncles and cousins—all stayed in Cleveland or some place near there.

As a single parent, I had no immediate family to rely on for support. I think this was as much my choice as it was my challenge. You see, my memories of my family of origin were overwhelmingly painful. I really didn't want my children to have a lot of exposure to the kinds of devaluing experiences that I had. As the only single parent in my family, I also felt judged and ashamed. Whenever there was a "must attend" family affair, a wedding or funeral, I tried not to go, or to make certain that I took a man (potential husband) with me. Somehow I believed I would be more acceptable to my family if I had a man (any man) with me. Therefore my children grew up without much association with or involvement with my parents—their maternal grandparents.

My second husband's parents lived in the same city, however. They have been an ongoing part of our support network.

Historically, single-parent families have used the extended family network as a key part of their support systems. This is very natural for African American, Native American and Mexican American families. It was a key to survival for formerly enslaved African Americans. Yet, today, as mobility has increased, the options for family support are reduced.

I recommend that you reach out to your extended family whenever possible.

However, be as selective about family members' interaction with you children as you are about others. If your family member has behaviors, attitudes or child-rearing practices that you feel would devalue or damage your child's self-esteem, don't expose your child to that person on a regular basis.

Extended family can include in-laws and former in-laws as well. Sometimes ex-spouses' or ex-mates' family members want to be supportive financially and emotionally even if their son or daughter isn't assuming full parental responsibility. Children also need the validation that grandparents and relatives can give. Our children need to know they are loved and cared for by as many adults as possible.

We need not wait till Christmas or birthdays for this demonstration of care. The successful single parents I know work out routine scheduled ways for extended family members to be involved with their families. Weekly respite breaks are one example. Relatives can keep children every Tuesday, or every other weekend, for example. One single parent sends out 50 copies of a letter that updates her family about her children's growth and progress twice a year. By keeping all her cousins, aunts and uncles aware of her children, she has increased the numbers of gifts and letters her children receive. A very creative single parent I know asks each of her more than 100 relatives to make a $5.00 investment annually in her children's college fund. Another family maintains a family clothing exchange so that children's clothes get recycled when children outgrow them.

Relatives can be good "emergency" support, too. But it's important to have maintained a good relationship through good times—phone calls, letters and invitations to dinner or lunch. People resent only being called in a crisis. They feel used.

Vacations With and Without Children

Planning vacations that include our children goes a long way toward sending messages of self-worth and value to our children, making them feel supported. It means a lot when children believe that we enjoy and like them enough to want to play or relax with them for an extended period of time. Part of our children's self-esteem comes from their belief that we find pleasure in them—in being with and sharing with them.

As single parents we are often so pre-occupied with surviving that we think we cannot afford the luxury of a "vacation." I'm not just talking about trips to the grandparents on holidays here. I'm talking about camping, state parks, scenic tours, Disneyland, Sea World, etc. Hotels and recreational parks are becoming more aware of the need to reach out to families. We can also motivate them to be more responsive to us as single-parent families.

Vacations Without Children

I also encourage setting aside at least three days to one week annually for a vacation without your children. Single parents can help each other here. Try offering to provide care for a friend's children while she or he takes a break, in exchange for the same favor when you take yours. I didn't give myself this gift of vacations until my son was 15 years old. That's right, I took my first vacation after being a single parent for almost 15 years.

I hope other single parents will learn that they deserve respite, vacations and relaxation earlier in their lives. It has a lot to do with self-esteem and support. It is possible, even on limited budgets. In fact, I suggest having a special savings account for recreation, vacations, fun!

Sometimes relatives want to help and they don't know how. The gift of a vacation can be life—or at least sanity—saving.

Twenty-Five

Dating

Support for single parents includes care for ourselves. We still have the need to have loving and intimate sexual relationships in our lives. That can often create a conflict with our own children. Who takes care of us? How much do we expose our children to about our lovers or intimate relationships? There are always the guilt feelings that arise if we expose them to a relationship thinking that it might become a permanent relationship and then it doesn't. This is a very complicated matter about which we as single parents have to establish our own unique guidelines. I'd like to share some basic rules that I think have worked and are important considerations.

Resentment

Did you ever notice how our kids show their worse side around the people we date? When we introduce them, they mumble instead of saying hi or hello. From the perspective of our child, we need to be mindful of the fact that they are always feeling a sense of connection to, and a sense of loss of, their natural, or biological parent. They usually resent the presence of any other person coming in, and feel that no other person could or should ever replace their natural parent. This resentment is going to be there no matter what we as parents try to do to fix it. Therefore, I think it's important to limit the exposure that our children have to that stress, unless it is absolutely necessary. In other words, give a relationship time to unfold and develop before we choose to expose our children to another adult, who in their minds may displace their parent. Don't generate a stress and adaptation syndrome that may not even be necessary. That is the first thing to remember.

I remember once, after my two marriages and almost a third, my son who was then 12 years old said to me: "Look, Mom. I love you and I want you to be happy, but please just don't bring me any more daddies."

Relating to Our Children

Another important relationship issue is to make sure that our friends or lovers value children and share our beliefs and our ideas about how adults should interact with children. They must also know their limits in terms of disciplining our children. This is a discussion that should be put on the table early on in the relationship. This is a very difficult subject for us as single parents, because there is a vulnerability. Often times, we feel a certain need for a mate, a father or mother figure, someone to help us with our families, particularly our boys. Because of that vulnerability, that sense of helplessness and sometimes even desperation, we may accept behaviors and attitudes that we really, in our hearts, don't feel are right. Children have a hard time forgiving parents for these kinds of errors and mistakes. I speak from personal experience, here. Our children have looked to us as their protection, as their comfort, as their Anchor and when they feel that this is betrayed, it causes a deep scar that may take some years to heal.

I almost married a man who had been raised by rigid parents. His father was a minister who believed "If you spare the rod, you spoil the child." I neglected to discuss my child-rearing beliefs with him. My children practically never misbehaved. Then one day my daughter disobeyed him and ran into the street. He spontaneously spanked her, hitting her twice on her legs. This was extremely difficult for her because 1) He was not her "real" father or parent; 2) She was not used to corporal punishment; and 3) She felt I had failed her. She felt that I should have prevented him from hitting her. She knew I would have talked to her firmly and made sure she understood the real consequences of her carelessness. She knew I would have honored her intelligence, her feelings and her spirit, and not humiliated or overwhelmed her because I was stronger and bigger.

Instead, because I was not there, someone else who cared about her safety used different discipline methods. His methods were not based on understanding the "whole" needs of my child. As a result, she learned to fear him, not to trust him. She also became unsure about my capacity to Anchor or "protect" her. It was very confusing for her. We've talked about this and she has expressed her feelings. My advice to single parents on this issue is— prevention is the best medicine.

Don't Be Manipulated

As single parents, we must make sure that our children and our children's needs for another parent are not used as a tool for manipulation in our own relationships. Sometimes the idea that people are taking on responsibility for our children is allowed to be used as a tool for making us feel a sense of obligation to them. And sometimes we do this to ourselves. We think that because someone would take on the responsibility of "someone else's children" or "another man's children," we are then supposed to have more of a subservient and grateful dynamic in the relationship with that person.

This is a common mistake. This kind of thinking comes from a very low sense of self-worth and self-esteem as well as from our residual feelings of guilt and shame about being a single parent in the first place. This only leads to less than desirable relationships, such as the replacement father syndrome.

Replacement Fathers

On the subject of replacement fathers, when I became a single parent and allowed myself to socialize, I tried on the last names of most of the men that I went out with after the first date. Clearly, my objective in dating was to find a suitable husband—to find someone who could fill in this missing role in my life, this gap. My kids needed a father figure. I was actually less concerned about my own needs. I was more concerned about the needs of my children. You see, I really didn't believe that I had the capacity to be a successful single parent, and I wanted to end this "problem" as quickly as possible. That was the message that I sent out, and ironically, it was kind of a subconscious demand on my part. I really wanted a new daddy for my children. And in so doing, I think I helped to push away appropriate men who might have come into my life who would have been eager to love me, and to love my children.

Companions, Not Replacement Parents

One of the greatest moments of my life as a single parent was when I reached a point of total acceptance of my role as the provider and the nurturer, my role as the head of my household. Then I began to date men not as potential replacement fathers, but as companions for both me and my children. Our children basically believe that no one can ever replace their father or mother, anyway. At best we can attract someone into our lives who becomes a good friend and a surrogate by mutual agreement, depending on the age of the children. The criteria by which we allow ourselves to form relationships should be both our need for an appropriate companion and partner and our family's need for another parent.

Once a person is selected that we think is compatible with us and our families, it is important to remember that that is exactly what that person is becoming. They are becoming part of our family; they're not just becoming our partner or mate. Many single parents who remarry never involve their children in this vital process. Children are often just told that "your mother is getting married and you're in the wedding." Or they find out after the wedding. This can cause a great sense of rejection on the part of the child. We are single parents with families, so anyone who comes into our lives comes into our families and I believe it's important to let children feel included early in the process of expanding the family. That's not to say that our children make the decision for us; this is always our own decision. But we need to find ways to make our children feel included in the process. We must take time to assure them that they are still going to be honored and respected.

How It Starts Is How It Goes

The way we start out the new family relationship is the message that we're giving our children about how the relationship is going to unfold. If our children are not included in the process during the beginning of commitment, then they are going to be fearful that they will be excluded throughout the relationship. Children will believe that this person is coming in not to add to their lives, but to take their mother away from their lives. Remember, too, that as single parents we are already pretty stretched and have limited availability to them. The issue of changing the family dynamic to bring in a new partner can have life-long consequences and impact on our children. Family counseling during this transition is a good idea. There are also several books and organizations designed to help blended families and step-parents. Some suggestions are listed in the resource section.

Background Check

As single parents, it's really important that we know about the character of the people that we date. We must take time to develop a real sense of trust. Today there are introduction services that do background checks on individuals before you get to the point of dating them. Those are useful. Another route is to make sure that the person that you meet comes through your network of friends and associates so that you have a basis for knowing more about them and learning about their history. It is very hard to undo scars that are caused by psychological and emotional damage. It's much easier to prevent them by taking the time to access needed information. Find out something about the make-up of the person who will now influence your home and your children. Ask about the new partner's own family history. Discuss discipline and childrearing practices and beliefs.

Beware of Married Men

I've noticed (as have many of the other single moms I've met) the abundance of "married men" who are available and who want to date single parents. Odd? A closer look at the hidden dynamics reveals both the reasons and the risks.

First of all, the rate of infidelity or playing around among married men has been estimated by some to be as high as 50 percent. Some researchers say it is even higher. But there seems to be a special vulnerability or attraction between married men and single women with children. My interviews with several single mothers over the years (as well as my own disastrous experiences) have led me to conclude that the ingredients for this cake are the single mother's great need—at times, desperation—for adult companionship and respect, and the married man's need to connect with a woman for whom the risks of "loss" are reduced. The single mother who perceives herself as really "needing this relationship" is less likely to date other men. She is also less likely to pressure him to leave home. All too often, we (as single mothers) feel "lucky" that someone spends time with us and/or our children.

The risks are enough to fill another book, or at least a chapter. Emotional entrapment easily develops. That's the state of hoping, wishing, believing he will leave his wife for you "someday" and compromising in the interim. The women that I've talked with usually begin to hate themselves for compromising. But the longer they're in it...yup...the longer they're in it. When anything (even a relationship) erodes our sense of our own goodness, particularly on an ongoing basis, we translate it into guilt and find ways to punish ourselves. This self-punishment takes many forms—chronic health problems, obesity, substance abuse, depression, economic problems, etc.

Usually the relationship has to be kept secret, so the children never get to see that their mother is being cared for, loved and supported. The need for secrecy also prohibits going out in public together. So the romantic and recreational experiences that we're really starved for cannot be part of the relationship. What it often boils down to is a relationship that meets primarily physical, sexual needs with only limited opportunities for needed emotional and psychological intimacy.

This discussion on dating married men is certainly not included as a form of judgement or condemnation. Rather, it is offered as heartfelt advice—another lesson that I've learned on my journey from low self-esteem and victimization to higher degrees of confidence and empowerment. I've directed this section to women, although the risks may be comparable for male single parents.

Introducing Children to People We Date

We should not be afraid to have loving relationships. Our children need to think and to know that we are desirable, attractive, loving human beings. We also need to model for them what a loving, meaningful, supportive relationship is all about. They are always learning from what we do. Our sexuality and our loving companions shouldn't be pushed under the table because we're single parents. We deserve a romantic life. But that life has to be managed in such a way that considers the innocence and the vulnerability of our children. We must be patient, careful and selective.

We should give our children notice—prepare them for meeting this person. The first meetings should be of short duration, always with us present. We should take time to ask our children later, "how did you feel when he (or she) was here?" Encourage the children to express their feelings and let them know their relationship with you is not changing. Once a new partner enters our home on a routine basis, he or she can have an impact on the psychological or subconscious terrain of our lives. Their interactions become more frequent and repetitious, and they are affecting both our own and our children's emotions. All sorts of monumental implications arise when someone comes into our home on a routine basis. Care must be taken to observe how our new partners interact with our children. This is wisdom that I share and it's wisdom that I learned the hard way. I've spent many years trying to heal damage that was inadvertently and unknowingly done in my own family experience.

Discussing Sexual Intimacy Issues with Children

Our sex life is our business. While we may choose to involve our children in an awareness of the fact that we have a special person in our lives, and that we have love in our lives, we should not over-expose our children, particularly our young children to these issues. They haven't had a chance to process and establish their own understanding of sexuality yet.

When space is limited, privacy can be a real challenge. It's not a good idea to make children become aware of our sex life before they are old enough to understand its meaning to them. There are those who disagree with this, but I find that children carry some very interesting notions about their parents' sexuality (like it doesn't exist), and it's a very gradual process by which we should open them to this issue. Remember that ultimately their sexual behaviors will mirror their own sense of value and worth. Our children will take cues from us and our behavior.

Risk-laden sexual behavior has, since the onset of the HIV virus and AIDS, become one of the most serious issues our children must face. Teenage sexual activity is astoundingly high. As single parents, we have a tremendous task of modeling by what we do, our value, self-worth and self-care of our bodies including our sex life. As in the case of alcohol use, parents' sexual activities and behaviors will influence children most.

The second greatest influence will be our communication and dialogues about sex. I was driving my eight year-old to school one morning when she almost caused me to run the car off the road by asking me a simple little question. She said, "Mom, do you think Daniel (her fourteen year-old brother) has had sex yet?"

I was stunned. I didn't know what was more disturbing—my eight year-old talking about sex or the idea of my fourteen year-old thinking about or having sex. It was a little reality therapy for me.

At eight and fourteen, sex was a real issue in my children's lives. They were seeing it on television, hearing about it at school, discussing it and maybe even being pressured by their peers and

I, prude that I was, hadn't yet initiated family discussions around this matter of life-and-death.

I started gathering books and resources, and decided to tackle the subject head-on. After dinner two nights later, we had our talk about sex. Well, my kids thought I was from a different era and anticipated that this discussion would be corny at best and embarrassing at worst. It was a little awkward, but it was a beginning.

My main emphasis was on love, and the importance of loving themselves enough to remain in control of their bodies, not to let someone else take charge of their most important resource— themselves. I tried to talk about what it was like when I grew up and I answered questions. But they made it clear that they didn't have a lot of questions and preferred not to talk a lot more about sex with me. Still, a door to conversation had been opened. I've included some sources for sex education and AIDS prevention education information in the resource section.

Since then, we've learned to talk more freely and I believe we share some values.

I also learned to use television as a teaching tool about sex issues. I constantly point out the violent, exploitive and unfair treatment that goes on at the expense of women's (and others') self-worth, self-respect, emotional health and physical lives. Television is such a pervasive force in our children's lives, particularly in the area of sexual behaviors, I think we must learn to use it to teach our children to think critically, to analyze and form their own conclusions. We must also help children to distinguish their own reality and cultural values from those that are projected on television or in the movies.

Twenty-Six

Discipline

One of the most important sources of support in my life as a single parent has been my children's "good behavior." I cannot imagine the course of our lives together if my children had been discipline problems, disrespectful or out-of-control. We have been a team. They understand what's needed and expected from them, and I try my best to do my part. We have created a comfortable life together, but the key is that we are a team. Everyone has a critically important part to play.

When my daughter, Charisse, was about three years old, I was feeling very stressed and she had just decided to behave "like a brat." I think she tried to have a kicking, screaming tantrum. Well, according to my beliefs about child-rearing and discipline, black children didn't have tantrums—and, certainly my children didn't! So, although I didn't generally practice corporal punishment or "spanking," I lost it and whacked her on her behind. She was shocked. She then began to cry, and cried for what seemed like an eternity. She cried and cried and cried. I became so frustrated I said, "Charisse, you can't still be hurting. Mommy loves you. Please stop crying. It's OK" She just kept crying for what seemed like forever. Finally, I asked her older brother, then eight years old, to talk to her.

He said, "Charisse, sometimes adults spank us. Not often, but sometimes. It's OK It's not the end of the world." She stopped crying for a moment and protested, "No, that's not true. Adults are not supposed to hurt children. When they do they go to jail!"

My son just hugged her and then told me, "Mom, that school she's in—I don't know." She was in a wonderful Montessori school at the time. Apparently she had received some instruction on child-abuse prevention and was crying because she thought I was going to go to jail! I never spanked her again—or my son. As I learned more about the fragile self-image of children, and about their fears, I chose to find other forms of discipline.

The Control Issue

I don't think it's wise to approach discipline by asking "how can I control my child?" If control is the only objective, we'll never succeed. The goal of discipline for children has to be the same as the goal for self-discipline—growth. Growth always requires education or learning. So when we plan to discipline our children, an important first step is to determine what we want our children to learn from the discipline act. First, what do we want them to learn about themselves? Next, what do we want them to learn about their environment or world? And finally, what do we want them to learn about us and our family relationship?

Spanking or hitting our children answers these three questions in this manner: About themselves: It tells them that they are helpless, subject to pain and humiliation and not in control of themselves, particularly their physical bodies. About their world: It tells them their world or environment is ruled by people who have more size, more physical strength and more power than they do. It tells them to learn to adjust their behaviors to escape or avoid this kind of harm. About us: Finally it tells them that we, upon whom they are totally dependent—are willing to hurt them, to inflict pain on them, if they do not meet our expectations.

These are confusing, inappropriate messages for children. Hitting and spanking teaches children to not trust, to expect pain and to perceive themselves as helpless, or that fighting or hitting is the way to demonstrate power. It also demonstrates less regard for their physical bodies and teaches them to do the same.

There are more effective ways to teach or discipline our children. I'm not suggesting that we allow our children to grow up without clear limits, structure and expectations. I am suggesting that we can teach our children how to behave according to expectations, reinforce their behavior and provide discipline without humiliating them or eroding their faith and trust in us.

Here are some general guidelines.

1. Read books on child development so that you know what are normal or expected behaviors at specific years and levels of development. For example, I've seen parents expect a two year old to sit still during a school play or program, or to not make a mess at a restaurant. Children need to be free to be children at different stages. We can prevent some discipline problems by having realistic expectations of our children's behavior at different ages.

2. Remember children who have lost a parent through divorce, death or separation may feel out-of-control and insecure about their world. They may need to express these uncomfortable feelings by asserting control in inappropriate ways (acting out, being belligerent). They may also seek security in relationships with friends or peers. Encourage children to talk about, write about, or somehow express their needs and feelings. Family counseling is always advised during times of separation and loss.

3. Revisit your own childhood memories and decide if you think your inner-child was disciplined or treated fairly. Take some time (through counseling or a support group) to heal your own inner-child. This is important. Research shows that persons who were abused as children seem to be compelled (unless they get help) to automatically (despite their determination not to) replay this abuse with their own children, or to marry people who do.

4. Avoid yelling and screaming at your children. It makes them think that you are out-of-control. This increases their anxiety level and makes them insecure.

5. Show them that their actions have consequences. For example, if they choose to ignore your rules about no company when you're gone, they lose television or other recreational options.

6. Be the boss. You should be firm, clear and consistent with your children. They need to know that you are in charge. If not, they feel "responsible" or that they must be in charge. This is a very frightening feeling for a child. Send clear messages that you're the boss, by your firm tone of voice and direct eye contact. Gently touch them to reinforce a point. Mean what you say and be willing to listen.

7. While you can treat all your children fairly, you may not be able to treat them the same. Each child is different and may require slightly different styles or responses from us. My daughter requires much more structure and limits than my son did.

8. As single parents, it's hard to monitor our children's behavior because we may often be away. Don't hesitate to use taped messages or friends and neighbors who stop by. Surprise visits from you are useful, as are regular phone calls. Reports from each child on his own behavior at the end of the day are useful. Also, asking teachers for weekly or daily notes can send a clear message to our children when needed.

9. Use telephones, beepers, letters, recorders, video tapes, etc., to remind children of your presence and your awareness. Children need to know about our efforts to be aware of their behaviors, even in our absence. This creates a feeling that they are always connected to you, and you to them.

10. Don't pass the discipline buck to the "other parent" or to other "mates." Don't allow school authorities to pass the buck to the "other parent" either. Make sure your children and your circle of people know and respect the fact that you are the boss—you are in charge of your family.

11. Praise, record, acknowledge and reinforce good, appropriate behaviors. Let your children know how much you love them and need them to do their part in making your family work.

12. Be clear about "their part." Prioritize their responsibility to succeed in school, to develop their bodies, to stay healthy and to have fun. Let your children be children. Clearly define their chores or work tasks, but don't give them adult responsibilities like constant care of younger siblings. Children cannot care for children appropriately on a continuous basis.

13. Seek out the reasons for behaviors. Usually children do bad things because of unmet needs for attention (security), out of frustration (the need to self-express), or to assert their personhood and identity (empowerment). Discipline can be most helpful when it provides alternative ways to respond to these basic human needs for security, self-expression and empowerment.

14. Don't be afraid to change. If a consequence or punishment doesn't work or if it fails to produce the desired effect, find a new consequence. Also, as a single parent, be careful not to create a punishment circumstance that makes life too difficult for you. Once I banned my son from the telephone, only to find that I couldn't reach him to check up on his behavior. Also, don't—in a moment of rage—create an exaggerated or extreme consequence that you later have to compromise or reverse.

15. Don't discipline in anger. Take time to calm yourself before taking action. It is more effective.

16. Learn to recognize signs of the need for professional help. Consistent or escalating discipline problems, self-destructive or violent behaviors, refusal to respond to communication, dramatic changes in school performance, ongoing sadness or hyperactive behavior—these are times when we should reach out to counselors who understand children and child development. Family counselors are also useful.

Twenty-Seven

Protecting Our Children

Today's youth are much more vulnerable to being taken advantage of in violence and sex, particularly teenagers. We need to maintain an open dialogue with our children, so that they learn to understand the boundaries of their own bodies and their own personhood. It is important to teach them that they don't have to allow anyone to cross those boundaries, no matter who that person is. The best way to make them understand that is to communicate it—with clarity and with certainty. We need to be able to check periodically—to simply ask them. Our children need not hold onto pain and secrets related to experiences over which they had no control. We're not with them constantly, so the best way that we can guard them is to teach them to guard and to value themselves.

Asking our daughters, "what would you do if..." and having fun with them during the discussion about sex are useful tools. Young girls need to role-play scenarios of interaction with young boys so they understand manipulation. This is probably as true for boys as it is for girls, today.

Friendship and Peers

We also need to talk about our children's friendships. Our children's relationships can become an important part of our own support system. Peers do have a tremendous influence on children. Knowing who our children's friends are and making sure that their friends *know who we are*, can go a long way toward making the parenting experience easier, particularly as our children move into adolescence. I opted to make sure that my son's best friends felt that they could spend time in our home. That was one way of having an opportunity to better know what was going on in his life. I learned who his friends were and developed very positive relationships with them. They call me "Mom." At one point I thought this would create an extra burden. But it actually took away the burden of concern about activities, values and the direction of my son's teenage life. Establish ways to interact with your children's friends in the context of your own home, if possible. This is an important step you can take in supporting your role as a single parent.

The next step is to create an opportunity (either by telephone or in person) to meet and interact with the parents of our children's closest friends. It gives the children a sense of continuity in their lives when they think that there is some communication of a positive nature between parents. They may act like they resent it, and they may, in fact, resent it. But again, the network of family and community makes them feel more connected and more involved with adults who care about them.

Adult Supervision

Several researchers have assessed adolescents' vulnerability to problems and looked for characteristics in the homes and families of children who have gotten into trouble, delinquent children. These children had mental health problems, suicidal tendencies and drug-addictions. Researchers wanted to find out what these kids had in common. Did they all come from single-parent homes? Did they all come from low-income homes? What happened? What were the risk factors? Surprisingly, it was not the single-parent phenomenon, nor was it poverty. What consistently seemed to put these children at risk was spending long hours without adult supervision. Long hours without account-ability to an adult or supervision by an adult—that's what puts our children at risk. As single parents, we must be ever mindful and vigilant—making sure that some adult person is aware of, and responsible for our children at all times.

I talked about the school system being a support network in our parenting role, but the school day ends long before the work day ends, which leaves our children vulnerable for many hours of the day. Children need activities, focus and adult supervision. Federally and state funded afterschool programs are certainly an option we need to be aware of when we enroll our children in school. An important question for the administrator or the school principal, is, "What options does the school have to offer for afterschool activities and care?" This area of accountability needs to be put into the school administrators' domain. As a community, we must be aggressive about providing structured activities and care for school-age children, including teenagers, while parents work.

Preventing Our Children From Using Drugs

I've often talked with single parents who feel that they have no control over their children's susceptibility to drug use. They feel that there is some unknown, outside influence that may get to their children and subsequently involve them in drugs.

Research done in this area shows that the child who uses drugs, in most instances, uses alcohol first. The child who uses alcohol usually comes from a family where they have seen alcohol consumed often. In other words, when we establish a pattern in our own household that says alcohol is OK, we are actually establishing a pattern in our children. We are establishing a feeling or belief that alcohol consumption is OK. Alcohol makes our children more susceptible to drug use.

One important step that we can take as single parents to reduce the risk of our children becoming involved with alcohol, and subsequently drugs, is to *not* model alcohol drinking in our homes. Even social drinking—even the simple, regular consumption of beer and wine—can give a mixed message to our children. Now, some of you may be saying, "Oh, come on, I can't be that rigid; I can't be that strict." You have to decide for yourselves what kind of boundaries you want to set in this area. I, for one, think it's better to omit alcohol use around the children. If it is used for parties, dinners and special occasions like entertaining guests, then it needs to be done in a very careful way. We should be mindful that we are modeling behaviors. We are establishing values and ideas that our children may be internalizing on a subconscious level.

There are resources that you can access to help you recognize signs that your children may be using drugs, and resources to help you intervene. Suggested sources for information about school-based prevention programs are listed in the resource section.

The best prevention is to help your child create family and future pictures—images—of a desired drug-free life. Our behavior can model hope of a quality future.

A Single Parent's Support Anchors

1. Believe in your right to a happy, fulfilling, family life experience and your right to have needed help and support.

2. If you are feeling overwhelmed, abandoned, deserted or victimized, reach out for needed support through individual or group therapy, or to a parent support group. Take time to express your feelings to your loved ones and to establish a loving relationship with the vulnerable part of you that felt more than you could bear as a child, or whose needs may not have been met.

3. Look into your family background to identify generational patterns of parenting, particularly discipline styles that you do not want to continue with your own children.

4. Discuss parenting concerns and issues with your closest friends and/or relatives and work together to problem-solve. For example, in the area of discipline: quiet time instead of hitting.

5. Learn to ask for and expect expressions of appreciation, love and affection in your own life from your family and friends.

6. Start planning for child care long before you need it. Monitor it closely.

7. Join a single-parent support group and help each other with needed information and activities. You may have to start one.

8. Preplan afterschool activities and work with your school authorities on this issue if needed.

9. Plan vacations with children, as well as respite without them.

10. Try to establish a relationship with a prima-ry-care family physician. Be creative even if you use a clinic or HMO. Don't rely exclu-sively on emergency rooms for your physi-cian support.

11. Begin to dialogue and discuss sex issues at home with your children. Let them know they can talk about "anything" with you.

12. Don't deny your own need for loving adult companionship and sexual intimacy. Just remember that our choices have a profound effect on our children's perceptions about their relationships to us. Take time and care to consider their feelings and needs.

13. Remember children tend to do as we do, not as we say. Model the self-discipline behav-iors we want our children to display, partic-ularly in areas of drug and alcohol use, sex-uality, and self-care.

Support Anchors for People Who Care About a Single-Parent Family

1. Show your acceptance and appreciation for this family as a single-parent family by establishing authentic caring relationships with the parent and, if appropriate, the children.

2. Involve them in recreation and fun activities like games, sports, athletics, exercise and vacation outings.

3. Pay attention to their expressed feelings and needs, and identify ways to support the parent and children emotionally by listening and talking—authentically.

4. If you know the generational and cultural parenting history, offer praise and affirmation about positive patterns. Reinforce changes or reinforce effective ideas that have been passed on.

5. Offer to provide respite for the parent which makes it easier for him or her to have an intimate relationship with an adult and not involve the children prematurely.

6. Focus on the single-parent family's functioning and identify concrete support activities for any areas of need. For example, can you provide tutoring or reading resources in areas of education? Or can you provide weekly or monthly respite to help improve the parent's nurturing capacities? Can you remind the children of the parent's expectations and reinforce the parent's socializing role?

7. Offer to be part of the family's "emergency plan." Share contact numbers. Let them know that in a crisis you are available for transportation, care, etc.

8. Be alert for opportunities to reduce stress factors in the single-parent family's life—such as transportation, child care, safety or security checks, listening, etc.

9. Remind yourself regularly of the positive functional aspects of their single-parent family.

10. Keep abreast of the children's lives in the single-parent family. Get acquainted with their peers and their friends as an extended network for "knowing" the child.

Solvency

Solvency is our capacity to
meet our financial obligations.
Chemical solvents are capable
of dissolving other substances.
Adequate financial resources
are powerful solvents. Having
enough money can literally
dissolve most of the risk factors
that single parents face. But in
order to become financially
solvent, we have to explore our
mental attitudes and
expectations about money.
These attitudes trigger the
feelings that dictate our habits
and behaviors that concern
finances.

Twenty-Eight

"Blood Out of a Turnip"

Sears left a note on our door-knob. My mother snatched it out of my hand, not knowing I had already read it. It said, simply, "We were here today to repossess (to take back) our washer and dryer." Although I was only nine years old at the time, I knew what that meant and why. Mom and Dad had argued a lot lately because he was in his "slow" or "off" season, and he wasn't making much money. The arguments always seemed to end with the same statement. He'd say in his high-pitched, stressed voice, "Look, they can't get blood out of a turnip. If I don't have it, they can't get it."

He'd usually leave the house on this note, and Mom would ramble on, tearfully, saying things like "What kind of man would let his family go hungry, just because he couldn't find work? What kind of man is he, anyway?" Her berating would make me want to throw up, so I'd leave and go to my room feeling sorry for him, but really fearing for our safety and well-being.

Children have a way of remembering scenes, events and conversations that concern money. They relate these issues to their sense of security. Young children, remember, already have an exaggerated sense of responsibility.

Now don't get me wrong. We never missed a meal. Sears never took the appliances back. We lived in a large, three-bedroom house and drove a late-model, almost-new car all the time. Our home was carpeted wall-to-wall and our drapes were custom-made to match the carpet. No, we were not poor. We were solvent—most of the time.

My parents had the capacity to pay our debts (maybe a little late, sometimes). Their income covered the costs and expenses associated with maintaining our family. Our basic security needs were always met. We had housing, food, medical care, clothing, transportation, adequate electricity and a telephone. This is what solvency means. It is our capacity to pay our expenses and debts.

It's a vital Anchor. If we are to succeed in raising our children, we must be solvent. Ironically, chemical solvents dissolve things. Adequate financial income helps to dissolve most of our worries and anxieties. In our society, life changes when we have enough money. Provide a single-parent family with adequate income, and risks for problematic outcomes decline by 90 percent. In fact, the barometer for success or failure for children from any type of family is the absence or presence of poverty and its attendant problems. Family and child poverty is the greatest risk factor this country faces. One in five children in America is poor. Among single parents, one in two is poor. If I could show single parents how not to be poor, I'd have given them the greatest gift of all. I can show single parents how I've moved from low income to comfort, and how other women have applied these same principles toward realizing more economic stability and success. I can also offer a systematic approach to solvency that starts with dissolving old patterns to create new attitudes about our finances.

Child's Pictures

As a child, the constant exposure to financial worry and stress imprinted me with a deep sense of my family's insecurity and with perceptions of "lack." Our emotional experiences concerning money are as important as our emotional experiences about anything else. What we see and feel becomes what we believe.

We tend to believe that money is magical in nature—available to those fortunate few and made to disappear by some unseen force.

National surveys of single-parent households have revealed that the leading concern or source of stress is financial. This is supported by economic indicators as well. But this book is about possibilities, and I want to focus on what has worked for me and the hundreds of persons with whom I've worked, concerning money or solvency.

Attitudes

Before we tackle "how-to's," let's consider attitudes. I was thirty-five years old before I realized that my attitudes and expectations regarding finances were identical to my father's. He was an entrepreneur, I was an entrepreneur. He had slow seasons, I had slow seasons. He believed in his heart that he had no control over his own finances—remember, "You can't get blood out of a turnip."

I did not know that I shared that belief, but in truth I did. I discovered this belief after ten years of financial struggles as a single parent. The insight came through a disturbing telephone call. I was in a transition time, having ended a relationship and recently moved. After a life-threatening illness, hospitalizations and surgery, I had fallen behind in my bank-loan payments, renegotiated and was giving every effort to make all payments. The main source of my income was through federally-funded programs via community agencies for which I provided services under contract agreements. This often meant delays. So I called my loan officer at the bank to let her know I'd be a few days late. She started yelling in a very judgmental tone "What's the matter with you? A professional woman like you should be able to keep a simple loan agreement. I don't understand, what's your problem?" and on, and on, and on. In shock and defense, I yelled back, "Look, I don't have any control over this situation. It's out of my control; I don't have control of my finances!"

The Neon Sign

The words flashed before my eyes like a neon sign. There, in this moment of emotional distress, I had unearthed a dominant belief about my finances. It was part of my father's legacy. Probably his father or mother's legacy to him, as well. As a child I had identified most personally with my dad, and had unknowingly taken on many of his patterns and attitudes about life.

I had studied enough personal-development books and taken enough classes in goal-setting and life management to know what to do to change or get rid of this erroneous belief. On that day, I began to retrain my thinking and to reeducate myself to accept control, to assert control, over my finances. I started (believe it or not) by simply writing an affirmation, one hundred times:

> "I, Gail Christopher, now allow myself to have control over my finances. You, Gail Christopher, now allow yourself to have control over your finances. Gail Christopher now allows herself to have control over her finances."

I wrote this affirmation 50 times, every day, for a week. I put little green pieces of paper all over the house as "triggers" to remind me of this affirmation.

We Deserve...

Like everything else, solvency starts with one idea: the idea that each of us—every single one of us—deserves to have enough income, to have the money that's required for a sense of comfort and well-being. We deserve enough income to have savings, a safe home, transportation, needed insurance, adequate food, clothing, furnishings, etc. The idea is that not only does everyone deserve this, everyone can have it, all of the time. The idea is a direct contradiction to two commonly held beliefs—beliefs I consider to be myths. These myths are:

1. Scarcity: There simply isn't enough to go around, because these are hard times; and

2. The poor must always be with us.

I'm always reminded that scarcity is a myth when I hear the daily/weekly lottery totals.

This idea can be stretched even further. Not only do we each deserve to have the security that comes with adequate income, but it's the right thing to do. Money is not bad, or the "root of all evil." And poverty is not blessed in my opinion and experience. In fact, poverty is the farthest thing from blessed that I have ever known or been. I say this because, in addition to family experiences, religious and ethnic group beliefs also shape our attitudes about money.

A relative of mine gave me a card that had been passed out at her church. One side looked like a $50 bill, the other side had a list of things that money can't buy. It said money can buy a house, but not a home; medicine, but not health; things, but not peace of mind. I guess the idea of this little card is to juxtapose money and God, implying that money is bad. Now, don't get me wrong—I'm not suggesting that we should be obsessed with or worship money. What I am saying is that when we are poor, we are usually "worried" about money (or the lack of it) all the time and in that sense we are obsessed with, or focused on, money. I believe that the thing we focus on constantly is our worship, in a way. The promise of most religions is that our "needs will be met." In our present society, this does require money. We need to give up old attitudes, beliefs or messages that attempt to distance us from our right to, and our deservedness of, adequate income and financial resources. No matter what their source, these beliefs were born of ignorance.

Take Responsibility

I think the first step to allowing the "blessings" of solvency and financial comfort to enter our lives is to adopt a positive mental attitude about money. If you adopted a child, you would choose to be responsible for that child, and to love it forever. When we adopt a positive mental attitude about money, we choose to be responsible for having good thoughts, attitudes, and expectations about money. We respect it, enjoy it, expect it and accept it! Amen!

So, based on our deservedness and our permission from the Almighty, what else stands between so many single parents and prosperity—or at least solvency or comfort? Most of us may say in a choral voice, "Dead-beat ex-spouses and 'other parents' who don't pay child support." Then we'll talk about the high costs and lack of affordable housing, child care, medical insurance and quality education. We're darn right! In the United States it costs from $157,000 to $300,000 to raise a child from birth to 18 years of age. Neither welfare benefits nor part-time employment, or even full-time minimum wage employment coupled with typical child-support payments, will cover these costs.

Be Your Own Boss

The simple truth is that, as single parents (for now anyway) we have to become entrepreneurial and creative about money—about income and expenses. To be successful as single parents, we have no choice but to devise a system that enables us to cross over the barriers—ex-spouses, lower wages and national policies notwithstanding—between us and our deserved financial stability.

For the single parents that I've known, it has meant multiple income sources and creative management. Or it has meant additional education and preparation for better paying jobs. Before they got to this, however, it meant examining and changing their attitudes—their thoughts and feelings. It meant changing their mental focus and expectations concerning finances and their relationship to money.

It starts with the capacity to believe—in our hearts, minds and beings—that we have the creative power to control our finances or incomes. It starts with the capacity to truly believe that the combination of our desires, thoughts, feelings and actions can and will lead us to solvency.

Years ago, I read a book by Phil Laut, called *Money is My Friend*. It appealed to me more than another good book of a similar nature, *Think and Grow Rich*, by Napoleon Hill. Frankly, I didn't believe I could grow rich. From poor to rich was a bit of a stretch for even my imagination. I'd have happily settled for just making money my friend.

What is a friend, anyway? You can count on a friend. Friends are there when you need them. Friends certainly don't desert you when you need them most. You trust friends. You have expectations and you enjoy your friends. Yeah, the more I thought about it, the more I could relate to this idea. Why not make money my friend?

I suggest you buy and read Phil's book. But let me share how it, and a few others like it, changed my circumstances.

Changing Our Focus

First of all, the ideas in the book made me stop focusing on the lack of money and gave me pause to contemplate, to consider my relationship with money. This meant revisiting my childhood, my ethnic heritage and my religious upbringing all of which constitute the root source of most of our beliefs. Upon quick analysis, I discovered that I believed some key things:

1. I could earn enough money to take care of my kids, but not enough to enjoy, save and have recreation and comfort;

2. No one would support me—I could only rely on myself for money;

3. And ultimately, I had no real control over money.

I discovered these deeply held beliefs through examining my parents' experiences and my interpretation of their money relationships. What are your attitudes and beliefs?

For my parents, their parents and their parents' parents, financial life was simply a struggle—a constant struggle. Even when it wasn't a struggle (in good times), the struggle monster loomed around the corner. Their struggles were real, but their struggles were cemented into attitudes, beliefs and expectations that were passed from generation to generation.

Savings

You couldn't save what you didn't have, so savings were rare, not part of our daily reality. If someone gave you credit, you could spend what you didn't have. But in so doing, you gave up your money, or control over it, before you even got it. You guaranteed that money would stay in your hands about 30 seconds—long enough to pass through.

Part of my solvency formula involved unlearning attitudes about saving money and creating a new relationship with money through saving it.

Years ago my first husband and I worked at the same institution. There was another young couple, who happened to be of a different race and religion, also working there. This young couple was Jewish. We had the same job classifications, although we had different responsibilities. So, our incomes, our paychecks were the same. We all decided to go out for lunch one day—we were probably one of the few sets of couples that were employed by this particular business—and this day was payday. My husband and I listened as the other couple discussed how much they'd have left after they deposited a portion of their income into savings. My husband and I looked at each other, but we didn't say anything. Then, on the way home, we said, "Savings?! How can they possibly save money on this little income?" We both kind of laughed and made light of it. Saving was a foreign concept to us. Neither of us had grown up in families that saved money. In fact, we'd grown up in families that focused on earning enough money to spend to meet their monthly expenses. Spending, not saving, was the primary rule about money.

But that experience stayed somewhere in my mind, tucked away, and I decided, "Ah, it's just a cultural difference. It's just a difference in the way people live." It was many, many years later, on the occasion of my 38th birthday, that I really began to understand that that couple had learned a lesson early—had in fact, been taught a lesson by their own parents, their own community. This lesson is a part of solvency. Indeed it is at the heart of not being poor. The lesson is that no matter how little money we think we have, we always have enough money to save some.

I've Got My Own

Why is that important? It's important because it establishes outwardly our inward beliefs about money. You see, if we believe that we have enough money to save, then we're saying to ourselves and to the rest of the world that we have. Do you remember the song, "God Bless the Child"? I think that can be taken literally, and God does "bless the child who's got his [or her] own."

> *Them's that's got shall get*
> *Them's that's not shall lose*
> *So the Bible says*
> *And it still is news.*

> *Mama may have,*
> *Papa may have,*
> *But God bless the child*
> *Who can stand up and say,*
> *I've got my own.*

In the words of this song, I think, lie the keys to solvency. The keys to solvency begin first with our focus. It goes back to the subject we discussed in the area of support. What do we think we deserve in terms of money? What do we really expect to happen? Can we stand up and say "I've got my own"? When we reach that point, we've taken a major step toward solvency which is a precursor to comfort and wealth. The same principle is at the root of tithing or giving 10 percent of your income to your church or charity. By giving, you are affirming the idea that you already have.

No Secret

How do you discover your own attitudes and beliefs? Our attitudes about money are reflected in our daily lives. It's no mystery. If we don't have enough money, therein lies our main attitude. Our main belief about money is that we aren't gonna have it and, in fact, somewhere underneath there is a belief that we don't deserve it. Because if that weren't the case, the circumstances would be different.

Now, I know, I know. I know there's the issue of jobs and job opportunities and community resources and there are a lot of external factors. But, what I want to share here is, I think, a turn-key idea that we must have in our consciousness if we're going to succeed. I've talked to hundreds, if not thousands, of mothers like myself who can attest to the fact that when they changed their attitudes, their relationships, their set of expectations about money, they began to see a change in their outward circumstances and in their lives.

Credit

Credit is like money. Single parents need to be able to access credit. This requires establishing a good credit history. It is common when marriages or relationships fall apart that related money problems damage the credit history of one or both parties. Since most divorced women experience a dramatic decrease in their economic status and income after a divorce, this can also mess up their credit history. Bills may go unpaid.

The key to credit is communication. Contact your creditors by phone and in writing. Explain your temporary circumstances. Stay in touch. When you cannot pay all of a bill, pay part of it. Ask them to work with you to help you protect your credit. But keep the promises that you make. Ask the credit reporting agencies for a copy of your credit history. If negative entries appear, write brief explanations and ask agencies to include these in the report. Always try to maintain three things: 1) A savings bank account; 2) A checking bank account; and 3) One creditor in good standing (credit card or store account).

Credit unions are very important sources of financial support for single parents. These are often work-related, church or union affiliated. If you can become a member of a credit union, do so. You can re-establish good credit, even after a bad credit history. It may require getting a secured credit card at first. Someone else may need to get it for you, as a second card on their account, or you may need to deposit cash to cover your line of credit. Keep up the payments—in advance if possible. Next, pay all old debts and get creditors to report debt satisfaction to the credit bureau. You will have to get them to do this. They won't unless you ask them in writing. Keep a copy of your updated credit report to show when applying for new credit. Explain your credit difficulties up front, so there are no surprises. Once you reestablish good credit, protect it. It is an important asset.

Other Financial Considerations

I recommend that as you become more solvent and your earning or income levels rise, you establish a relationship with a financial advisory group to help you make important decisions about insurance, wills, retirement, investments and college savings plans. All single-parent families need at least three forms of insurance (if they can afford it)—life, health and disability. All single parents need a will and all single parents should have some form of savings.

Twenty-Nine

Demystifying Money

The next step to changing our attitudes and our relationship with money is to demystify it. We begin by getting over the fear of lack of it and focus not on the lack, but on the presence of money. A good step in that direction is to establish a budget to identify exactly what it costs for us to maintain our family and to fulfill our functions as the head of this household, as the "boss." What is the income? How does it compare to your expenses? Use this chart to calculate one month's budget.

We want to estimate, at least on a monthly basis, what it costs us to live—what our expenses are. Once we've taken a realistic look at what it costs, we then need to look at our income. How much money is coming in to help us meet those expenses?

Use the chart below to look at your sources of income and in-kind support. If, for instance, you live with family and don't pay housing costs, put that in under housing support. If we find that there's a problem and the expenses are in excess of the income (which is the case in most situations), then we have to sit down

Cost of Living Budget Work-Sheet

Regular Monthly Payments :		Personal Expenses :	
Payment	**Amount**	**Expense**	**Amount**
Savings		Clothing (cleaning, laundry, etc.)	
Rent or House Payment (including taxes)		Medication	
Transportation (including insurance)		Education	
Furniture		Service Fees (beauty, health)	
Loan Payments		Travel	
Health Care		Gifts/Contributions	
Child Care		Spending Money	
Life Insurance		Taxes	
Other Insurance		Federal/State Income	
Maintenance		Property	
Utilities		Other Taxes	
Telephone			
Food Costs (at home)		Total Regular Monthly Expenses	
Food Costs (away)		Total Personal Costs	
Miscellaneous		**MONTHLY TOTAL**	

and become very creative about how to change that situation—how to increase the income or decrease the expenses. But the decision to do that has to be based in a real belief that we can, and that we deserve to have enough money to meet our needs.

Monthly Income and Related Support

	Source	Amount	Date	

	Source	Type of Help	Dollar Value	Date
	Total Dollar Value: Income and Support			

Thirty

The Big Four

In short, solvency or financial success for single parents begins with gaining control over any or all four of the biggest expense areas: housing, transportation, child care and food. The degree to which we can save on or reduce these expenses is the degree to which we can overcome our biggest financial threats. However, it may mean changing behaviors and sometimes compromising. It almost always means reaching out for help to family and/or friends. Remember, too, that most states have special hardship or emergency crisis programs set up to provide assistance with housing, cash or food stamps. State or city human service, children and family service and/or public aid offices should be contacted during times of financial crisis.

Begin by picking one area—transportation or housing. Look at what percentage of your income is being consumed here. If it is too much, then affirm the outcome you desire: a) To reduce the expense; or b) To increase the income. Now begin to brainstorm (use a friend) and throw out several (at least 10 or 15) different ideas for consideration. Use a process of elimination to narrow your choices down to five. Make your plan. Try it.

Don't let a negative outcome get you down. Look at is as feedback—information upon which to build a better approach next time.

Expect a miracle. I remember one single parent who had four young children. Housing was a big issue. Suddenly, to her complete surprise, her father retired, moved to an apartment and gave a four bedroom house to her and the children. With her biggest expense and worry reduced to almost nil, she decided to start her own business. At first, it supplemented her "day job." Within two years it became her full-time work and income. She is now a professional story teller who owns her own business that distributes her audio and video tapes, as well.

Housing

Since housing takes up the largest percentage of most of our income, it's probably a very good place to start considering our income versus expenses. In low-income families, housing can take 70 percent of the income, leaving little for food, child care, transportation, etc. Identify creative strategies for decreasing expenses while we work to increase our income. This is where the extended family can play a key role, as can forming partnerships and friendships with other single parents in similar situations.

The reality is that we are living in a country where affordable housing stock is not adequate to meet the needs of the people. There just aren't enough affordable houses around. When our country faced similar situations in history, the government moved to build more affordable houses and people used creative strategies within their families and communities. The great migration, for instance, of African American families from the South to the North was a time in which many relatives opened their homes and created spaces for other people to live with them. Times are not that different today. We need to look back at some of those values of extended family and find ways to help to reduce that tremendous cost that eats up a big part of our budget in the early stages.

Don't be afraid to ask a relative or friend to share housing space on a temporary or interim basis, until you can change your income level, or purchase a car which frees you to re-locate to an area where costs may be lower and/or jobs are more abundant. Here's where single parents could collaborate more. I know several single-parent families who have rented or purchased larger houses or apartments jointly to reduce costs and create a better quality space arrangement.

Housing issues are single parents' greatest financial strain. When we look at why families disintegrate and children end up in foster home situations, it's often due to lack of space in which to live, or adequate, safe, housing. When we look at the homeless situation we find that the fastest growing number of homeless families are mothers with young children.

In addition to finances, we may face other barriers to appropriate housing. Some realtors discriminate against families, particularly single mothers with young children. This is illegal. Landlords cannot legally deny housing based on the presence or absence of children. There are fair housing agencies to assist in situations like this. You can contact the national office to determine a local housing resource near you. The phone number is listed in the resource section.

Here are some creative housing strategies to consider:

1. Share living space with another single-parent family and use physical space creatively.

2. Take in boarders—students, elderly—to defray some of the costs. Remember to always make safety your first priority. Check out personal references and background information carefully. Be a careful observer at first and monitor closely. It is usually safest to work through networks like churches or close friends when accessing new people.

3. Insist on help with housing from the "other parent," sometimes instead of child support. One single parent I knew forced her ex-husband to get his parents to provide housing support for her and the children during the first two years after the divorce.

4. Access housing cooperatives or small community living arrangements through churches or community agencies.

5. Use extended family—generational sharing. Some experts believe that part of the increase in numbers of reported single-parent families is due to the fact that more young mothers now use welfare benefits to move away from parents and grandparents than in the 1950s and 1960s. Extended family living arrangements can help to reduce child care as well as housing costs.

6. Barter or exchange services for reductions in living costs. Some single parents have agreed to work as care-takers or janitors in return for lower rental costs.

7. Use university or college housing while in school. Many colleges offer housing for "couples" and will make similar offers for single parents.

8. Protect your housing credit history. Pay your rent on time. This history follows you. If you fall behind, clean up the arrears and make sure the rental agent doesn't give you a bad report.

9. Pray! All of my miraculous housing solutions have come to us after I've prayed. I am convinced that our family must have a special Angel for housing.

Seriously, when I mustered the courage to leave my second husband, I had no idea where we would live. One of my clients came into my office that day and asked, "Do you know anyone who could rent a house for a couple of years while my aunt is out of the country? She has waited until the last minute and is worried about finding the 'right' people." A miracle? Yes! The rent was affordable, the neighborhood safe and the space ideal.

There are no real panaceas for this housing dilemma. My advice is simple:

> Don't accept less than decent housing. Know up front that this is your greatest financial challenge and reach out for support immediately. Whenever possible, involve your ex-mate or ex-spouse in this key aspect of planning for your children. Housing issues include utilities—especially telephone. For single parents, a telephone is a necessity.

Transportation

Another critical area of expense is transportation—being able to get to and from child care, as well as to and from work. National researchers estimate that we, as single parents, spend as much as 25 percent of our income just on transportation. On the average, we spend as much as 35 percent to 50 percent on housing. So, just in living and in getting to and from those things that are essential in our lives, we have already spent almost two-thirds or more of our income.

Inadequate transportation is again, a potential source of vulnerability, particularly for our children. There is a safety factor in some neighborhoods. Of course bad weather compounds transportation issues. I've tried strategies from shared transportation to working at home. I know single mothers who use creative strategies to help deal with transportation needs—car pools for child care and living near work. Using school bus services and weekly or monthly passes also helps. Asking relatives and friends to help out with specific transportation routines can be useful. A dear co-worker agreed to take me to my child's child care center each day because he passed it on his way home. At one point, right after I left my second husband, my marriage problems had led to credit problems, so I could not get credit needed to buy a car. My kids were in a school that was located a good distance from our new home and my work required that I go from site to site. I really needed a new car. After being denied credit, I worked out a deal with a livery service. I paid a monthly fee and in exchange had a personal driver to handle our specific pre-arranged transportation needs. The driver was a good person who was an important part of our support system during that time. It cost me less than a car payment, gas and insurance—and helped reduce my personal stress.

Child Care and Solvency

A single parent who works full time for minimum wage could easily spend 90 percent of her income to pay for child care for two children, 49 percent for one. Child care is an important expense area in which single parents have to be very resourceful and creative. While we addressed related quality and child development issues in the "Support" section, it is important to look at cost-saving aspects now. If you are like half of all single parents and living with a poverty-level income ($9,890 for a family of three and $12,675 for a family of four), you may access federally or state funded child development and family programs such as parent/child centers and Head Start programs. If you receive AFDC benefits, recent welfare-reform laws may require that you enroll in a job readiness or skills-training program. Your state may provide subsidized child care while you are in training.

Some areas have special school-related infant care programs for young teen-parented families. Some states have also given block grants that can be used for state-funded early childhood programs. Congress passed a national child-care bill that will help states subsidize child care for working parents and provide more child care for AFDC recipient families, as well as to provide tax credits for low-income working families with children. Contact the office of your local elected official, congressman or senator to find out how your city or state is benefitting from the legislation and what you can do to access needed assistance. All of these options relate to young or preschool-age children.

Care for School-Age Children— Latch Key Kids

We must remember to consider the costs of afterschool care for school-age children. While some federal and state money may be available for supporting afterschool care, it is limited. You may, in fact, have to pressure your school or local park district to establish structured, supervised afterschool activities for children. By gathering a group of parents together who are willing to share in the management and/or costs, you can sometimes create a parent-cooperative afterschool program at the home of a parent or in the school. Public libraries are now becoming more involved with afterschool care because children are often using libraries during these hours, rather than going home to an empty house. I found myself advertising for, interviewing and hiring an "Afterschool Companion for School-Age Child." When I stated that I wanted a companion, instead of a baby-sitter, I found the correct person. She was eighteen and understood her job as being a friend for my ten year-old daughter. This meant going to activities with her, reading, helping with homework and sometimes shopping. It meant listening to and engaging her for the few hours between school and the end of my work day. Relatives, ex-spouses or ex-mates and other children's parents can all be resources for afterschool care. This is an important matter that is too often overlooked. The "latchkey kid," the child that comes home and spends 10-15 hours a week without adult supervision is at risk—real risk.

When I found myself with two children who were six years apart in age, I promised myself and my oldest son that I would not burden him with the responsibility of "taking care of his younger sister." And for the most part, I did not. During a transition time, however, after ending a live-in relationship, I was functioning in a "survival" mode. We had just moved, started over, and I was working long hours. My son was twelve and my daughter was six. Legally, leaving her in his care for a few hours was not neglect. Yet, a twelve year-old boy has a lot on his mind. A twelve year-old who has just moved into a new community has even more on his mind. One afternoon while walking with a friend his age, he forgot that his sister was walking with them. In their conversation, the boys simply lost sight of her, turned a corner, and looked back to find that this six year-old girl had disappeared.

The next two hours were very traumatic for the two boys, particularly my son, and very traumatic for my daughter. When she realized she was alone—abandoned—left by her brother and his friend in a strange neighborhood, she panicked. She began to cry and ask for help. She did not get it, however. By the grace of God and her own wit, she found her way to the home of a friend of mine, whose sixteen year-old daughter was home. She let her in and called me at work. The lesson: children cannot take appropriate care of other children.

Reducing Food Costs

Much to my children's dismay, I can take a basic rice or pasta dish and add (according to them) everything but the kitchen sink—melt some cheese over it, put it in the oven, bring it out, and call it dinner—a casserole. At one point, we had a very well-intentioned neighbor who would come upstairs to chit-chat after her long day at the office, which would usually be about dinnertime for us. As she observed me serving these cheese-topped casseroles on several evenings during the week (along with a big salad) she began to feel sorry for my children. I noticed that periodically, she would wink at my daughter and say, "Why don't you come downstairs, Charisse, I have something to show you." Little did I know that upon arriving in her apartment, they would gorge themselves on hamburgers, french fries or hot dogs.

My casseroles have remained a running joke in our family, although I have subsequently stopped preparing them (and anything else) with the same frequency. But my casseroles were economical, and the art of stretching a food-dollar while providing quality nutrition, is probably one of the most important solvency lessons that we have to learn as single parents.

The Department of Agriculture estimates that for single-parent families, purchasing food takes up the third highest portion of our income. There's rent, then transportation and then food. Now, as we become magicians with money, one key is to reduce expenses. We can reduce expenses for food and, at the same time, improve the quality of foods that we consume. Some single parents experience some relief by participating in the federal food-stamp program. The discussions that follow apply whether purchasing food with stamps or cash.

Meats

Let's start with meats, for instance. Meats can make up the largest part of the food budget and by choosing to have a diet that is not high in expensive meats, which are usually too high in fat, we can reduce the cost of groceries. Solution, increase other sources of protein in the diet. These will include beans—like lentils, navy, black, that provide adequate protein when combined appropriately with rice and other grains.

Good ideas for planning diets and menus that are still very adequate in protein, that cost less, and that provide better quality nutrition are found in these recommended books: *Diet for a Small Planet*, by Francis Lappé and *Let's Have Healthy Children* by Adelle Davis.

The grain and bean combination also provides needed dietary fiber. Fiber reduces our risk for cancer and for other conditions that are associated with what's commonly known as constipation or bowel stasis.

Convenience Foods

Pre-cooked, pre-sweetened and pre-cut foods are generally more expensive. We, as consumers, have to pay for the time and effort that went into packaging them for "our convenience." I know that this is an inherent conflict, because as single parents, we have less time than we do money. So, the question is: Is it better to use the convenience foods, and therefore save on time? I have been convinced that we can prepare foods in a more wholesome way and still not spend a lot of time in the kitchen. Begin by making sure your weekly menus contain lots of salads and whole grains and beans.

Here are some ideas:

1. Plan menus on a monthly basis.

2. Include lots of whole grains like brown rice, oatmeal, millet, whole wheat pasta products and whole grain breads.

3. Include lots of beans and seeds—lentil, mung, navy or red beans; sesame and sunflower seeds.

4. Pre-prepare these types of items at least twice a week—meat loaves, casseroles or soups.

5. Invest in both a pressure cooker and a crock pot. They save lots of time and can be used for soups and stews.

6. Use a microwave for re-heating and preparing single-food items like baked potatoes, quickly.

7. Offer fresh fruits and dried fruits for dessert.

8. Include salads each day. Pre-wash vegetables and store in crispers. Create your own "salad bar" effect each day.

9. Make breads—both quick and yeast—often: e.g., corn bread, whole wheat bread.

10. Pre-arrange at least two meal-sharing events per week. For example, a weekly pot-luck or a Sunday dinner or brunch exchange with friends.

11. Include green or yellow vegetables daily. In summer months, grow your own or purchase from farmer's markets.

12. Along with friends, visit small farms that allow you to pick your own fruits and vegetables. The savings can be tremendous.

Water, Water Everywhere

Water is always an important beverage and we need to encourage the consumption of it. Fresh fruits and fruit juice contain water. Making pre-sweetened beverages like iced tea or lemonade, or sweetening them using artificial sweeteners instead of sugar, can be an appropriate substitute, although many children don't like the taste of artificial sweeteners. There has been some progress made in that area with the newest forms of artificial sweeteners. There are some cautions about excess use of artificial sweeteners or any use if you have certain metabolic problems. Check with your pediatrician about the newest artificial sweetener. Avoid purchasing excess caffeinated, carbonated and sugar-sweetened beverages. It is important in not only reducing our grocery bills, but increasing our intake of wholesome foods.

Weekends

The weekend can be devoted to pre-preparation of meals that can be used during the week, and children can simply heat these meals in the microwave. Often our work schedules necessitate that the children or child-care workers heat these meals easily. I know, you're thinking, "Weekends! When is my day of rest?" Quite often as single parents we don't have full days for rest every week. We might only have an evening for rest and one weekend out of the month for rest. But, I've found that many successful single parents use their Saturdays or Sundays for pre-preparing the meals that are to be consumed during the entire week.

Coupons

Research suggests that people who live in inner cities simply don't clip coupons and use coupons as readily as people who live in suburban areas. But, as part of reducing expenditures for foods, coupons are often useful. I have found savings are greater on non-food items like cleaning supplies, soaps, and household items, than they are on food items. Typically, coupons on food items tend to be on pre-prepared and prepackaged food items. As our family uses more natural items, there are less food coupons available. I have worked with other families who have become very creative in their use of coupons and find they help to reduce costs. Once again, it takes time to clip the coupons. Some single-parent support groups make this one of the group activities.

Thirty-One

Time is Worth More Than Money

We've discussed money-saving strategies, and one of the things we've noticed is that they require time. Since 90 percent of single parents with school-age children work, the challenge of finding time to implement these strategies, be with our children, and for that matter, be with ourselves—is a major challenge. I am including this time management discussion because today perhaps more than ever before, time is money.

And how we manage our resource of time has a lot to do with the quality of our lives and our income. I need to clarify something here. We really can't manage time. It is always the same—24 hours in a day, 60 minutes in an hour, etc. What we have to learn to manage is ourselves and what kind of activities we decide to put into our limited time. First we need to be aware of how we're not managing our time, or how we are being managed by the reality of the lack of available time in our lives. We must take a good look at what we're doing with our days right now. Use the following chart to assess how you're spending your time. Using color-coding may help.

24 Hour Time Review Chart

	SUN	MON	TUES	WED	THURS	FRI	SAT	most time spent
6–7								
7–8								
8–9								
9–10								
10–11								
11–12								
12–1								
1–2								
2–3								
3–4								
4–5								
5–6								
6–7								
7–8								

	SUN	MON	TUES	WED	THURS	FRI	SAT	most time spent
8–9								
9–10								
10–11								
11–12								
12–1								
1–2								
2–3								
3–4								
4–5								
5–6								

Personal Activity Codes:

S:	Sleep	M:	Me	SC:	School
TV:	Television	F:	Food or Eating	TP:	Transportation
PW:	Prepare for Work	C:	Children	*	Create Your Own Additional Categories
W:	Work	HW:	Homework		

A Matter of Habit...

Now that you see how you're spending your most limited asset—time—you may want to make some changes. You may need more time for yourself, or time with your children. Remembering that time can't be managed, only we can be managed, we need to look at some of the principles of effective self-management. Self-management is usually a matter of habit. Habits are easily formed and hard to break. What "habits" keep you from doing what you know you need or want to do to improve your income or level of solvency? Single parents who have worked at home have identified some time drains:

- Excessive telephone time;

- Soap Operas and other forms of TV;

- Excessive travel time;

- Interruptions by friends, including boy-friends or girlfriends;

- Fatigue; and

- Fear of failing.

It often helps to set specific goals, or to have a focus for the day or hour that allow us to take charge or better manage our activities. Use the following Self-Management Work Sheet for starters.

Monitoring our own use of time in relationship to our own goals is a good exercise to do about once every three months, or whenever we are feeling overwhelmed.

Here are some general ideas to help us manage our time better.

1. Divide big jobs into smaller tasks that can be handled one at a time.

2. Prioritize according to desired outcomes. If the outcome is to have more money, then focus on related activities like creating a business, finishing school or preparing a resume.

Self-Management Work Sheet

Start by stating: My goals for today are: (state in terms of outcomes, not just activities, e.g., "To complete Chapter Four in the math book in preparation for my GED class." Not—"To study math."

My Goals for Today:

1. _____

2. _____

3. _____

Time	Action	Important to Which Goal?	Comments

I Learned This About My Activities Today:

_____

_____

_____

3. Maintain a daily calendar or appointment book. It says your time is important to you.

4. Do periodic time logs to review how you're doing.

5. Impose deadlines on yourself.

6. Schedule your television viewing. Limit yourself to specific programs. Otherwise, turn the set off. Don't let it watch you.

7. Schedule recreation—relaxation and play time for yourself.

8. Keep a daily record of your accomplishments. Make to-do lists and check off what's been done.

9. Learn how to delegate. Some portion of what you are doing can always be done (just as well) by someone else. Identify what others can do. Ask them to do it. Follow up to see that it's done, however.

10. Anything that's important to us will require some of our time. However, it's up to us to decide what's important. Then we have to write it down as a goal and make a list of related activities that we must make time for. Goals can be anything—weight loss, better muscle tone, more friends, finding a new mate, improving income, helping children succeed in school, getting a car, moving, etc.

11. Schedule quality time or focused attention moments/hours with each and then all of your children.

Enough Time

When I was executive director of a national organization that represented families and support groups for families, we commissioned the Gallup Polling organization to assess a representative sample of the country to answer some key questions about parenting and family issues. We asked parents what they valued most and what their greatest challenges were. Suprisingly, what they wanted was more *time* to spend with their children. As single parents, that's probably the resource we have the least of. Giving ourselves and our children focused attention and special time is, indeed, an ongoing challenge. Because their happiness helps us to be free to work, to remain "solvent," part of our solvency has to include making sure our children still feel connected to us, and that they know how important they are to us.

As our children reach the school-age and adolescent stages, we tend to pay less less attention to their need for us to be with them. Let me just suggest some things that may be helpful in making sure that our children get enough of our time. First, if we have more than one child, we need to plan to give each child their own special evening or their own special day on a regular basis. They can look forward to this time, knowing that it is their day with you. It helps to reduce the tension between brothers and sisters—sibling rivalry.

Rituals, Again

Another important way to devote time to your children is to make sure that there are some rituals that you share on a routine basis. One of our primary rituals became watching the Bill Cosby Show every Thursday night together as a family—laughing, interacting and discussing some of the important issues that were raised in the program. Your ritual may be worshiping, going to church together or having a special kind of meal together once or twice a week. Invariably, as the children get older and move out to their individual schedules, you will find that you're unable to have everyday meals together. Other rituals include bedtime activities—reading or telling stories, baths, gardening or games. A ritual is a practice that has special meaning to you, that is repeated and enjoyed. Create your own. Even chores can be turned into sharing opportunities/rituals. You can also involve other families in these activities.

Use Transportation Time

The time that you spend going to and from school is valuable, too. I often drove my children to school and found that these moments were special moments if we made them special. If we let ourselves get caught up in the hectic pace and the sense of stress of getting to places on time because we overslept, etc., then those moments were not special sharing moments, they were moments of anxiety. Learn to steal those moments together that you do have, in a mind-set that is relaxed and calm, for the purpose of interaction. This is an important way of meeting our children's needs for our focused attention, as well as our needs for their love and appreciation.

I remember, while I was directing the family organization, we were preparing for a major meeting and the phone rang early in the morning. The call was about the upcoming board meeting. I was busy talking while preparing breakfast, and my daughter became belligerent and angry. She stormed out of the room. I was infuriated with her because she wasn't respecting the fact that I was taking care of important business. As I began to chastise her for her seemingly outrageous behavior, she just looked at me and said "Mom, I thought families were your business." And I got it, loud and clear. She, in fact, was expressing her disappointment in my having allowed our brief time together, our morning ritual of breakfast, to be interrupted by a business-related phone call. Those meals together, although brief, need not be hurried, and they can be used as special times, special opportunities for listening and sharing with our children.

Make Bed Time Special

I've found that the bedtime ritual still is an important ritual in our family, although I am often exhausted. Back-rubs, stories, jokes, games, songs, prayers together—can all be important rituals that we build into our lives to give our children a sense of stability and reliance on our presence. That's what makes them feel valued and that's an important part of our solvency—because if they're thriving emotionally and physically, we are free to work without anxiety.

Thirty-Two

Education and Solvency

In this society, as is becoming the case all over the world, literacy through education is the precursor, the necessary element for being able to earn an income that creates solvency. I don't know of any state in the country in which income from public aid will generate a state of solvency, as we have defined it in this section. AFDC benefits simply will not generate enough income to pay the bills and to meet the expenses that are necessary for raising children. We have to be literate, educated and employed. The more educated, the greater our income potential. Education is an important part of our and our children's future financial success or solvency.

Our children's education presents some special challenges to us as single parents. This was dramatically revealed to me shortly after I moved to a suburban area in search of better schools for my children and in an attempt to reduce the risk factors that my children, particularly my son, would face as a teenager in an urban area. I was attending parents' night. I waited in line with the other parents and finally made it up to the table where I sat down. The teacher glanced at me and then began to read from the page.

She said, "Let's see now, Brenda. She is getting a B here... and Brenda is doing..." and then she looked at me and said "You're not Mr. & Mrs. So & So, are you?" I remained calm.

After she found a new folder which was, in fact, my daughter's file, she began to read from it, again failing to make eye contact with me. She began to recite, "Um, hm, Charisse is getting a C here, she's not a problem in Math. Um hm, she's not a problem in English, she got a C. She's not a problem here in History and in Social Studies, either." By the third "not a problem," I was becoming angry. I said "Excuse me, I'm not here to discuss whether my daughter is a problem; I don't expect her to be a problem. That is not why she is in school." That broke the ice. She then looked at me. We made eye contact and for the first time communicated on a deeper level. We began to cut through her stereotypical expectation—that my daughter, a black child from a single-parent family was going to be a problem in her classroom. The mere fact that Charisse had not presented any behavior problem to her was the highest expectation this teacher had of my daughter. This was devastating, but also revealing.

I took the time to be at that parent meeting and to confront this teacher's prejudice and her negative expectations. But, how many thousands of us as single parents never make those meetings and never have those interactions with teachers? It is up to us to help them move past their own misperceptions. Our relationship with teachers can help to determine the quality of the teacher/child relationship.

The irony is that my daughter, who was reported to have been doing C work and to have been "not a problem," brought home a report card the following month, that was almost all A's with one or two B's. What happened in that month, following my visit with her teacher, that hadn't happened in the weeks that preceded it? I believe the teacher began to value my daughter more, because she knew that my daughter had a parent at home who was deeply invested in her success and in her education process.

She then began to relate to my daughter, not as just another child who she was thankful was not a problem, but as an individual with capacity and potential and needs. Ironically, this teacher turned out to be the teacher that my daughter valued most in her middle school experience. At least two years have passed, and she still corresponds with this teacher on a regular basis. This story reflects how our children become symbols of society's negative projections. Many teachers expect poor performance from children from single-parent homes. We must learn how to support our children's educational and academic success.

Be What We Want Them to Become

The best way for us to support our children's educational success is to model for them that we, in fact, value the education process and literacy. When we model within our homes and within our lives a high respect and value for learning, our children develop the same values. No matter what our education level is, we are always engaged in learning and improving. If we didn't graduate from high school, it's a real inspiration for our children when they see us make a commitment to get a GED and finish school. If we are having trouble reading, we can acknowledge and admit that and learn to read along with them. Our education success has a powerful motivating impact on our children.

I believe that the real key to changing outcomes for children from single-parent families lies in optimizing education experiences. As single parents we can reduce our own, and ultimately society's, costs by making sure our children get the best possible education.

School Choices

There is talk these days about school choice and providing vouchers that would enable all families to select their school—public or private. While I am not sure that vouchers without associated transportation and/or funds to assure better quality schools in all neighborhoods would really result in equal choice for all parents, I do know that single parents need to use any means they can to be selective about schools, classrooms and teachers. From my children's earliest grade school on, I have tried alternative schools, magnet schools and private schools to assure quality education experiences.

In the large urban areas in which we lived for most of their school-age years, most public schools were inferior by my standards. My son's middle- and high-school years were spent in a private day school which offered him a full-tuition scholarship for most of those years. He was about to enter ninth grade when the public school system teachers went on strike. This was the third year of strikes. As a single parent, I was in big trouble. The thought of my now-adolescent son being out of school without adult supervision for a month or more was upsetting, to say the least. I had already decided to put my daughter in a neighborhood Catholic school that was comparatively low in tuition costs. But I was really feeling pretty desperate about my son's education, and quite frankly, his safety. I had to go to work and so did all the other adults I knew—except the teachers on strike. I thought for a moment about asking a friend who was a teacher, but changed my mind. Then, as I usually do in times of crisis, I prayed.

My son asked if he could attend a former classmate's going away party. The young girl was about to go away to a private boarding school out East. I said yes. The next morning the girl's mother called me and said "I just had to talk to the parent of that fine, well-mannered young man. Your son was a delight to have at our home. You should be proud of him. Where is he going to high school?"

I said, "If they open, he's going to Whitney Young, a magnet high school." She said, "Yes, that's a fine school, but have you ever considered a private prep-school?" I said, no, I couldn't afford that. She said, "Well, there are private schools that offer scholarships to exceptional students. Your son seems pretty exceptional to me. Here, take this number and call this school. It's here in the Chicago area, and I know they're looking for students like your son."

I took the number and called the school. Even though their semester had already begun, they agreed to interview us. We made the bus ride (at that time we had no car) for two-and-a-half hours to a north suburban neighborhood. When my son saw the school setting—the college-like campus with landscaping and its own library building—he was speechless. He eventually said, "Mom, I really want to come to this school." I said, "You know you'll spend four hours a day on busses." He said, "That's OK, it's worth it." Well, the admissions officer called us two days later and said that something unusual had happened the day after we left. A delegation of about 20 students who had spent time with Daniel on his tour had come to her office as a group and signed a petition requesting that he be admitted to their school—this semester.

Whatever was the source of this miracle—Daniel's charm or my prayers, or both—Daniel started school the following Monday. This school was ideal for our needs at the time. The program included daily athletic or sports activities for all students. Class sizes were small and teacher/student ratios were small, too. He ate three meals there and stayed in school until about 5:00 each day. Although he didn't get home until after 7:00 in the evening, he was not idle or without adult supervision. He was safe. In his second year, we moved to within 35 minutes of his school.

Boarding Schools

Some single parents, who have the financial resources, consider boarding schools for their older children. Don't forget about scholarships and financial aid. Many private schools want to diversify their student population. I made this choice for my daughter at a comparatively early age—she was entering the seventh grade. We searched for a school that had a small, intimate family-like atmosphere and found one which had only 20 or so boarding students. Here are some reasons why today's single parents may want to consider the boarding school option:

1. The movement back and forth between two separated parents homes may create chronic stress in highly sensitive children.

2. The parents' work schedules may require constant travel and unpredictable hours, which despite child-care arrangements and telephone parenting, still leaves children feeling frustrated and insecure.

3. In the absence of other siblings or years of residence in one neighborhood, children may feel isolated without needed peer support. Boarding schools can provide important peer support and a pseudo-family atmosphere.

4. Some children thrive in highly structured settings and need more focused attention than one working parent can afford. Dorm parents and boarding-school staff have this—attention to children—as their primary function.

5. Excellent study habits and academic skills require time and resources that some single parents may choose to delegate to the staff of a private-school setting.

6. Peer pressures and environmental risks can be reduced in more monitored, controlled settings.

If you choose this alternative, remember to involve your child in the choice. Let them help to select the school. Above all, work to maintain a close emotional bond with the child even while they're away. Write, call, visit, observe classes. Try to take your vacations while they're at home and spend quality time with them then. Also, ask the boarding school to send regular reports to the non-custodial parent, as well. Encourage the non-custodial parent to maintain a relationship with the child who is away in school, too. At this point, I believe that the decision to let my daughter attend boarding school was the smartest parenting decision that I've ever made. Each child and each parent must make careful, individualized choices about education and school. Here is a letter written by my daughter from school while she was in the eighth grade. Its content reassures me that we made a good choice. It may help other parents who are considering the value of boarding schools. Books on boarding schools are included in the resource section.

February, 1993
Dear Mom,

I am in science class, writing a letter home for an assignment. We've done this before, and I enjoyed doing it, but I got a bad grade. So I'll try a different approach. The most interesting thing that we learned, to me, was about Venus and the other planets. The planets Venus and Saturn were the most curious. Venus was neat because of its hellish environment. Although it used to be thought of as a beautiful blue heaven, we now know that the planet has experienced the Greenhouse effect. I thought that was cool since we (Earth) are, too. Could you imagine that thousands of years from now, aliens would look at our planet through a telescope and see the beauty that Neil Armstrong and the other astronauts described? Then they would actually land, and not be able to stand the harsh winds, atmosphere, rain and temperatures! All they would find would be the remains of an ancient civilization. Cool, huh?

Saturn caught my attention because of its beauty, of course, but the actual planet itself is not what I'm writing to you about. The second largest moon in the solar system, Saturn's largest of 21 moons, Titan, is what interested me. Titan, which has a substantial atmosphere, has had no life found on it yet. But its current atmospheric make-up is similar to that of proto-Earth and life could evolve on Titan. If it did they'd have a beautiful view of Saturn! An even more interesting thing happened...

Right after reading this, I had a dream in which I was grown up and I lived in our house alone, and lived off royalty checks. I had been to college— Brown. (I know because I remember seeing the degree on my wall.) I had majored in English and History with a minor in Astronomy. My most recent book had taken place in the future, hundreds of thousands of years ahead. There was life on Titan, and my story was about a girl who lived there. I was in the process of writing a book about Venus, about a family who lived in the civilization there, until the Greenhouse effect killed them all. When I woke up, I went straight to my desk and wrote down my dream, like you taught me.

Even more dreams of mine have been occupied by my science project, "Stonehenge: The Timeless Mystery of the Ages." I've never cared so deeply about a science project before. I think it's partly because before my science projects were just gathering previously known information. In my Stonehenge project, I read theories and chose the one I believed in, adding a little bit of my own. Another reason I'm so into Stonehenge is because it keeps taking me back to The Mists of Avalon, the book both of us read. There are references to Stonehenge in it, and to Avalon in Stonehenge books. My theory was called Worldwide, and it stated that people from Atlantis built Stonehenge. I didn't know this until recently, but The Mists says that, too. By the way, my science partner, Evelyn is reading The Mists, too. I now believe, through both Stonehenge and The Mists that there is not only one truth for anything, and that all the Mysteries (as with everything in the world) are connected.

That's why sometimes science frustrates me. The teacher and the book tell us things that have been scientifically proven to be true to their knowledge, but what does that say? In my opinion, what you believe is a reality for you, and that rule applies to everything. If Catholics believe in Jesus Christ dying for our sins and that if they do not repent they're damned, then that is their truth, or if Muslims believe in Muhammad, that is their truth. So be it. It is neither my place to force my beliefs on them, nor viceversa. The same goes for science, especially in things I cannot see, touch, hear or come in contact with. If Einstein believed that E=MC², then to him, "E" did equal MC². But I don't believe a science teacher or a science book can force that belief on us and say it is the only one truth. For the belief in one truth is dangerous and fool-hardy at times. If the belief is forced and accepted outwardly but not completely, it can never be a reality.

I don't know why I'm telling you this, Mom, because you already know how I feel on this subject, as it applies to other things. But you did not know, and as a matter of fact, neither did I, until I put it in print, that this belief applied to science and that was my problem.

Well! You learn a new thing every day! Lots of love,

Charisse

8th grade
Science Class

I put education right up there with housing and transportation as a budget priority, although when my income was low, we were blessed with school scholarships.

As single parents we must be reminded and remind our children that education is the key. Find ways to monitor, observe and advocate for your child. Children need to know there's a bond between home and school. Whatever choice you make regarding your children's school setting, here are some suggestions to help assure that they will have a successful school experience.

- Always meet and establish a relationship with the teacher(s) and the principal.

- Let the teacher know that you want to be informed about your child's progress—good or bad. Talk by phone and write notes.

- Make sure your child is in on some of these discussions.

- Ask the school's principal about the school's student success rates and challenges in academic and discipline areas. Find out about the "culture" of the school. What are the expectations?

- If the school is doing poorly and plagued with violence, find another school. You can do it. Don't settle for less than what you know your children deserve and need.

- Find out about magnet schools or special programs. One single parent I know enrolled her daughter in a special agricultural high school. She chose it because bus service was provided, it was in a safer neighborhood and it was recruiting minority children who had a science aptitude. Call your board of education and find out about your options.

- Find out about afterschool activities and pre-arrange these, if possible. Ask for referrals to programs in your neighborhood if the school doesn't have them. Work with other parents to help the school set up supervised after school activities.

- Find out if your children feel welcomed, respected and safe in their classrooms. If they do not, go to the school and observe their classes. Discuss your observations and concerns with your child and the teachers. If after trying you don't see improvement, take steps to change the class or school.

- Set up structured, uninterrupted time for homework—no TV or telephone.

- Ask sisters and brothers to review each other's homework.

- Give lots of praise to children. Give lots of praise to teachers. Never suggest (or allow anyone else to suggest) that your child is stupid or inadequate. Always encourage and support their willingness to try.

- Help your children plan their future and show them how education fits into that future.

- The smaller the class sizes, the better the possibilities for success. If the classes are too large, more than 25 students per teacher, discuss your concerns or look for alternatives.

Public schools in low-income communities are facing tremendous resource inequities. This lack of funds usually impacts the standard of education that children from single-parent families can receive. That reality will only change when we change it. Think about it. Suburban and better functioning schools usually know that they are accountable to the parents in that community.

Schools that work—public or private—feel a strong degree of community and parent involvement. The same is true on an individual basis. Children that succeed, despite terrible odds, do so because a caring adult invests in their success. When a caring adult lets a child know that their educational success is the most important thing in the world, that child will probably succeed.

How do you let a child know that their education is the number one priority?

1. Make learning (reading, exploring, writing, discussing) your whole family's number one priority. Use everyday activities like cooking as opportunities to learn about math or measuring, etc. Use transportation time to learn about geography, space location, etc. Use games and television to teach about social and life-skills. Take time to discuss meanings and messages. Use mail to teach about reading. These are just a few examples. Help children see that learning is life—and life is learning. Tell your child you care about their school experience.

2. Ask your child about school and show excitement, interest and joy each day.

3. Point out a school success factor every day.

4. Share your children's school stories with other friends and family members.

5. Make study time a routine part of every evening, with no television or interruptions. Help your children set goals for that time and monitor outcomes. As single parents, we must work harder to model and reinforce a "learning environment" in our homes. It's a key to beating the odds.

Thirty-Three

Child Support

My single parenting experience began in the 1970s. I have to be frank and relate that it was not until 1992, while writing this book, that I actually made a firm commitment to myself about my deservedness to receive financial support from my children's fathers. I recently asked my attorneys to take legal action to recoup 16 years of unpaid child support and 6 years of unpaid child support. I had lived most of my single-parent years like 75 percent of the single parents in this country—without child support.

There was not even an order for support in my first divorce. This was common up until the 1980s. Many divorce decrees did not include support orders. I did not use state agencies to enforce the child-support order in my second divorce, because at first he paid for child care, which was worth more than the award in real dollars. But, I finally realized that by allowing them to ignore their responsibility, I was continuing a pattern that started in my own childhood—a pattern of negating my own self-worth and my own deservedness, and passing on that legacy...i.e., negating my children's self-worth and deservedness.

Let me share with you the thinking that had allowed me to do this. I was protecting everyone else. Rather than to feel that pain, I chose to ignore it. I found "fifty ways" to rationalize this inaction. I thought "it was their responsibility and if they didn't own that responsibility willingly, then they would have to deal with their own conscience." I thought, "I can handle it, and I will handle it." It hurt too badly to face the fact that these men that I trusted, loved, made commitments to, married and had children with, were now abandoning their children financially. Once I faced these rationalizations, I was able to choose to take action and pursue the support my children deserve.

Use The Laws

I can certainly say to all single parents out there today, that we finally have laws in this country that protect the Innocent. It is the responsibility of any able-bodied adult who has committed to bring forth another life into this world, to care for that life. It is our (father and mother) primary responsibility in life to care for that child.

Keeping Kids Out of the Money Struggle

I didn't want my children to become pawns in a monetary struggle. Often times, in fighting over money, innocent children are pulled back and forth and feel as if they're to blame for their parents' pain. They readily take the blame and the responsibility.

We have to avoid this type of abuse and manipulation of our children, but that doesn't give us permission to disregard our deservedness and our children's deservedness. This issue doesn't mean we should ignore the laws that are there to protect them. Every biological father, and every biological mother who is able-bodied and mentally capable should, I think, accept the full responsibility, the partner responsibility, for seeing their children through the critical developmental years.

Unemployed "Other Parents"

Many of us have ex-spouses or "other parents" of our children who are not employed and we see that as a reason not to hold them accountable financially. I recognize the inequities in our society in terms of employment opportunities for all. Unemployment rates for all have risen since the 1960s. It has been astoundingly bleak for African American males. With the exception of the Vietnam War period, unemployment rates for African American males has been more than 20 percent during the 1970s and since. This has also been the period of the most dramatic increases in rates of single parent households within African American communities. While scholars debate the significance of these statistical facts, single parents, the majority of whom are women, are facing three realities—fewer marriages, more divorces and less income and related resources for their families and children. In short, absent fathers. Part of the American maleness scheme is that father means provider. In the absence of employment opportunities and/or income, it seems almost logical that the father/provider role is aborted, although sadly: "If I cannot provide, I cannot father," or "If he cannot provide, he cannot father."

I have learned that when we don't expect support from the "other parent," we give our ex-spouses and ex-mates a very demeaning message, which further erodes their self-worth and their self-esteem. By not asking for and demanding their support, the message that we're giving them is "We don't believe you can give it to us. We don't believe that you are a decent, capable, functioning parent." We are also devaluing ourselves and our children. And even though we may not say that, that's the implication. Sometimes, out of what we believe to be care, we will say "Well, we'll just let them go, because they can't do it." But that's not really very kind to any human being. It is not right to give our children, ourselves and the "other parent" a message that they aren't worthy or capable. I firmly believe that one of the clearest messages we need to give to "other parents," to all parents, is that we believe they are capable and we expect them to meet their financial responsibilities, or at least to try.

Rejection

We also have to deal with the feelings of rejection from them when they don't pay child support. So often I've talked with single parents, particularly with fathers, who somehow confuse the issue of child support and think that they're giving money to the mother with whom they are still angry. That is mixed-up thinking, and fortunately, the law helps them to get past that. My bottom line message to all single parents is that you will feel better about yourself if you're receiving some form of financial support. I feel better about myself, knowing that I am using the law to support my deservedness as a parent, my children's fathers' deservedness as parents and my children's deservedness. That's essentially what we're talking about—the fact that we all—our family—deserves the commitment.

I recognize that the outcome may not be money. My children may not receive any new financial support right away. But, by exercising my right (and my children's rights) to ask for it and using the law to enforce that right, I'm sending a clear message to my children, to myself, to their fathers and I hope to all single parents. It is our commitment, our promise to Anchor the Innocent.

Child Support in Other Forms

Some successful single parents ask their former mates, "other parents" to contribute support by taking care of the children. Some have asked for this type of support instead of money. This is particularly useful if he or she is unemployed. Former in-laws can be supportive in this way, as well.

Our decision regarding who is to care for our children, while we perform the other vital role of bringing in resources that maintain the home, is the most important decision we're going to make in the lives of our children, because that person is shaping their self-perception, and that person is shaping their attitudes about life. That special someone is responsible for seeing to it that our children's innocence is protected and that our children know, believe in their hearts, they are truly cared for. This important decision cannot be handled quickly. If the "other parent" has the skills and wants to offer this kind of support it may be equal to or more valuable than money.

Steps to Help You Access Back Child Support

As of 1974, Title IV-D of the Social Security Act created a national child-support enforcement program. There are also private agencies that charge a small fee up front, and take a percentage of the money that is obtained from the absent parent. Whether using a public or private agency to get child support, be aware of the following:

The agency or attorney needs your help to:

    a. Establish who the absent parent is;

    b. Find the absent parent; and

    c. Establish or enforce a support order.

They also need these pertinent facts from you:

    a. The absent parent's name and address;

    b. The absent parent's social security number;

    c. The children's birth certificates;

    d. Your child-support order;

    e. Your divorce decree or separation agreement;

    f. The absent parent's employer—name, address, phone number;

    g. Other contacts—friends, relatives, etc.;

    h. Asset information—tax returns, bank accounts, etc.; and

    i. Any other related information regarding the absent parent's location, etc.

To find the absent parent's social security number, use hospital records, old insurance policies, credit cards, bank accounts, pay slips, tax returns, past employers, or military records. Private attorneys can only work with FPLS through State D&S.

Once you give this information to the attorney or enforcement agency, they will contact the absent parent and ask them to come in for an interview. They are notified that legal action may be taken.

If you receive AFDC—Aid to Families with Dependent Children—or federally assisted foster-care payments, you automatically receive child-support enforcement services. AFDC recipients do not pay. For others, states may charge a small fee.

If you are using public agencies, there is usually a case backlog. The process will take time. If you are using a private agency or attorney, the more information you can provide, the better. Always save divorce decrees and legal documents for this type of use.

It is best to work out parent-support issues privately through mediation and have them entered into the decree and then enforced. The new federal and state programs make it possible for various means of enforcements including wage assignments, credit reporting of arrearages, garnishment of wages and, of course, prosecution and incarceration. For a booklet that answers all your questions on child support, write to the addresses included in the resource section.

I believe, however, that punitive enforcement strategies, while partially effective, are treating the symptom. The causes of unpaid child support cannot be corrected through legislation or enforcement mandates alone. The causes are in the hearts, minds and values of this society that are embodied in parenting and education practices that devalue women and children. One single parent I know, waived child support because she only had custody in the summer. After learning the cost of day-camp and other child-care alternatives, she asked her ex-husband to help with the expense. His response was "I support the kids 46 weeks a year, why should I support them in the summer?"

Absent, non-supportive parents are abusing their children and the custodial parent of their children. This is passive aggression. It is displaced cruelty, anger and hatred that began in their own childhood. Absent, non-supportive fathers need help— psychological help—to heal the wounds and scars that block their capacities to demonstrate care and empathy for their own children who are, in reality, an extension of themselves.

Thirty-Two

Silk Purses

You've probably heard the expression, "You can't make a silk purse out of a sow's ear." Well, I've seen single parents do it. Many have managed to make something of value out of what appeared to be nothing. In most cases these were women who had some sort of business or small enterprise of their own. These micro-businesses generated important supplemental, or at times primary, income for their families. These women were, in fact, entrepreneurs. What does it take to be a micro-business owner? It takes self-confidence, imagination, hard work, lots of energy, organization and persistence for starters. It also takes a great idea.

Ideas for Micro-Businesses

I've seen women turn ideas like story-telling, braiding hair and making cookies into sources of income that lifted their families out of poverty. In some cases, the confidence and skills gained from the self-employment or micro-business translated into skills that could be marketed in the traditional job market. One single parent started out doing foot reflexology, or foot massage, for senior citizens. She built on this success, emphasizing her people skills and organizational skills to land a job as a receptionist at a local medical center.

Self-employment can be an important option for single parents because: 1) the hours can be flexible enough to provide needed time for children; 2) work can often be done from the home, reducing transportation costs; and 3) income can be increased in relationship to business volume. Self-employment can be a disadvantage because: 1) it may not be a reliable or consistent source of income; 2) it requires excellent organizational and record-keeping skills; and 3) some housing codes do not allow businesses to be conducted from the home.

Like anything, self-employment has its pros and cons. Yet, I've seen it help many women move away from welfare or AFDC benefits to an above-poverty income.

More and more cities and states are offering assistance to micro-business owners. Contact your local department of economic development or your Chamber of Commerce to see if such micro-business development centers exist in your area.

Some ideas for self-employment ventures are listed here:

Catering—meals or specialty items	Clothing Retail—Specialty Items
Word Processing	Cosmetic Sales
Bookkeeping	Nutrition Sales
Resume Writing	Tax Assistance
Braiding Hair	Library Research
House Cleaning	Massage
Child-care	Nail Care
Elder Care	House Painting
Crafts	Landscaping
Sewing	Laundry Service
Image Consulting	Afterschool Care
Party or Wedding Planning	Direct-Marketing Sales

A Single Parent's Solvency Anchors

1. Discover and then undo your self-defeating attitudes or beliefs about yourself and money. Make money your friend.

2. Use imaging and affirmation techniques. Write your deserved outcomes/goals down.

3. Open savings accounts (or if you don't have enough money yet, put money in special savings places at home).

4. Never, ever let yourself be without some money.

5. Discover the power of your own mind and thoughts. Look back to times in your life when you got exactly what you "imagined"—imaged and created.

6. Create your family budget.

7. Find creative strategies that impact the big four expenses—housing, transportation, child care and food. Set goals in these areas. Take related actions.

8. Take measures to establish, clean up and/or protect your credit. Don't be ashamed or intimidated—credit problems are normal.

9. Education and solvency are partners. Become a life-long learner and model that for your children.

10. Literacy is essential. Make words, stories, images or sounds, and books an important part of your home environment.

11. Control and monitor television viewing. Use it to achieve your educational goals. Don't let it use you to merely achieve it's "ratings," or advertising goals.

12. Make sure that you have a will and insurance. Make sure someone you trust knows your financial arrangements for your children.

13. Establish two key relationships:

    a. With a banker; and

    b. With a financial planner or advisor.

14. Exercise your and your children's legal rights to financial support from their "other parent."

15. Keep good legal and financial records. You may need them.

Solvency Anchors for People Who Care About a Single-Parent Family

1. Establish a trusting friendship.

2. Take advantage of special opportunities to give in ways that equate to monetary value or expense reduction, child care, back to school shopping, transportation and/or recreation.

3. Agree on predictable routine types of support—respite, access to laundry facilities, afterschool sharing, reading, or story telling, etc.

4. Provide services that relate to financial management—accounting, taxes, bookkeeping, business planning, etc.

5. Help the single parent to explore entrepreneurial ideas. Enter into shared money-making projects or ventures—sales, special events, etc.

6. Point out attitudes and behaviors that may work against solvency, being careful not to be insulting, condescending, or patronizing. All communications must be built on a foundation of respect and trust.

7. Contribute to a college or education fund for the children.

8. Offer the children opportunities to earn money.

9. Remind the single parent of their successful financial strategies. Affirm their solvency.

Strength

As single parents we draw strength from our commitment to our children—to life—and from our choice to love and sustain our families. Strength is our capacity for effective action, our capacity to exert required force or to resist attack. Individual strength comes from our physical well-being, our power of concentration, our emotional balance, and ultimately from our own sense of a connection to the source of all good, all life—our spiritual awareness.

Thirty-Five

Boundaries

It was 6:00 p.m. and time to check in with my answering service. The workshop had gone well. Daniel was with his best friend this weekend and by now Charisse was enjoying a family picnic with her father's parents.

"Dr. Christopher, we're so glad you called in. We've been trying to beep you for hours. Isn't your pager working? We received an urgent message about 1:00 this afternoon. It was an anonymous caller who said he and his wife had chased off a man who was trying to molest your daughter. They said they had taken her back to her dance school and informed them about the incident. Apparently they heard her cries and ran to help her. They said that they tried to catch the man, but he got away."

The next three hours were the longest hours of my life. I could not get an answer on the phone at the dance school. When I got there, there was no note, no indication of my little girl's whereabouts. I was frantic. Where was she? Was she alright? Why had she been alone? Why wasn't she with her grandparents? I screamed "God, please not my baby! Please not her!" I didn't know what to do.

Everywhere I called there was no answer. Finally, at 9:00 someone answered at my ex-in-laws' house.

"Yes, the school director just dropped her off here. We were
amazed that at age six she was able to direct them to our house.
We were told this morning that she had been picked up by
someone else, so we went to the picnic without her. We're sorry."

"Is she alright?" I asked.

"Yes, she seems to be OK. A little nervous."

"Did they tell you what happened? Did the school people say
anything?"

"No, they said she'd been with them for hours."

"Let me speak to her. Put her on the phone. ... Baby, it's me, it's
Mom. I'm on my way, honey. I'll be there as fast as I can."

"OK, Mom."

When I got there, she was sitting alone in the bedroom. Apparently, no one else knew. Neither she nor the school had told her
grandparents about the incident. I just hugged her and she began
to cry. I held her and we cried together. I was so worried.

I felt guilty, angry, frightened, frustrated and just sick. When
would it stop? Hadn't I had enough pain? Hadn't I been raped,
violated and abused enough? Why my daughter, too? Why my
baby? She was only six years old! My God, what kind of animal,
what kind of beast would hurt a child? I wanted to find him; to
kill him; to kill him over and over and over again! But, I could do
nothing—nothing but be enraged, helpless, and try to help my
daughter.

Charisse didn't tell me what happened, I told her about the phone
call. She cried more. God, I'm so thankful to that couple, whoever
they are. Had they not helped my baby—I don't know what
would have happened to her. Had they not left a message for me,
I might never even have known. Charisse was ready to block it
out completely—to make it go away by believing it never happened. She didn't want to talk about it, even to me, her mother.

I tried to figure out what to do next. Should I call the police?
Should I take her to the hospital? Should I call a lawyer? I talked

to Charisse again. It seemed that physically, she was alright. Apparently, that couple had gotten there before he damaged her body. She didn't want to talk about it, though. She did say that the man had forced her into a corner under the stairs, and that he had put his hands on her body. She said she screamed and kicked and that the people came to help her.

So—wisely or unwisely, I didn't call the police. I didn't take her to a hospital. I guess I felt that she had been through enough. I felt she just needed to be loved, comforted and to go home. The next day we would find a psychologist who specialized in sexual abuse and children, and we would take her for counseling.

But, the next day Charisse refused to talk about it. She said, "Mom, can't we just forget about it?" I tried to explain that we couldn't, that she needed counseling. She finally agreed to go.

She saw the therapist a few times, drew pictures of the incident, and convinced the therapist that she didn't need additional help. Apparently she asked the psychologist "Did this ever happen to you or to any of your children?" When the therapist said no, she said, "Well, how can you help me? How can you know what I'm feeling if you've never felt these feelings?" When the therapist called me to discuss my daughter, she said that she didn't think my daughter needed many more sessions with her. She described their first meeting and said that Charisse really had one key question for her: "Why did God let this thing happen to me?"

In Charisse's question was the heart of the matter. Why had this young, innocent girl been molested? Why had she been exposed to such emotional trauma? Why was the pattern of sexual abuse and violation being passed on? As a female, but particularly as an African American female, some form of intrusion, violation and rape were probably in her enslaved great-grandmother's memories, her grandmother's memories, her mother's memories and now in hers. Would it ever stop? Would we as women ever have appropriate boundaries, lines of definition around ourselves and our bodies that prevent such violation? As single parents we are particularly vulnerable, here. We often feel that we are weak, without support—isolated and vulnerable.

In my own way, I tried to explain to her that divine protection had, in fact, been there. That it was the presence and protection of her own inner power of divine love that enabled her to scream, to fight back and to summon help.

The therapist had told me what changes to listen and watch for in Charisse's behavior that would indicate more professional help was needed. She said that if Charisse seemed sad or depressed, if her sleep patterns changed or she began to act out aggressively, we should seek intervention. But she felt only time and love would heal this wound. She said that from her conversations with my daughter, she believed we had the strength within our family to work through and heal this painful experience.

Family Strength

What strength? What strength, as a single-parent family, did we have for coping with this crisis? Had the therapist meant our ability to communicate, our trust? Had she meant our faith and our beliefs, or our ways of handling stress? Had she learned from my daughter about our system of emotional insight that we used as a self-help technique to help change our behaviors and our focus?

She had learned from conversations with my daughter that we felt empowered; that I and my children believed that we were always connected to the divine creative intelligence—God—and as such, through our everyday thoughts and feelings we were co-creators of our reality. She learned from conversations with Charisse that we knew how to take an unpleasant experience and look through it to find related childhood memories or programmed images that may have contributed to its creation.

In the end, this therapist who specialized in working with abused children, a seasoned therapist, said she felt privileged to have had an opportunity to work with such an insightful child. She had no doubts about our family strength, our capacity to process and heal this trauma.

Self Help

Despite her assurances, I watched my bright, confident, competent little girl's self-esteem erode day-by-day. The incident had happened in June. By August, Charisse had gained over twenty pounds and had become less outgoing, less interactive and a very different child. Each time I looked at her, I saw her slipping away into a shell—a physical shell as well as an emotional one. And, as her mother, I had become obsessed with her safety. Every decision, every plan centered around making sure she was protected and always with an adult. I transferred her to a Catholic school. I knew and trusted the principal, and he agreed to pick her up and drop her off for me. She went everywhere else with me. Still, as I watched her change before my eyes, I felt helpless. I could do nothing.

She refused to use our family's system for emotional self-help. She refused to talk about or revisit the incident. She refused to talk about seeing another counselor. She quit dance class and reduced her activity levels. Her body became less defined. In fact, she was using her body (as I had done) to protect herself from what she now saw as an unsafe world. She felt less and less attractive. So she withdrew from her friends. We relocated. We moved to a suburban area in hopes of "starting over." I thought it would be safer and she might develop a new set of friends.

Then, it happened. Her father re-married and he and his new bride went to Mexico for a vacation. This experience of perceived loss triggered a week of bad dreams—actually nightmares—for Charisse. She would wake up in the middle of the night screaming, but she wouldn't talk about her dreams. Finally, on the third consecutive night of disrupted sleep, she said, "OK, Mom. Let's talk about this. Let's work on it."

Unlearning

Both of my children, Daniel and Charisse, have attended enough of my workshops and have learned to listen to their own feelings, to use them to determine which of their emotional needs were not being met and to talk to their inner child in assuring, empowering ways to change their beliefs and focus. The technique is my own adaptation of self-help methods developed by others, like Ken Keyes, Bradshaw and others. It's a step-by-step process of re-visiting past experiences and using our rational mind to change our perceptions, thoughts and feelings about their meaning and impact. Self-help and professional help often work best together. One should not be substituted for the other.

The Process

Using this technique, I asked Charisse to describe her dream. I asked her how she felt in the dream. She said she was afraid. She felt it in her stomach and her knees were weak. She knew that fear was a security need. When she is afraid, she knows that she needs to somehow find a way to feel more safe, secure. I asked her what did she want to have happen in her dream? How would she have it change? What was her "demand"? She wanted him to "leave her alone." At this point she broke down and cried. I held her and asked her to say "I'm OK. Even though that man was chasing me, trying to hurt me, I am OK." She kept crying as I held her. I kept asking her to acknowledge that she was really alright—she, her whole self, was not damaged—she would be OK. I asked "What else did you want to happen?" She finally said that she wanted her Daddy to help her. At this point, she cried out in desperation, "Why wasn't he there to protect me, Mom?"

In that moment she voiced one of her deepest hurts. She expressed her feelings of abandonment, of helplessness and vulnerability because her father was gone. This perception of abandonment and helplessness is common in children of divorced parents. It needs to be addressed as it can affect their behaviors and future relationships. Eventually with support she acknowledged that she could be safe, OK, even though her Dad was not there. Again, she cried and I held her while she repeated these words.

Finally she breathed a deep, whole-body sigh. She became calmer and said that she felt better. Later that night she awoke again. This time she came into my room, shook me and said "Mom, I had another dream. This is a security issue, too." I sat up and said "Charisse, I think we've done enough work for one night. Write your dream down and we'll talk about it tomorrow."

Reflections

Truthfully, I was exhausted. I tried to go back to sleep, but instead I thought about how her father's absence, our divorce, and her feelings of vulnerability were related.

I thought about my own status as a single parent. My mind was filled with images of my own lifetime of painful interactions with people—particularly men—that didn't honor my personhood or respect my boundaries of self and human dignity. In my own spiritual belief system, I believe that I am made in the image of God and as such, I accept my role as a co-creator of my life and experiences. I had to take responsibility for my world. So, I searched for the images, the mental patterns and beliefs that contributed to this pattern of vulnerability and violation. As I searched, I recognized its beginnings in my own family background—in my parents and their parents.

My promise to my children, and to myself, was to try to break this cycle. More than anything else, I did not want to pass it on, even unknowingly, to yet another generation. Yet, here we were, a single-parent family of three having to function, to move beyond chaos and insecurity and to establish order, routine and above all, feelings of safety, security and boundaries. How were we to live in ways that would generate new mental images, new perceptions in the minds and hearts of my children?

For a few moments, the feelings of guilt and inadequacy overwhelmed me. What was so wrong with me, anyway? Why couldn't I create a "normal" two-parent family for my children so they would be safe, protected! I'm sure many single parents feel this kind of guilt and desperation at times.

My Mother's Beliefs

In that moment of self doubt, a basic misperception—wrong belief—flashed across my mind like a neon sign. Somewhere in my experience, in my heart, I truly believed that our safety, our well-being as a family required, depended on, the presence of two parents in the home. Somewhere in my belief system, I felt inadequate—abnormal—as long as "we didn't have a man in our house to take care of us."

This was my mother's belief, and no doubt, her mother's belief, too. It certainly is a clear message that society reinforces through television, novels, movies, etc. If I was going to succeed in anchoring my family and raising my children, I had to change, to undo this wrong belief! My children's safety and well-being was not dependent upon the presence of a man. We were not vulnerable, fragile, helpless victims. We did not have to live in fear. *We were strong and capable of being a healthy, functional family.* I had to reach back and remember my true lineage, including family patterns in which women were honored, respected and valued as equals and as strong. I had to trace my heritage back to a culture that allowed men and women to share responsibility more equally. This culture counted on the strength of a community of relatives to assist in child rearing. It was important that I remember how to be resourceful, how to gather a community of support and allow myself and my family to be a well-functioning family.

I had to help my son and daughter to move into a new way of thinking, feeling and believing. My task was to create images and perceptions of our strength, our power, our boundaries and subsequently, our safety.

Her father's re-marriage and vacation trip had triggered feelings of abandonment that allowed my daughter (on a subconscious level) to pull up her experience of violation, to look at it again, to face it with me and to talk through it to unearth the root emotions and fears that were draining her energy. This process helped me to identify my own related thoughts and feelings, too.

As single-parent families, we must explore our perceptions, thoughts and feelings about ourselves. We must be clear about who we are. We cannot allow others to impose their values and judgements on us. Nor can we allow people to project low value and "abnormal" or "at-risk" assumptions onto us arbitrarily. We must take charge and define and assert ourselves and demonstrate our family strengths.

The Summer

Our lives changed after that night of sharing and healing. Charisse became more social, more outgoing again. Emotionally, spiritually and mentally, she had grown. But her physical appearance, her body image, still reflected her defense, her hurt. It was now two years since her painful encounter, and summer was approaching. Because we were new to the area, I was concerned about the summer. What would I do to make sure both children were safe and engaged through the summer months? With the added expenses of our move, I had increased my work load. I was spending even less time at home. The summer could be a disaster. With Daniel now a teenager, I was concerned about gangs, drugs, sex—all the normal risks. And, of course, I was always concerned about Charisse.

In desperation, I got down on my knees that night and prayed. You see, I save the kneeling prayers for major, major needs. I usually pray in a less formal manner. But I was feeling really desperate. I remember my prayer:

> "I need help with my children. It's important that their needs are met this summer. It's important that they grow. I need the freedom and peace of mind of knowing that they're safe. Please help me."

The next morning at 8:30, I rushed into an early meeting. One of my friends and professional associates said, "I just put my two children on a bus, and I won't see them again until late August." I asked where they had gone, assuming that, like other married friends I knew, she had a strong extended family-support system and they were going to spend the summer with grandparents.

She surprised me by saying, "Oh, they're off to a wonderful summer camp." I asked what they did there. Her children were nearly the same ages as mine. "Oh, they do all kinds of sports, crafts; they learn to canoe and to camp out. It's very rustic, but very good for them."

My inner voice told me this was a blessing. This particular friend was the daughter-in-law of a former state governor. I said to myself, "if this camp is safe enough for a former governor's grandchildren, it's good enough for my children." I asked her, "Do you think I could send my kids?" She said, "Well, maybe. It's expensive, but here's the number of the camp director. Call him. Tell him I referred you."

The next 24 hours was part two of this miracle. I had to prepare them, psychologically and literally, for going away for two months to this "camp." We had to purchase equipment, airline tickets, clothing and supplies. But we did it. Within 48 hours of my kneeling prayer, my two children were in an ideal, perfect setting that provided the growth they needed, and gave me peace of mind.

This camp has been around for 47 years. It is owned and operated by a family. Year after year kids from around the United States and the world work with counselors (ratio is 1:4) and live in cabins. They have individual programs for athletic skill development and learn important lessons about sharing, caring, responsibility and self discipline. At the end of the summer, parents come for a two-day celebration weekend. Kids perform and receive awards for their accomplishments.

When I arrived in time for the skit night and saw my daughter on stage, my heart and eyes overflowed with tears of joy. There before me was a slim, confident, proud little girl, singing and dancing with her peers—joyful, self-expressive and assured. In just eight weeks, she had lost all the excess body fat and weight she had gained in two years, and she had re-gained her self confidence and inner strength.

As single parents, we must pre-plan for summer experiences that support our children's needs for ongoing structure, stability and focused attention. Summers can be opportunities for growth or chaos. I strongly recommend structured camps. Find out about programs offered through local YMCAs, YWCAs, churches or the local park district. You may need to work with community leaders to organize appropriate summer camps. Whenever possible, urban children need a rural experience. It helps them connect to nature and to their inner strength. Here's where you may want to get relatives to help financially. But don't wait until the last minute like I did. Please pre-plan.

New Learning for our Minds and Bodies

During the fourteen hour drive home from camp I kept crying, looking at her and crying. She finally said, "Mommy, what is it?" I said, as I held her hand, "Well, Charisse, I'm crying because I'm so thankful and so happy to have my daughter back. You're you again. You are back in your body." She said, "I know what you mean, Mom. I am back."

My daughter had healed an old woundedness. Charisse felt abandoned before her negative experience. She felt alone and vulnerable. Charisse felt my fears which were my mother's and grandmother's fears. Charisse also felt her own sense of loss. Children depend on both parents (if they have exposure to both parents). They have deep feelings of loss when one leaves. Even when children have never known their "other parent," they receive messages of loss through relatives, friends and/or the media. They learn about the "expectation" of the presence of two parents. These thoughts and feelings impact them on deep inner levels. When these feelings are not expressed and worked out consciously, they may get stored unconsciously and dictate body reactions and stress-related behaviors. This can lead to confusion, conflict and, ultimately, to a sense of poor control and low levels of trust of their world and themselves.

Charisse was becoming free of the entrapment caused by violation, trauma and loss. She had been given opportunities to move, to use her body in new ways through successful physical-play experiences like swimming, basketball, running, climbing and fun with accepting new friends. Her body received new mental, emotional and spiritual messages. Her body learned that she was safe. She need not be afraid and she no longer required the insulation, the fatty tissue, to protect her. New messages were being sent through her body, messages of worthiness and competence—of strength.

Body Muscles:
Natural Sources of Strength

All children, particularly children in single-parent families, need to optimize their natural sources of support and strength, their natural boundaries. These are, to a large degree, their body muscles. This amazing group of body tissues responds instantly to our experiences. We feel our muscles grow tight or tense in preparation for action, or at the end of a stressful day. When we are excited or joyous, our heart (a muscle) seems to flutter or the muscles of our stomach may jump. Even the adult sexual experience and child birth are based on muscle responses. Our muscles give us immediate contact with our world—on an external level, through patterns of skeletal action and on an internal level, through the increase or decrease of our heart rate and activity of our digestive system. Our muscles support us and they tell us we are alive. Muscles, and related hormone levels, help define our bodies as male or female, and subsequently our social roles. Our very postural shapes, our self-identity, and boundaries are supported by muscles. Yet, we seldom think about our muscles on a daily basis or allow them to provide the natural strength that is there for us.

Optimal tone and muscle activity is a critical factor in overall strength, vitality and healthy-body physiology. When the largest body muscles, our hips and thighs, are active and toned they act as "engines" that help ease the load of our internal life-supporting organs like the lungs, liver, heart, bones and even the pancreas in maintaining metabolic efficiency and health. High levels of muscle tone and fitness are associated with assertive personality traits and fewer episodes of depression as well as with reduced pre-menstrual syndrome (PMS) tension and symptoms.

Women, until recently, were not expected to maintain high levels of muscle tone, fitness or body strength. Unless we were athletic or in the beauty industry, we simply ignored our muscles. While my daughter's change in fitness levels was important to her as a growing girl, fitness is just as important to my strength as a single parent. Sometimes I look in on my children as they are sleeping, and think "I'm really the one person in life they can count on. I really am their anchor, their support. It is a matter of life, their lives, that I maintain as high a degree of wellness and fitness as possible. As single parents, we simply have to exercise every day.

As Charisse's innermost responses to her world changed, and she began to believe that she was strong and safe (even without her father's presence in her home every day), she gave her body muscles permission to serve their true purpose. She also changed her breathing patterns and relaxed chronic tensions. This new awareness was coupled with sports and athletic activities that allowed her to move freely with purpose and balance. She was becoming strong from within.

Healing + Self-Esteem = Strength

During that summer and in the months that followed, her inner strength and self-esteem were dramatically affected. She received care and respectful treatment, coupled with opportunities for success and socialization through play. She learned and practiced skills needed for minimizing the impact of devaluing situations. This process, starting with her dream and addressing the feelings it revealed, helped her to recognize that her innermost needs for a sense of security, self-expression and empowerment were being addressed on physical, emotional, mental and spiritual levels. In this sense, her healing and growth were holistic.

Charisse returned to this camp each summer for several years. Her summer friends and this rural environment became an important balance to her urban life and to her sense of herself. She has never lost the esteem and strength gained through processing and healing this childhood experience of violation and she has given me permission to share her story in hopes that it may help others.

This story from my family's life illustrates how our legacy of beliefs, experiences, fears and feelings had an impact on our development as a family. In addition to our parents and family of origin, many of our beliefs come from our religious or spiritual upbringing and culture. These beliefs determine our outlook or world view and ultimately the quality of our lives—certainly the strength of our families.

Thirty-Six

Not Living in Fear

This Anchor of the single parenting experience—*Strength*—also relates to our capacity to give ourselves a sense of hope and inspiration. It is a natural outgrowth of the other anchors—*Self-Esteem, Support* and *Solvency*. From our trust in ourselves and in our capacity to create desired outcomes in our lives, we gain needed strength, needed hope. By focusing on what we have, we are able to create more. Yet our over-all expectations and world-view are very important, too. How we view the world, how we believe the world is ordered or structured, has a lot to do with our sense of helplessness or our sense of empowerment. If we believe the world is doomed and there is no order and there is no force that's guiding and directing and loving the world, it's a pretty frightening place. I think that we each need and deserve some set of beliefs that gives us a sense of hope and faith that there is a transcendent power or force that is operating for the well being of humankind, and all life on Earth.

Grains of Sand?

The next thing that we have to consider is how are we relating to that force? Does that force love us, or are we just sort of a grain of sand on the beach that doesn't matter. This is essentially what I think constitutes a basic religion or spirituality. Do you have a belief in a force or power that orders the universe? What is your relationship to this force for good in the Universe? For me, it was very important that I find a belief system that let me think of that relationship as one of love, acceptance and appreciation. I had to filter out any aspects of a belief system that condemned me, or separated me from that force for good. My capacity to parent is enhanced because I have a deep sense of being connected to the essence of all life. I have a deep sense of spirituality. This sense gives me hope. Hope supports our strength—our individual and family's strength.

One of the saddest occurrences in our society, is the epidemic of homicide and killing among teenagers today. One of the reasons that many teenagers are willfully placing themselves in lifestyles (gangs and drugs) in which sudden death is a real risk is that they don't have much hope, much belief about their future. They've somehow begun to place such a low value on themselves, and on their lives, that they're willing to take a chance and to give up, to throw away their very precious gift of life. This has something to do with not being able to believe, to have faith in something or someone who cares. Effective spirituality and religious practices can give us the capacity to believe we are cared for, to know that we do matter at all times and that we are always connected to the power that sustains life.

As single parents we must believe in the possibility of wholeness and health for our families and for our children. It is important that we not live in fear but be strengthened by faith and hope. Our strength comes from our ability to see ourselves and our children's lives as we would have them be. Even when crises arise, we must envision and focus on our desired outcomes. By accepting our strength as single parents, and believing that we can create safe, supportive family environments for our children, we model strength for our children and the world.

The Power of Prayer

You'll find throughout this book that I have referred to prayer, and how prayer has worked in my life. How we pray is, I believe, as important as our willingness to pray. To me, prayer is an affirmation. It is an opportunity to acknowledge our connection to the source of all life. It is a moment in which we can rise above the problem or pain and be in touch with eternal truth, eternal wisdom. If we waste that moment, we may well end up with static on the line—with what seems like a bad connection.

When affirming your strength through prayer, use this holistic approach.

	Action	Impact	Focus
1.	State	Being	Spiritual
2.	Acknowledge	Thought	Mental
3.	Accept	Thought	Mental
4.	Allow	Feeling	Emotional
5.	Experience	Feeling	Emotional
6.	Affirm	Sense	Physical
7.	Release	Relax	Physical

These seven steps work for me. When praying I always state, acknowledge, accept, allow, experience, affirm and release. This approach to prayer embodies the holistic philosophy presented throughout this book. This chart shows how this holistic concept relates to prayer.

Spiritual Power of Prayer	**Mental Power of Prayer**
State—Truth of Being Whole.	Acknowledge Loving Thoughts
Focus energy on wholeness	Accept Loving Thoughts
Emotional Power of Prayer	**Physical Power of Prayer**
Allow Feeling	Affirm Sense of Goodness
Experience Feeling of Love, Goodness	Release — Let Go of Fear

Spiritual Growth

How do we take actions that nurture and support our own balanced spiritual growth? What helps us to continue to believe and have a faith that gives us hope and strength? I think that giving ourselves time to do so is the first step. We must take time to read and to participate in activities that support our belief system. It is important to pray or to meditate—to make a decision to put a spiritual or religious ritual into our lives on a daily or weekly basis. This activity should be designed for the sole purpose of reinforcing our relationship, our connection to a loving presence, to a loving God. These practices help to reduce stress, feelings of victimization and feelings of helplessness. These practices strengthen us. The example on the following page illustrates this idea by using the 23rd psalm from the Bible.

As a Christian, I believe the best connection to divine love is a personal connection, a connection through thought and prayer and our own daily intimate relationship with life's goodness. In this sense I am also remembering some of my ancestors' spirituality. For to them, Native Americans and Africans, religion was

The Power of Prayer Chart

	Step	Example (From the 23rd Psalm)	Illustration (Personalized Prayer)
1.	State the truth about yourself and your relationship to the source of all good.	*"The Lord is my Shepherd, I shall not want."*	I am always connected to—a part of—divine love. Love flows to me and through me all the time. God is where I am right now.
2.	Acknowledge that your need is already met.	*"He maketh me to lie down in green pastures. He leadeth me beside the still waters. He restoreth my soul. He leadeth me in the paths of righteousness for His name's sake."*	As God is where I am, my needs are known. There is a perfect outcome for me. The goodness (whatever you're praying for) that is for me is available to me, right now.
3.	Accept the good, the fact that your need is met.	*"Yea, though I walk through the valley of the shadow of death, I will fear no evil, for Thou art with me."*	I accept my good and let myself receive and experience the love that is here with me now.
4.	Allow the image of the specific manifestation desired to become real for you. Receive it in your heart.	*"Thy rod and Thy staff, they comfort me."*	My need (state specifically) is met.
5.	Experience the feelings, joy, sensation of your answered prayer—your victory.	*"Thou preparest a table in the presence of mine enemies. Thou annointest my head with oil. My cup runneth over."*	I now experience that joy. Right now, as I pray, I am receiving, "It is done."
6.	Affirm the eternal truth as goodness—divine love as the ultimate power.	*"Surely goodness and mercy shall follow me all the days of my life."*	God is love and so am I. God is the source of all good and that loving source embraces, supports, guides and nurtures me right now—always wholly.
7.	Let Go of Fear	*"And I will dwell in the house of the Lord forever."*	For this love, I am eternally thankful.

enmeshed in everyday living. Every activity and ritual had a spiritual meaning—a celebration of connectedness with all life. Even Native American houses were often built in shapes to honor their concept of God—a never-ending, connected circle.

In this excerpt from John S. M'Biti's book on African religions and philosophy, we are reminded about the importance of religion and spirituality in traditional African belief systems:

> "Both birth and childhood are a religious process, in that the child is flooded with religious activities and attitudes starting long before it is born. A child not only continues the physical line of life, being in some societies thought to be a re-incarnation of the departed, but becomes the intensely religious focus of keeping the parents in their state of personal immortality. The physical aspects of birth and the ceremonies that might accompany pregnancy, birth and childhood are regarded with religious feeling and experience—that another religious being has been born into a profoundly religious community and a religious world.

Children are so important in some of the diverse groups in African society, that social status and honor are often equated with fertility, birth and the care of children. An elder is given more respect—more authority and power—when they have more children.

I believe we need to degenderize our perceptions of God, however. So much of my life, for example, was an experience of abuse, abandonment and neglect by males, it didn't help me on a subconscious level to relate to God as a male. Part of me didn't have any experience of blessings, of goodness, from males. So, when I said "Father God," I automatically, unconsciously established an expectation of rejection. When I began to love and to worship God in spirit as an intelligence, a force, and not to picture God as having *any personification or gender* (male or female), but rather as a power, a force for good and for love, it was much easier for me to believe and to relate to that intelligence or perception. Again, my point in writing this book is to share the lessons that have been particularly important in my life and in the lives of the single parents that I've helped. If relating to God as He, as the Father, works for you, then by all means, use this image or perception. Removing all barriers (conscious and unconscious) to an intimate relationship with the whole of life—love—is the most important lesson. This relationship, this belief, can be our source of unyielding strength. For some, degenderizing their perceptions of divine love may seem to be in conflict with their religious teaching about Jesus Christ. My own early background has been the Baptist faith and the central role of Jesus is key. There is no conflict, really, in degenderizing divine power and still accepting Christian teachings about Jesus.

Women have been devalued and undervalued, and all those things associated with women (like child care, nurturing, emotions, feelings) have been devalued and undervalued historically as well as in our current culture. The need to have created an image or perception of God as male is, I think, an extension of that need to devalue that which is feminine. I don't really think that this devaluing of women was ever God's intent. It certainly conflicts with biblical stories about the ways in which Jesus related to women in those times. There are several examples of how he valued women. In fact his ministry was about the rights and inclusion of those who were traditionally excluded or held outside of the then religious-elite. He blessed the poor, blind, disabled, gentiles (ethnically different) and women who were otherwise outcast.

Beliefs for Today

An effective, sustaining belief system does not burden us with excessive guilt, shame or expectations of punishment. We need to know that if, in fact, we are made in the image and likeness of our Creator and our Creator is good, then so are we. We need to accept our own inner strength. It is important that we surround ourselves with people who share this belief in our basic goodness, and not allow ourselves to interact with and to be influenced by those who would judge, condemn or give us shame because we don't share and practice their same beliefs or lifestyles.

Our religious or spiritual beliefs must allow us to live this life experience to the fullest—to believe that our bounty, our good is manifesting in our day-to-day experiences. Historically, a focus on the hereafter has been used to justify misery in the present. Religious or spiritual beliefs should help us cope with today's realities and not sedate us into passive acceptance of pain or suffering.

Most Important for Single Parents

This issue of a positive spiritual base is, perhaps, more important for us as single-parent families than for others. There are really two basic emotions and all other emotions stem from these two. There is the positive emotion of love, the feeling and the experience of love, and then there is the opposite emotion and the feeling of fear. Spiritually we're either operating from one or the other. Having a connection to and a relationship with a force for good that loves us unconditionally, is an important element to bring into our home and to instill in our children.

Remember, the primary role of the family is to create a perception of security, to make us and our children feel safe. Helping them to believe that they are loved and protected by a transcendent force or power adds to their, and to our, strength and security. We need a conscious and a subconscious acceptance of such love. We need to be clear about our connection, as well as our children's connection, to the intelligence that orders nature and life. Without this we may indeed live in fear. If we live in fear, then our children live in fear and we have a cycle of stress and anxiety that predisposes us to problems—health-wise, socially and financially. It is ironic that the motto of the early American institution of slavery was to "make them stand in fear." Fear is the root of tyranny and of limitation. Its opposite, love, is the basis of freedom and growth—of strength and true inner power.

But what if you don't believe in God or any transcendent power? Then find a way of believing in life's goodness and see yourself as part of it. Allow yourself to receive the loving energy of life. Research on healthy families has shown that, even during the Great Depression when families faced incredible economic and emotional stress, the strong ones that stayed together and functioned well despite the odds had one thing in common. These families had an unshakable belief, faith in a transcendent power or force for good, that was real to them. These families had hope and the strength it provides.

Thirty-Seven

Avoid Religious Tyranny

A recent national survey revealed that fully 78 percent of Americans pray every day! Yet most books on parenting, and certainly most psychological counselors, don't even mention prayer as a key to healthy parenting and family function. There is a reason why many scholars and professionals involved in counseling avoid religion or the issues associated with it. It is because such belief systems are often misused—and become the source of tremendous psychological suffering, particularly among women and children. Religious and Biblical tyranny have been used to justify cruel treatment and denial of human rights throughout United States history and the history of the world. It was the rationale for child-beating—"spare the rod and spoil the child." Religious beliefs were used to condone or justify enslavement of millions of people based on the color of their skin, their culture and country of origin. It is still used by hate groups to justify racism, anti-Semitic activity and all manner of inhumane beliefs based on condemnation of others.

Since helping professions do not validate most religious and spiritual beliefs, when healing we must bring our own spiritual awareness into our lives by using other resources. We can turn to church groups, to community, to family and to spiritual literature to enhance our growth and strength during the separation and loss crises that precipitate many single parenting situations.

When I advocate a strong spiritual foundation for single parents, I am aware of the risks and caution individuals to be empowered and assertive as you formulate or chose a set of religious beliefs that support your growth. Major religions carry a legacy that is unjust to women. It goes back to the Creation story and Eve's reported role in bringing the forbidden apple to Adam. Most religions were also formed in a time when medical and health knowledge and practices were limited. Childbirth, sexual or reproductive disease and tragedy were common causes of great suffering. Societies found ways of associating sex with these evils—which they attached to women. Sexual acts were considered unclean, dirty. Children who came from the sexual act were actually considered evil, born in sin. Rigid child discipline practices grew out of this belief. Remnants of these collective beliefs still remain in our society. Such beliefs are associated with feelings of guilt, shame, self-hatred, judgement and projected hatred in the form of violence.

Religious organizations that center around the supreme authority of one person or individual authority figure and forbid questioning that authority are potentially harmful to individual esteem and freedom. Be cautious about joining any group or community that does not encourage your critical questions and dialogue. Beware of any group or set of beliefs that demands some form of absolute obedience or submission and threatens you with condemnation, eternal damnation, punishment and/or soul destruction for non-compliance. A careful review of the perennial truths that pervade all the world's great religions reveals promises of happiness, joy, freedom and love. Persons with specific political and social agendas have distorted many of these universal truths and created dogma used to justify violence, forms of tyranny, oppression and many inhumane practices.

I recommend using this test to assess any set of religious or spiritual practices and beliefs:

1. Does it make you feel fear? Or does it make you feel love?

2. Are you burdened with feelings of shame, unworthiness and guilt? Or are you free to accept your whole self, to grow and to evolve?

3. Are your forced to rely on someone outside of yourself to gain access to or connection with your source of strength and divine love? Or can you, as an individual, be connected to or have direct access to that which you believe is the ultimate source of good or power?

4. Does the belief system cause you to think about, focus on and dread the worst of society—its evils? Or does it free you to focus your thoughts and mental energy on life's great good—on hope and optimism?

5. Does your belief system condemn you in various ways and cause you to spend your life proving your deservedness as a woman or a man? Or does it assert your value as an individual and affirm your worth?

6. Finally, does your belief system condemn and judge others who believe differently? Does it promote acceptance, tolerance, compassion and equity for all human beings regardless of race, gender, class or orientation?

Using these questions can help you to find the most successful, inspirational truths inherent in most belief systems and can free you to simply not accept any aspects of systems that could be harmful to your self-esteem and your capacity to create families that impart hope and stability to your children.

There is an irony that in religious beliefs, potentially a key source of inner power and strength, we also have the potential to encounter great psychological harm and risk.

The challenge is to sift through the ancient literature, the cultural myths, the prejudices and mis-truths to find a universal truth that speaks to the equality and deservedness of all. One of our country's founding figures felt he accomplished this by creating his own book of the words and direct sayings or teachings of Jesus Christ. A non-conformist in many ways, Thomas Jefferson is also quoted as saying "I have sworn... eternal hostility against every form of tyranny over the mind of man."

Jefferson and many of his contemporaries (despite the gender and ethnocentricity of that time) knew the power, the strength, of the human mind. The genius and gift of our society—our system of governance "by, for and of the people" is that it honors the mind of each person and suggests that each individual has the capacity to participate in governance. This capacity is based on respect for the individual's creative intelligence.

Care must be taken not to devalue or limit that creative power through abuse or tyranny in any form, even religious.

Thirty-Eight

Mind Over Matters

Ultimately, the mind, the psyche, is at the heart of our personal strength and capacity to cope, to parent and to be resilient. If we are to succeed, and raise our children to succeed, we must not allow anything—any person, personality, belief system, drug or technology—to have authority over our own creative ability, our minds, which are in many ways like the drops of water in the waterfall—part of the whole river—of creative intelligence. Each of us is a part of the intelligence that energizes and enlightens the world. As such we are part of the creative whole, of all life.

Relationships derive their tremendous power in life from their impact upon the individual's mind or psyche. Family relationships because of their intimacy, have the power to impact how we think, how we feel and the subsequent actions we take—the combination that makes up who we are—our personality. The critical lesson of the single-parent experience is about relationships and the healing of relationship patterns that have been, and too often continue to be, harmful to the minds of the people involved.

How Others Influence

As we attempt to prepare our children for effective interaction with the larger society, it is important that we understand some of the dynamics of destructive relationships. The escalating gang phenomenon is an example of how a "pseudo-family" relationship can entrap, immobilize and sometimes destroy a person. High vulnerability to teen pregnancies is also associated with destructive relationships. What makes today's youth so vulnerable? The influence is in the mind of the participant, as is the case in cults and any form of abusive, risk-laden emotional entrapment. This story helps to illustrate the workings of this kind of entrapment and indeed, our own and our children's potential vulnerability.

One woman in our workshop was "entrapped" in a destructive relationship with a man who was abusive to her. She had divorced her first husband twenty one years ago and raised her now-adult daughter as a single parent. Now she had married again and within a year it seemed the relationship was failing. Her new husband used drugs and had begun to steal from her, but she could not seem to pull herself away. When he treated her terribly and they fought, she would make up her mind to leave him. Sometimes, she actually did leave him. But, within two weeks she was back in his arms again. Those of us who knew her and cared about her could not understand how a forty-three-year-old, professional, intelligent woman who had achieved so much could let this person take over her life, her strength, and make her so unhappy. Why was she tolerating this?

Destructive relationships, abuse, and neglect are often part of the circumstances that lead to the single-parent experience. Children from single-parent homes may also be vulnerable to these kinds of relationships. It is important to explore some of their implications particularly as they relate to the mind. Jan Kennedy in her book *The Touch of Silence* gives the best explanation about this type of challenge and healing that I've ever read. She explores the complex ways we have of coping with overwhelming traumas and the emotional pain of abusive situations.

Cruelty and abuse dehumanize people and they become less conscious of reality. When people are terrified, it is natural to dissociate, distort reality and deny what is actually happening. We may begin to fantasize safe realities. We become conditioned to alter our behavior to avoid the cruelty, the punishment, in a desperate attempt to gain some control and predictability for our safety, to gain some strength. Our very attempts—our altered states of awareness, consciousness, and feelings of fear—make us highly suggestible and open to being more controlled by the abuser. We may eventually behave like a person who has no will of our own. We lose our spirit and will to live. We lose our strength and our ability to create our reality. Instead, we feel dependent on the abuser (the gang, the cult relationship) for safety, reality and self-worth.

Abuse and victimization are more powerful than any drug. Like drug or alcohol dependent persons, victims of abuse may blackout during terrifying moments and may have no conscious recollection of what actually happened to them. They do, however, recognize (at least believe), that the abuser or the intimidator has the power to dictate their reality. As a result, the abuser becomes the only one who has the power to restore their sense of self-worth and good feelings, and to say when they have been "good enough" for the cruelty and abuse to end. The abused person behaves as if they are in a hypnotized state, unable to control or, for that matter, to account for their own behaviors. In this state—frightened, battered, abused or entrapped—people are compelled to do what appear to be "crazy" or self-destructive things just to hold onto, or to be affirmed by the individual, or group, to which they are attached. In this vicious cycle we are weakened to a point of extreme self-hate. Such victims, particularly children and teens, have no capacity to exert individual strength or to resist.

Denial

It is this state of self-hate that often dictates our systems of denial and suppression. Denial during and after a terrifying abuse and dehumanizing experience is a tool of self-protection. Some suggest that it has four stages or levels:

1. *Denial of Fact*: This is simply choosing to assert that something didn't happen or *not* to say that it did happen. Often we think people are lying when they deny the fact. In truth, part of their minds really believe the apparent lie.

2. *Denial of Consequences*: If the individual can face the fact, sometimes it is too painful to face the consequences. We admit that the event or act or loss occurred, but seem numbed, oblivious to its consequence or result. Moving past denial of consequences means accepting the effects and then looking at the next level—implications.

3. *Denial of Implications*: What does it all mean to me, to my life, to my world? Does this require action, change, healing or taking control? Some people never get past level two because level three is too overwhelming. But you'll find that the strength and energy to cope with level three, the implications, comes through level four which is moving past denial of feelings.

4. *Denial of Feelings*: Underneath the denial of fact, consequences and implications is our need to not face the painful feelings of anger, hurt, resentment, guilt and shame—and in victims of abuse and neglect, extreme self-hatred—that lie beneath the layers of denial and dissociation from ourselves. But denial or suppression of feelings does not reduce (in fact it may actually increase) the power of the feelings to generate bodily stress reactions. And these somatic or bodily stress reactions create symptoms, most of which are behaviors that let us know our "energy", our life vitality, is low. Yet, in the absence of needed resources, we either ignore or self-

> medicate the symptoms, failing to unearth, uproot or address the feelings that were automatic responses to the pain of unmet needs.

How do we move past these self-destructive relationships and self-protective mechanisms? How do we move out and on to better things? Most critically, how do we move past the generational cycles of dysfunction and destructive relationship patterns and behaviors that are so commonly seen within families? Experts in the field of family therapy as well as those in the area of child abuse repeatedly observe the generational patterns of dysfunctional and destructive relationships. Adult dynamics of abuse and neglect are passed on to children and children repeat these learned patterns of relating in their intimate partnerships and pass similar patterns onto their children.

These generational cycles of poor relationship patterns can be found within all family structures, not just single-parent families. They have often, however, precipitated the dissolution of marital or cohabitation commitments. Clearly these kinds of poor relationship skills are at work when parents absent themselves from the young child's life and abandon the other parent with total responsibility for child-rearing.

Breaking the Cycles

People who are successful and do break the cycles of ineffective, painful relationships do so when they begin to believe that they have the resources—the strength to change. This strength is usually an inner spiritual strength. Their minds become free to grasp the truth of their own innate capacity to be loved, wholly—and subsequently to give love, wholly. This freedom to love and to be loved is the essence of true spiritual strength and inner power. It is vitally important to today's single parents.

Many approaches exist within our society to help people move toward this type of inner strength and power. There is an extensive network of Twelve Step programs which are designed to assist people in breaking destructive relationship patterns with things (alcohol, drugs, food, money) and people. At the heart of these programs is spiritual renewal and total self-acceptance.

The Co-Dependency movement is another self-help network that helps adults revisit and heal destructive relationship patterns that had their beginnings in families of origin. Many professional counselors and clergy are skilled in supporting people through needed self-healing.

As single parents we must be aware of and alert to these factors that influence our thoughts, feelings or actions, so as to free ourselves and our children from potentially negative patterns. Families and people within families are key influences because they impact how we use our minds. The importance of mind (thought, feeling, action) influences cannot be over-emphasized. In the most critical area—health, for example—thoughts that trigger feelings causing the stress (fight or flight) reaction impact several body systems and organs simultaneously. Eyes (pupils) dilate; glands involved in digestion constrict releasing their chemicals and related movement decreases; heart muscle activity speeds up; the liver releases stored glucose or sugar; the kidney decreases its output; and adrenal glands speed up. All of these bodily reactions are unconscious, automatic—in association with degrees of perceived stress triggered by thoughts and feelings.

Confidence Leads to Well-Being

If, as adults attempting to parent, we are holding onto (through denial and depression) a warehouse of stress-triggering thoughts and feelings about ourselves and others, we are reducing our innate capacity for effectiveness. The opposite of fear is confidence which is associated with believing we are loved and cared for—not vulnerable. Confidence is associated with a more relaxed, energized state of being. Since many of our deepest fears are carried over within our subconscious or unconscious from childhood, recognizing and minimizing them may require accessing that part of our mind. There are many ways of influencing the subconscious.

There is agreement, at this point, in both the world of medicine and psychology—we have a conscious mind that directs and filters information and which we control through our will.

Hidden Influences

We also have a subconscious mind that dictates our automatic responses, the involuntary aspects of our body functions like heartbeat, circulation, digestion, etc. The concept of hypnosis actually has its basis in finding ways to reach our subconscious mind, bypassing in some way, our conscious thought or will.

In terms of strength as a single parent, we want to increase our awareness of our conscious thoughts and look for clues in our environment that might help us to better understand what is going on in our subconscious—our hidden thoughts or attitudes about ourselves and our lives.

Somewhere in our brain, in that part that relates to our subconscious, we have stored the sights, the sounds, the colors and the feelings of everything that's ever happened to us. But, of course, we are not consciously aware of all of this. Those actions not under our conscious control are being influenced by our subconscious, particularly our emotions. Remember many vital body functions, like our breathing rate, our circulation, our digestion and our elimination are affected by our automatic reactions which are directly tied to our emotions which are tied to our subconscious reactions. Psycho-somatic medicine is based on the link between our emotions and automatic body functions that are under the control of the "autonomic" nervous system, which is one reason why stress affects our health.

The Important Subconscious

The subconscious is also the seat of our imagination or our creativity and our dream state. Those things that become habitual or automatic, those behaviors that we don't have to think about in order to execute, have been moved to the realm of the subconscious. You may remember when you first started to learn how to ride a bike, for instance. You had to think about pressing down the pedals. You had to think about holding the handlebars, keeping the wheel straight, balancing and how to stop. But after you learned those behaviors, you put them on automatic and you gave them to your subconscious mind. You no longer had to think about riding a bike, actually you could think about any number of things while riding a bike. This is also true of driving a car. Most of us don't think about driving cars while we're driving them—which may have something to do with the number of accidents that occur. But seriously, we've learned to move certain information to the subconscious mind because the behaviors have become automatic, habitual.

It Reacts... It Doesn't Think

The subconscious really doesn't think, it reacts to what we think consciously, and what we give it to do. The subconscious is the automatic pilot, if you will, and it's job is to carry out our orders. Remember, too, it directs the body. The world of media and advertising is very aware of the role of our subconscious mind in affecting our behaviors and many times advertisements are designed to get to our subconscious so that we have less conscious control over the decisions that we make as consumers. There's a whole science that has evolved around accessing the subconscious mind. One very important technique used often is repetition. I can remember, I was a vegetarian, but I heard the advertisement that said, "Aren't you hungry? Aren't you hungry? Aren't you hungry? For a Burger, burger..." so often that I began to find myself hungry for a burger even though I didn't eat meat. Repetition is a very common tool used by the advertising industry to affect our behaviors.

Through Group Identity

Another way advertisers access our subconscious mind is through our sense of identification with our own ethnic or racial, ancestral, gender or age group. That sense of identity is somewhat automatic. It's something that is deeply embedded in our experience. Group identification and belonging relates to a basic human need, and it has been relegated to our subconscious. There are certain automatic responses we have concerning our group identification as women, as males, as members of a particular race—whatever the case may be—even as children. As such it provides a way to reach our subconscious mind—by relating ideas to our sense of identity and/or affiliation.

Authority Figures Have Power Too

As children growing up, of course, our relationship to our parents was that they were authority figures and they have had a powerful impact on our perception of ourselves. They had direct access to our subconscious and as a result, throughout life, authority figures remain very important. Sometimes messages given to us by authority figures go right through and affect our automatic levels of functioning and access that part of ourselves that we don't have much conscious control over. Religious leaders often have tremendous authority in our lives because of our subconscious beliefs and needs. Teachers can have a great influence over our children too. Their judgements or blessings can powerfully impact our self-esteem and individual capacity.

Through Feelings

A vital avenue to our subconscious mind is through our feelings. Once again, we realize that feelings are of primary importance. In times of great anxiety or moments of fear or moments of great joy, we record and hold onto those memories in a very special way. We've seen how childhood traumas are remembered, stored and re-ignited by related incidents in adult life. The emotionally charged moments of romantic passion are times when our subconscious may be influenced, or at least accessed. When our extreme emotions are involved we go on "automatic" and we are not thinking rationally.

Through Sex

Another final way of reaching or affecting the subconscious mind is through the sexual or orgasmic response. That may be tied to the emotion that's involved there, but psychologists have known that sexuality and the sexual response are directly linked to our subconscious (involuntary mind). This is one reason why our young people should not be exposed to sexual actions and behaviors prematurely. That is a point of vulnerability for them and for all of us. It's a point of significance for us as single parents to recognize that sexual intimacy is a level of sharing our being and our personhood that can access (override) in some instances, our conscious or willful control. It's another reason to delay the sexual involvement phase of a relationship until there's a high degree of trust and knowing because we're opening a special part of ourselves to someone else's influence—a part that we may not have as much conscious volition and control over.

The Mind is the Essence of the Person

Families are people-makers. The mind is the essence of the person. Therefore, families shape and influence the mind—the thoughts, feelings and actions of all members, particularly the children. Every day interactions (words, hugs, etc.) shape children's conscious and subconscious awareness. This is the power of parenting and the ultimate responsibility we have accepted when we said yes to the universe and agreed to become a parent. We have agreed to create circumstances that will help to shape the minds and human capacities of our children.

We will be more comfortable with the outcomes when we are more aware of and intentional about the process. We can also be more forgiving of ourselves and others as we learn more about hidden influences in our own lives.

As single parents we will be more successful in our parenting roles when we learn to limit negative mental influences. This can begin by understanding the subtle factors that may be dictating our own responses and/or increasing our own vulnerabilities within relationships. From the strength that comes with this understanding, we can better Anchor our families, no matter how turbulent the waters. We can reduce our children's susceptibility to gang involvement, drug use or premature sexual activity by recognizing their basic needs and helping them to understand the power of their own basic emotional needs for feeling safe, for expressing themselves and asserting control. We can also help them to understand how their relationships can affect their lives now and in the future.

Our strength as single parents is often related to our capacity to heal the wounds of separation and/or abandonment. It is also related to our capacity to foster a state of mind—conscious and subconscious—that is peaceful and without chronic stress. This may require deliberate ongoing work to discover our deep unmet needs and/or perceptions, baggage from our own childhood. It may also require daily disciplines in the form of deep relaxation, meditation, prayer and emotional reflection or insight work. There are several books included in the end notes that can be used to help you choose and develop needed discipline in these areas. Peace of mind—inner peace—is a great source of strength, because it enhances our physical, mental, emotional and spiritual reservoir of power—personal inner power.

Thirty-Nine

Images

Images and symbols play a central role in how we store and how we hold onto memories, both on a conscious and subconscious level. We need to be very selective about how we allow images, symbols and information to enter into our mental environment. Choosing what to watch on television and what we allow our children to watch on television (and at movies) is a part of this. The average American family will watch more than six hours of television every day. Most children have watched more than 6,000 hours of television by the time they enter kindergarten. The word television is very revealing. In many ways, by giving it such a large percentage of our waking hour focus, it does "tell us what to envision," what to image or imagine. It becomes the source of our images. For children, this is particularly destructive because they are learning how to image—to use their imagination. Television teaches them to turn that power over to something else.

According to the American Academy of Pediatrics, repeated exposure to television violence makes children more prone toward violent behavior and more accepting of real life violence.

As a society we are becoming desensitized to the horrors of violence and the destruction of human life.

Learning to take control of our own minds and images, as well as teaching our children to use their minds to image creatively, may require limiting the hypnotic input of television and learning to use it for specific educational and entertainment purposes—not as the household companion, baby-sitter and/or link to the world of imagination. Start by pre-planning a limited number of shows and times for viewing television and post the schedule. Stick to your schedule. Videotaping programs to watch during scheduled viewing time can help.

Telling stories and reading are better ways to train our children's minds to create, to image desired outcomes. Remember that emotion, repetition and authority figures all have a way of getting to our subconscious and television programs provide plenty of each.

Goals—Direction

Now that we recognize the importance of our mind as our strength and as a key to our spiritual growth, how can we take charge of, or take control over, our own mind—conscious and subconscious. One way is to establish our own sense of direction. Operating without goals is like starting out on a journey and not having a destination.

I suggest that a very important tool for self-management and self-control, and ultimately for maintaining our mental and spiritual strength, is to establish our own goals and our own sense of direction each day in our lives and for each phase of our lives. This will, in turn, dictate our focus. A very useful tool for us as single parents is to establish our goals for the week, or the day, in a notebook or journal. When we write things down they take on more importance to us. We see them and remember the importance of those things.

Communication and Imagination

Another very useful and important tool for gaining conscious control over our lives and our thoughts is to learn the art of listening, observing very carefully and paying close attention to what is going on within and around us. We need to evaluate how we are reacting. In other words, we must learn to look at and listen to our own thoughts, being aware of what we are thinking and what those thoughts are triggering in terms of feelings, such as worry. Worry is a series of negative thoughts that trigger a series of negative feelings. And those negative feelings tend to be stress-inducing. When we worry, two facts are clear:

1. There is something that we want, that we desire;

2. We're not looking at what we want, instead we're looking at what we don't want.

Imbedded in the word imagination is the word "image." The images and the pictures that we create in our minds are very important tools. There was a popular book published a few years ago called *Creative Visualization*, by Shakti Gawain. I recommend it because it tells you how to use your mental power to help get what you want from life, not what you don't want.

When we worry, we're actually giving the power of our thoughts and feelings to bad outcomes. Many world-class athletes—those that participate and win in the Olympics—use the tool of imaging, or imagining themselves going through the winning act. Can you picture an athlete centering their mental energies on seeing themselves lose? That's absurd, but that's what we unknowingly do when we worry. So, I'm suggesting that, as single parents, we must use our mental energy to picture ourselves doing and receiving what we want from life. Deliberately picture ourselves winning and deliberately create pictures of our children winning. This strengthens us.

Habitual Thoughts and Spiritual Strength are Related

My own thought control is probably the most important discipline that I have had to develop to help change the quality of my, and my children's, life experience. It is the most important key to strength. If I had to determine one thing that was most important to me as a single parent, I would say it is how I use my mind to manifest my true strength, my capacity, and to remind me of my connection to the source of all life—all good. Yet, the mind operates within our bodies which are influenced by feelings and our overall spiritual beliefs or expectations.

I was particularly strengthened when I was able to revisit my own spiritual or religious beliefs and to find words within it that validated my commitment to using my mind more deliberately. There is a perennial wisdom that suggests human-kind is made in the image and likeness of God. "Reflecting as a mirror the glory of the Lord" and being thus "transformed into the same image from glory to glory." (II Corinthians, Chapter 3) Our mind is a mirror reflecting that toward which it is turned. We become like what we contemplate. We create what we focus upon. Focus (conscious and subconscious) is, in many ways, the essence of faith.

Forty

Wisdom of Single Parenting

The ongoing, seemingly never-ending challenges of single parenting require that we grow to a point of being able to value ourselves as single parents. Yet they do strengthen us and enable us to exercise unique freedoms and joy.

I became aware of my personal strength when, a few years ago, I was on a dinner date. We had been seeing each other for about a month. Maybe it was his second glass of wine that gave him permission to speak freely, but he began to talk about his concerns for our relationship. At one point he blurted out, "I'm not sure I'm ready to be a parent again. I'm not sure I want the responsibility of raising someone else's children. They need..."

I got up from the table, quickly, and as I turned to leave him sitting there then and forever-more, I said, "I don't recall ever inviting you to take on a parenting role, or any role, with my children. I don't need you, nor do they." As I walked angrily to my car, I realized how much I'd grown. Just ten years earlier, I did view the men that I dated as potential replacement fathers. I would try on their last names after the first date. I wanted to be rescued, to be saved.

I never dated that man again. He had devalued what I had learned to value most—my successful role as the head of my household.

To meet challenges as successful single parents, we have to become very creative, very resourceful and highly skilled at getting the results that we want and deserve from life. This requires walking out of the everyday molds of our society and learning to tap into a reservoir of deep inner strength. In the United States today, society and family molds are based on traditions that automatically give authority and strength (implied and real) to males, and male-dominated systems, like corporations. As single heads-of households, most of whom are women, we must learn a lot about other kinds of strength and wisdom, and learn to honor the validity of aspects of life that are not always valued in today's world.

We need to appreciate and master the art of reaching out to others and forming bonds of connectedness, not walls of competition or control. We must awaken our hearts and recognize our inner strength and our mental power to transform our lives from within, to literally create something out of nothing, releasing fear that comes with a focus on lack and scarcity.

We also have to recognize and tap into the positive power that this society terms as an assertive provider, strong doer quality within ourselves—while we maintain our capacities to nurture, create and receive and express tenderness. As single parents, we have to define our own strengths and identities as women and as men. This lesson became crystal clear to me when my son, then a sophomore in college, shared one of his deepest fears with me. He said, "Mom, I haven't had a masculine role model and I am trying to learn 'how to be a strong man'." I was prepared this time. If he had said this years earlier, I would probably have been overwhelmed with guilt. But, I had grown.

What Do You Mean by Strength?

My reply was both a question and an answer. "What do you mean by strong, son? Do you mean the positive aspects of the masculine role in our society? Do you mean how to be a strong provider? A person who makes things happen, who builds, who creates, who protects and whose presence tells the world that there is a power here that can do? Do you mean a presence or model for perseverance, strength, fortitude and success? If that's what you think you're missing, then think again. You've had a good model of those qualities right here within me. Furthermore, you've seen that so-called male energy balanced with my female-ness. You've learned to honor connectedness. You've learned about caring, tenderness, sensitivity, feelings and inner power. And you can also choose role models in many of the males you meet in life through school, work and play.

"You, my son, are as prepared for manhood as the next young person your age, as long as you believe that you are strong and are made in the image of God and exercise your capacity to create the life that you want. That power is within you. It is not only male or female. It simply is. It is life. You are a man and have the freedom to define what that means to you."

He said, with a chuckle, "I guess you're right, Mom. I never thought of it that way before."

Strength Anchors for A Single Parent

1. Put your spiritual peace first; from this, all else will follow. It is your ultimate strength.

2. Maintain a mind-set and focus on goodness. Be appreciative and expect more good. Fill your mind-space with images—pictures that support the quality of life that you are now creating.

3. Relaxation—physical relaxation—is required before you can feel or experience spiritual peace. Fear and love cannot occupy the same space at the same time.

4. Establish activities, practices in your everyday life that remind you that you are connected to a source of inner strength. Use prayer, meditation, inspirational reading, etc.

5. Seek strength through groups or counselling to identify the unconscious thoughts and feelings that led you into a less than fulfilling relationship so you can identify and integrate those experiences, rather than allow them to drain your energy.

6. Take control of images in your life. Limit television viewing to desired input.

7. Affirm each day that you have or are creating a healthy, happy, family life, and that you appreciate your life. Talk to other successful single parents.

8. Affirm your own inner strength and power, and your right to exercise that power.

9. Make sure your children believe that you are not living in fear, so they can live in faith and experience the normal joy of childhood.

10. Listen to and observe your own mind—feeling state—and the factors that influence it. Note how many factors influence your behaviors and desires—unconsciously. Then assert your own volition or control more each day. Use your goals, your purpose and chosen direction.

11. Rely on aspects of your spiritual or religious belief system that respond to your innate needs: for a sense of security, of being loved unconditionally, for expression of yourself—your identity (female, black, hispanic, white, etc.) and for a sense of empowerment or capacity to create a fulfilling, happy life. Discard aspects that cause you to fear or be stressed, that devalue your identity as a person, or that make you feel helpless.

Strength Anchors for People Who Care About A Single-Parent Family

1. Share activities and events that provide spiritual strength.

2. If beliefs are similar, involve their children in your spiritual activities, too.

3. Provide concrete support of their spiritual practices—rides to church or related activities. Share inspirational publications, literature, tapes or books.

4. Use your mental energies to focus on their strengths and successes—not weakness and needs. When and if you pray for them, affirm their strength.

5. Acknowledge the family and parent's need for time and support to heal any loss.

6. Encourage open communication and honesty about their real day-to-day experiences. Take time to listen and share.

7. Avoid judgement, comparing and criticizing based on your own beliefs and family experiences.

8. Remind single parents that you believe in their strength and capacity and that you are there if needed for support.

9. Work on maintaining a friendship. Offer to do normal things—recreation, shopping, etc., together. Try not to let their marital or relationship status interfere with your friendship. Real friendship, fellowship, is the best demonstration of spirituality. It is a vehicle for unconditional love and as such it is a reminder of our inner source of strength.

Part III

Conclusions

"Family life not only
educates in general but its
quality ultimately
determines the individual's
capacity to love."

Martin Luther King Jr.

Forty-One

Single Parents and the Whole Society

We cannot allow society to continue to simply view single-parent families as abnormal, disadvantaged minority families. It is not OK to limit resources and books on child care and family structure to those that presume the presence of two custodial parents when (if current trends continue) more than half of all children born today will spend some time during their childhood years in a single-parent home, and single-parent families have been a reality throughout history. I've reviewed hundreds of books and articles on family life and parenting. A very small number consider the one-parent family as normal or acceptable. This condemns millions of wonderful families and children to a lifetime of "not good enough" struggling and pain. It is time for this nation to move beyond the stubborn state of ignorance and judgement that was epitomized by one of our country's elected national officials who recently made well intentioned, but disparaging comments about the single-parent phenomenon after viewing a TV situation comedy in which a financially successful career woman chose to become a single parent.

Neither the situation comedy's writers nor the elected official have a clue about the reality of single parenting in this country. Television news departments rushed to interview model single parents. Most of their examples mirrored the TV show's character. They were financially secure women (most in their 40's) who made the choice to become single parents and not to marry. They also showed one or two divorced younger mothers who receive child support and share parenting duties with their former spouses. All spoke in very positive terms about their experiences and their lives. I know the interviews were well-intentioned, and the objective was to project a positive, non-stereotypical image of single parents.

Exceptions, Not the Norm

But the fact is that those examples were the exceptions, not the norm. They had resources that most single parents do not yet have. Most of the millions of single parents, like myself, woke up in horror one day to find ourselves alone—with the lifetime responsibility of caring for one or more children. We faced poverty, rejection, feelings of guilt, helplessness, fear and shame at some point along the way. We struggled to find affordable housing, safe child care and decent schools. We prayed every minute that the children wouldn't get sick, because if they did, and we had to miss work, our whole world would fall apart. We couldn't allow ourselves to "get sick" despite the debilitating stress of fulfilling multiple roles simultaneously within bodies whose needs went unmet. In most cases our ex-spouses and ex-lovers have turned their backs on us and on their financial responsibility in some way (as well as their emotional and spiritual place in our children's lives).

Most of us were knocked unconscious by the brutal hand of abandonment, and came to only to find a menacing shadow standing over us. The shadow stays to haunt us each day, whispering constant reminders, subliminal messages—"You don't matter. You're so unimportant that I'll pretend you never existed, and seduce the rest of the world to join me in my dance of hatred and abuse of you." Many of us became magicians and learned to make soup from stones to feed our invisible children, who were betrayed by their "other parents." These absent parents have somehow found permission in their own souls to deny their most sacred trust and say no to life's plea for continuation through children—children that carry the light of eternal love and innocence.

The Capacity to Love

Nobel Prize Laureate and Human Rights Leader, Dr. Martin Luther King, Jr., once addressed the important function of families in our democratic society. In a speech delivered in 1965, in New York City, he stated that, "Family life not only educates in general but it's quality ultimately determines the individual's capacity to love. The institution of the family is decisive in determining not only if a person has the capacity to love another individual but in the larger sense, whether he is capable of loving his fellow men collectively. The whole of society rests on this foundation—for stability, understanding and social peace."

What is the whole society? It is all of the social relationships among and between human beings. These relationships become our institutions—schools, churches, corporations and communities.

The escalating rates of dissolved marriages and aborted relationships in which children have been born suggest that something is missing in our capacity to love or to bond with, and to relate with empathy and compassion to the needs of children—even our own children. Since it is the men, primarily, absenting themselves, the single-parent epidemic suggests that too many men are lacking in their capacities to relate empathetically and compassionately to the needs of children and, indeed, to their children's mothers. As a group, American men are now spending fewer years in homes with children than they did twenty years ago.

Psychological research reveals that our individual and collective capacities for caring, empathizing or giving and receiving emotional support are formed primarily during childhood and infancy. We learn how to love from our parents, or our care-takers. Part of our country's masculinity myth discourages male involvement with child rearing and male expressions of feelings and emotions. From an early age, boys are taught "not to cry" or to like girly things. Indeed, consider the name-calling using a variety of "female" terms as negative reinforcement for behavioral adjustment—"You run like a girl," is used to ridicule even girls! These and other masculinity expectations teach men that theirs is the superior role in society—meaning that the woman's role is inferior.

Too many children have been taught that men should control and expect subservience from women. Women are expected to give up their identity, even their names upon marriage and are conspicuously absent from positions of public power, authority and leadership. Women have been taught to devalue and not to expect nurturing qualities from men. Men often learn that physical violence—and even abuse—are concomitant, necessary parts of male self-expression. This does not mean that all men are violent or chauvinistic, or that all women are subservient. However, symbolic violence is often a part of boys' and men's play, and women are most often victims of symbolic and real violence.

These societal values when reinforced as childhood learnings make it harder for today's men and women to sustain caring relationships based on mutual strength, care and esteem. These learnings make it easier for divorce, abandonment, neglect, desertion and denial of basic emotional needs for security, self-expression and empowerment. As such, they may be the seeds of the spiraling single-parent phenomenon.

The Will to Parent

The jury is still out on all of the causes of changes in family structure and the escalating numbers of single-parent households. I am suggesting that increased involvement of both men and women in the day-to-day realities of early childhood and human development—through awareness, experiences and feedback—may help to address more of the needs of our children and our future society. We can no longer take parenting for granted and trivialize or minimize its value, or for that matter, its risks to society. We cannot, however, legislate or mandate capacities to care. People—men and women—must value the process of supporting the development and growth of other human beings.

This life-sustaining parenting capacity must emerge from within us—from within our whole selves—as a reflection of the care, compassion and empathy that supported us through our own dependent, vulnerable years. Our capacity to parent is both learned and acquired. The will to parent is, too. While we may change public policies to reduce the barriers to effective parenting, we must also change public attitudes, and expectations about the critical value of parenting (and all families) and the need for both men and women to participate in this process in compassionate, involved ways.

As a society we need to create more humane ways of relating to and within families that truly understand and value all of the members. The women and children who have historically been devalued, must be valued. We must also find more ways to offer fathers full esteem and a meaningful sense of place within the home and in the daily lives of their children. Infants and children are very fragile and are so easily wounded by omissions and commissions, by accidental and deliberate acts. Remember, child abuse means that as children we have felt too much to bear. Child deprivation means that we have been exposed to too little to meet our needs.

All families (single- and dual-parented) need to abandon old parenting beliefs and practices based on ignorance. Ideas such as children are inherently bad—or "born in sin"—or the admonition to beat children—to not "spare the rod"—are not appropriate in light of recent understandings of human and early childhood development needs. Infants and children have a unique set of developmental needs and tasks—physically, emotionally, mentally and spiritually. Their rapid period of growth between birth and four years of age provides an amazing lens for viewing and appreciating the wonder, yet fragility of the human personality. Issues and capacities for dependency, pleasure, love, intimacy, assertiveness, curiosity, exploration, restraint, anger and self-discipline emerge in the child's early life. As parents our responsibility is to provide environments that support optimal development and evolution of these and other related capacities. The child is complex and unique. But it is our relationship with the child that is the catalyst—like an enzyme. The parenting relationship, our day-to-day interactions with our children, sets a series of interactions and events in motion that can lead to whole children who become whole adults.

The parenting relationship can also set a series of interactions and events in motion that lead to wounded children and adults. Such children and adults, like myself and millions of others, spend much of their adult lives un-learning and/or healing the scars from childhood. Many, however, don't even know about the wounds and cannot see, cannot feel the scars.

Families that struggle in the face of poverty; or families that use whipping, spanking or beating as discipline; chaotic families and families that have rigid attitudes and/or encourage children to "be seen and not heard"—many of these families unknowingly subject children to abuse and/or neglect. Whenever our parents were constantly preoccupied with fear, struggle and stress, we as innocent children were vulnerable to feeling more than we could bear, or to having less than we needed. This was true in all families—those with two parents in the home, or one parent. Single-parent households are even more vulnerable.

Barriers That Divide Us

We have to "unlearn" negative behaviors and relationship patterns that began in our families of origin. This "unlearning" is a requirement if healthy new relationships are to be formed and sustained.

As we learn more about our whole selves—the physical, emotional, mental and spiritual aspects within each of us—perhaps we can heal some of the barriers that divide us as men and women and contribute to the escalating rates of divorce and dissolution of relationships.

The sharp increase in numbers of single-parent households in the United States since 1970 parallels an interesting and, I believe, related set of domestic or family policy developments. First, the national movement to expose and to end abuse and violence within families took shape during this era.

Later marriages, declining fertility, increasing rates of divorce all contributed to a drastic decrease in the number of years that men spend in our families with our young children. Between 1960 and 1980 the average number of years men between the ages of 20 and 40 spend in active fatherhood roles dropped from 12.34 years on average to 7.0 years. That's a 43 percent drop.

Some say that the women's movement has contributed to the absence of mothers in the home. As a society we are ignoring the pain caused by the escalating absence of fathers. As roles have changed and we have been called to better value the equality and strength of both men and women, we are challenged to create new ways of relating within families and more effective ways of modeling relatedness for our children. Many old models of family functioning simply do not fit today. Today's family models require authentic caring, partnerships and shared roles. They must be built on genuine regard, respect and love. But they can only be demonstrated by persons who have learned to value—to love or esteem themselves, and this begins in infancy and childhood. The cycle is circular and generational. These kinds of relationship issues are central themes in the lives and hearts of single parents.

Seven Models for Relatedness

1. Children have to be shown through parental modeling how to truly value their bodies. They need to appreciate the wonder of their own healing capacity and the innate intelligence of their body cells and systems.

2. Children have to learn to trust their minds and feelings from parents that honor their minds and feelings through daily sharing and heartfelt communication.

3. Children have to be taught the history of our nation and their own cultures, as well as to be helped to think critically about beliefs and values in a historic context. This will keep them from ever being oppressed or tyrannized by attitudes from the past that were steeped in ignorance.

4. Both male and female children have to be taught how to empathize, to demonstrate care and compassion, and need to receive messages from parents, teacher and media that caring is valued more than violence

and/or destruction of life. From this, they may be better prepared for bonding with and parenting their own children.

5. Children need to learn that they are connected to a source of divine intelligence and power that is reflected in nature and the order of the world around them. They need to develop a heartfelt sense of connectedness to all life.

6. Children need to feel a sense of responsibility that comes from confidence and their capacity to contribute to the development and well-being of their own families and communities.

7. We must point out and help children dismiss degrading and devaluing messages in our society that suggest inferiority or superiority of any one gender, ethnic group or other status, and help our children to accept the equality and interdependence of all.

Our Society—Of the People

Our failure to address self love, gender and parenting issues has helped to move couples apart and threatens the very fabric of our democratic society. Within our society that is "governed by the people"—the family is of primary importance because it is where "people" are made, literally where people are prepared for their roles and their responsibilities in adult life. The emphasis should not just be on how families are structured, but moreso on how parents can best fulfill their functions, and why. We must learn from our diversity and build on the strengths that we all bring to life. This appreciation of all families and the parents that sustain them is the essence of our continued growth and is vital to our nation, as a whole.

Forty-Two

Afterword

Afterword by My Daughter, Charisse, Age 12

Existence
Depends on the Unit
The Family
Together
Yet Alone
Parent
We do not fall
But Prosper
In Love
Insignificant Numbers
Block
Ideas of
The Family
The Deep Rooted
Myth

Of Four
Two Parents
Two
Matters Not
We have been ripped
From Our Families
For too many years
Now it is time
For healing
With more powerful potions
Known to man
They Are Three
They Are Love,
They Are Trust,
And They Are Understanding.
For Conflict Tears Us Apart
Opening a Deep Chasm
Splits the Earth Between Us
For Conflict Arises From
Hate
From Deceit
From Ignorance
Now it is time to draw
From Our Strengths
To Heal Our Weaknesses
Now It Is Time
To Call On The Family
And Numbers Won't Matter
There Is No
Number
There Is No
Factor
In the Family
But
Love

Afterword by My Son, Daniel, Age 18

When we think of family we must think of a story—a story much greater than the familiar bed-time tales of childhood that begin and end with the turning of a page. For family is of a never-ending nature that weaves and spins itself in and out of existence. Family is made of memory and dreams. And where they start or stop depends on who's telling the tale. In truth, no matter who's voice is bringing the forgotten into the relative light of remembrance, there can be no beginning or ending. There can only be continuance; a re-embarkation on a journey through a vast network of rivers and lakes and streams who's source is the collective family consciousness. In this ever evolving mind what we call beginnings and endings are merely bridges that connect the present to the future, the future to the past, and the past to the present.

As children we spend very little time on these bridges, darting from one reality to the next, only taking notice of where we are, and paying little, if any, attention to how we got there. Time and life have very little to do with one-another early on, for life seems to be a timeless adventure in which we are guided from one moment to another by the loving and brutal force of existence. For some it is a long journey of painful isolation across a psycho-spiritual and emotional wasteland. For others it is a voyage through a forest of possibility and expression, where day and night are but reflections of each other as they are both illuminated with an ever-present light. This is a light of understanding and nourishment, a light of compassion and wisdom. This is the parental light of unconditional love and the presence or lack of it determines the nature and intensity of the storm we must all brave: childhood.

From my own experience, I can recall moments of blindness due to the intensity of my mother's love for me, while at the same time, feeling surges of pain that remind of the times in which I cried because the darkness enwrapped me so tightly and so thoroughly that I could not breathe. Strangely enough, these were the times in which my mother tried to provide her only son with the male role models which society deems "critical" to the proper development of a young boy. The idea of masculine and feminine role models is without question one of the most prevalent socio-cultural gender myths perpetuated in our society. For the light of which I spoke, the light of unconditional love, is not dependent upon or determined by the biological limits of gender or the expressive energies of sexuality. One must recognize that as human beings we are comprised of both masculine and feminine energy. Only through cultural programming and socialization is the individual taught to express one component of their being while suppressing the other. This process must be replaced by a program of whole-self understanding and development.

When the holistic transformation occurs, the single parent will no longer have to feel inadequate or guilty that they are somehow failing their children by not providing a proper role model for their son or daughter. Likewise children will share that sense of wholeness and develop an inner strength and sensitivity to themselves and other people.

Having grown up as a single-parented child, I can say that I've learned more about strength from my mother than any man that has been significantly involved in my life. My mother's journey toward wholeness is shared by her children and will hopefully inspire other families, regardless of their structure, to embark upon that same journey together. We can no longer spend our lives ignoring pain for it is understanding our pain that facilitates our growth and evolution; both as individuals and as a collective. As we commit to the health and evolution of our own families, so too will we commit to the health and evolution of the world family. So let us move toward re-defining family and toward re-defining ourselves. Now is the time to heal! Don't submit to fear! Commit to love!

End Notes

Introduction

1. E. Alderman and C. Kennedy. *In Our Defense: The Bill of Rights in Action.* (New York: William Morrow and Company, Inc., 1991.)

   The Bill of Rights or the first ten amendments to the United States Constitution outline the most comprehensive protection of individual freedom ever written. The First Amendment begins by protecting the individual's right to free choice in religion. *In Our Defense...* offers readers a view of how the grand principles of this and all other aspects of the Bill of Rights affect the lives of Americans.

2. *Statistical Abstract of the United States Population, 1992, 112th Edition.* (Washington, DC: US Department of Commerce, Bureau of the Census, 1992.) p 58.

   The Statistical Abstract of the United States is the standard summary of statistics on the social potential and economic organization of the United States. According to the latest data available on religious preference covering the civilian population, 18 years and older, indicates that 89 percent report some religious preference, while 81 percent report a Protestant or Catholic preference. Eleven percent said they had no religious preference, two percent preferred the Jewish religion and six percent claimed other religions. Of the 89 percent, 65 percent were actual church or synagogue members. These data represent averages of the combined results of several surveys during the year and are subject to sampling variability.

Part I: The Innocent
Single Parents Today: Who Are We?

1. United States House of Representatives, Committee on Ways and Means. *Green Book*. Washington, D.C., 1992.) p 1078.

   Provides up to date population statistics for legislators.

2. S. Kamerman, and A. J. Kahn. *Mothers Alone: Strategies for a Time of Change*. (Denver MA: Auburn House Publishing Company, 1988.)

   Most of today's single parent families occur as a consequence of divorce, separations and birth to unmarried parents. Prior to the 1920s, most single parent families resulted from mortality and subsequent widowhood. As causes changed, perceptions about and attitudes toward these families have changed.

3. I. Garfinkle and S. S. McLanahan. *Single Mothers and Their Children: A New American Dilemma*. (Washington, D.C.: The Urban Institute Press, 1986.) pp. 17-29.

   Sixty to seventy percent of total income for any family (two-parent or one-parent) usually comes from earnings of the breadwinner. Consequently, the ability of single parents to earn income is the critical determinant of the economic status. This book offers an insightful view of the earning and income dynamics of single parent (mother only families).

4. S. Minty and S. Kellogg. *Domestic Revolutions.* (New York: The Free Press, 1988.)

   In the late 1800s, the Federal Homestead and Timber Culture Acts provided cheap land to families. During the 1950s the Veteran's Administration and the Federal Home Loan Mortgage Administration, sponsored by the federal government, made low-interest mortgage money available to support families and the suburban housing boom.

5. Kamerman and Kahn. *Single Mothers and Their Children* Bumpans. *"Children and Marital Disintegration: A Replication and Update,"* Demography, Volume 21 (February 1984), pp. 71-82.

   Predictions vary slightly concerning the numbers and percentages of single-parent families in the United States. This demographic study suggests that 60 percent of all children born in the 1980s will spend some time in mother-only families. Whereas 45 percent of white children and nearly 86 percent of black children will (if current trends continue) spend part of their youth in families headed by women.

6. Mellman and Lazarus, Inc. *The Mass Mutual American Family Values Study.* (Springfield, MA: Massachusetts Mutual Life Insurance Company, 1989.) pp. 15-20.

   This public opinion research firm was commissioned to conduct a national public opinion survey regarding families and family life perceptions. They questioned a nationally representative sample of 1200 people.

Who Values Families

1. S. Coontz. *Reconceptualizing Family History in the Social Origins of Private Life: A History of American Families 1600-1900.* (New York: Virso Publishers, 1988.)

2. E. A. Mulroy. *Women as Single Parents: Confronting Institutional Barriers in the Courts, The Workplace and the Housing Market*. (Dover, MA: Auburn House Publishing Company, 1988.)

Often violence in the home precipitates a woman into divorce and single parenthood. The U.S. Department of Justice reported in 1986 that approximately 2.1 million women were victims of domestic violence. The Massachusetts Department of Health reported in 1986 that in that state a woman is murdered by her husband or boyfriend every twenty-two days. Mulroy offers insights into this phenomenon.

3. K. Phillips. *The Politics of the Rich and Poor*. (New York: Random House, 1970.) p. 17.

The 1980s introduced new political economics with intensified inequality and pain for the poor while it assured unprecedented growth of wealth for the upper bracketed.

4. Kamerman and Kahn. *Clarifying the Options: Insights from Abroad on Mothers Alone*. pp. 70-102.

Escalating rates of single-parent families is an issue in all industrialized nations.

Compelled

1. C. Bruner and M. Berryshel. *Making Welfare Work: A Family Approach*. (Des Moines, IA: Child and Family Policy Center, 1992.) p 17.

The Iowa Family Development and Self-Sufficiency (Fa DSS) Demonstration Grant Program is one of the four state welfare programs which has a vision for families that includes goals not directly tied to employment. This program recognizes that family instability has a strong correlation to welfare dependency, but it looks for the deeper causes and relationships that lead to this instability. For example, they note that: "In the State of Iowa, ADC families contribute more than half of all children in the foster care system, and nationally it is estimated that eighty percent of all foster-care cases come from the twenty percent that are single-parent families, yet they also represent that "the stress of poverty, lack of social support and single parenting all contribute." This perspective motivates program workers to look for the factors within individuals' backgrounds that increase vulnerability to family instability and poverty.

The Legacy

1. A. Miller. *For Your Own Good: Hidden Cruelty in Child Rearing and the Roots of Violence.* (New York: Farrar, Strauss and Giroux, 1983.)

   Explores the origins of violence within harmful and cruel principals that guide "traditional" child rearing practices.

2. A. Miller. *Thou Shalt Not Be Aware: Society's Betrayal of the Child.* (New York: Farrar, Strauss and Giroux, 1986.)

   This book explores the innocence of the child and the devastating consequences of betrayal of that innocence.

Parenting Begins with Pregnancy

1. G. S. Brewer with T. Breiver, M.D., Medical Consultant. *What Every Pregnant Woman Should Know: The Truth About Diets and Drugs During Pregnancy.* (New York: Penguin Books, 1979.)

   "Nutrition is the most important of all environmental factors in childbearing whether the problem is considered from the point of view of the mother or that of the offspring." Sir Edward Mellanby, 1933. The book contains research as well as menus and guidelines that are needed by expectant mothers.

2. D. R. Shanklin and J. Hardin. *Maternal Nutrition and Child Health.* (Springfield, IL: Charles C. Thomas, 1979.) pp. 44-46.

Love

1. D. Chopla. *Quantum Healing: Exploring the Frontiers of Mind/Body Medicine*. (New York: Bantam Books, 1989) pp. 39-43.

2. M. Lloyd Jones. *Healing and the Scriptures*. (Nashville: Oliver-Nelson Books, 1987.) p. 24

   Dr. Jones presents some of the known facts regarding Kathryn Kuhlman's healing ministry. He notes that the authenticity of her work was documented by what he calls "balanced, sane men, elders of the Presbeyterian Church as well as by certified medical men." Ms. Kuhlman has reported her healing work in two books: *I Believe in Miracles*, published by Lakeland Publishers and *God Can Do It Again*, Marshall, Morgan and Scott Publishers.

Part II: Anchors

Anchor One: Self-Esteem

Frogs Into Frogs

1. N. Branden. *Honoring the Self, The Psychology of Confidence and Respect*. (New York: Bantam Books, 1983.)

   The author asserts that "the greatest barrier to happiness is the wordless sense that happiness is not our proper destiny." His chapters Self-Esteem and Child/Parent Relationships, and Generating Positive Self-Esteem are highly recommended for all single parents.

2. S. Coopersmith. *The Antecedents of Self-Esteem*. (San Francisco, CA: Witt, Freeman and Company, 1967.) pp. 37, 98, 113.

   In this landmark work, the author reviews the theoretical and mystical literature dealing with the antecedents of self-esteem. From it, he developed a study which obtained information from three sources: an 80-item questionnaire compiled by mothers on their parenting practices and activities; 2-1/2 hour interviews with mothers; and responses of children to a series of questions about parental attitudes and practices. Among his many findings is the conclusion that mothers of children with high self-esteem tend to be high in their own self-esteem (p. 98). He also notes that dissatisfaction is greater among the mothers of children with low self-esteem and conflict is more pronounced among their families (p. 113). He concludes that there are four major factors contributing to the development of self-esteem (p. 37).

3. *The Holy Bible: King James Version.* (United States: World Bible Publishers, Inc., 1989.) Matthew, Chapter 19, verses 6-9.

Self-Esteem is Shaped by Our Families

1. Anderson et. al. *Nutrition in Pregnancy and Lactation in Nutrition, Health and Disease.* (Philadelphia, PA: J. B. Lippincott Company, 1982.) p 318.

2. F. Caplan and T. Caplan. *The Power of Play.* (Garden City, NJ: Anchor Press, 1974.)

   The power of play is both extraordinary and supremely serious. This book is a valuable resource for all families—particularly for single parents whose stresses may reduce emphasis on play.

3. K. Keyes. *Handbook to Higher Consciousness.* (Coos Bay, OR: Love Line Books, 1978.)

   This self-help guide and accompanying workbook offers readers a step-by-step guide for exploring conflict situations to find the underlying inner child needs and perceptions.

Low Self Esteem and Chronic Stress

1. M. Horowitz, M.D. *Stress Response Syndromes.* (New York: Jason Aronson, Inc., 1976.)

2. R.H. Holmes, and R.H. Rahe. "The Social Readjustment Rating Scale." *J. Psychosomatic Research* pp. 11 and 213-218; 1967.

3. D. W. Allen. "Hidden Stress in Success", *Psychiatry*, (May 1979) pp. 92 and 171-176.

4. K. W. Sehnert, M.D. *Stress/Unstress: How You Can Control Stress at Home and On The Job.* (Minneapolis, MN: Augsburg, 1981.) p. 66.

The Nutrition Connection

1. J. Bland, Ph.D.; ed. *Medical Applications of Clinical Nutrition.* (New Canaan, CT: Keats Publishing, 1983.)

2. J. Bland, Ph.D. *Your Health is Under Siege: Using Nutrition to Fight Back.* (Brattlebow, VT: Stephen Greene Press, 1981.) pp. 80-81.

3. C. E. Woteke, Ph.D., R.D. and P. R. Thomas, Ed.D., R.D., editors. *Eat for Life: The Food and Nutrition Board's Guide to Reducing Your Risk of Chronic Disease.* (Washington, D.C.: Institute of Medicine; National Reading Press, 1992.) pp. 6-7.

The Spell

1. G. C. Christopher, D.N. *The Body Owner's Workshop: An Introduction to Health Preservation.* (Chicago, IL: Nutrassessment Centers, 1979.)

2. R. Friedman. *Body Love: Learning to Like Our Looks and Ourselves.* (New York: Harper and Row, 1989). pp. 28-30

Breathing: A Matter of Life and Death

1. S. Keleman. *Emotional Anatomy.* (Berkeley, CA: Center Press, 1985.) pp. 42-48.

2. Goldthwait, et al. *Essential Body Mechanics.* (Philadelphia, PA: J. B. Lippincott, 1952.) pp. 148-151.

3. A. Montague. *Touching: The Human Significance of The Skin,* (New York: Columbia University Press, 1971.) pp. 52-64.

4. H. Benson, M.D. *The Relaxation Response.* (New York: Avon Books, 1975.)

5. J. Levy. M.D. *The Baby Exercise Book.* (New York: Random House, 1975.) pp. 25.

Winners

1. J. Bland. *Your Health is Under Siege: Using Nutrition to Fight Back.* pp. 81-82. (Previously cited.)

   The diet of most Americans is too high in sodium content. Dr. Bland depicts how this pattern contributes to high blood pressure and can actually increase the dimensions of the heart.

2. S. Baker and R. Henry. *Parent's Guide to Nutrition.* Boston Children's Hospital. (Reading, MA: Addison-Wesley, Inc., 1989.) pp. 63-69.

3. C. Moore. *Keys to Children's Nutrition.* (Hauppauge, NY: Barton's Educational Services, 1991) pp. 133-135.

4. National Dietary Council. *Recommended Dietary Allowances, 40th Edition.* (Washington, DC: 1989). This book reflects the concurrence of scientific opinion about the levels of intake of essential nutrients to meet known nutrient needs of practically all healthy persons.

Sex and Self-Esteem

1. N. Wolf. *The Beauty Myth: How Images of Beauty Are Used Against Women.* (New York: William Morrow and Company, Inc., 1991) pp. 159-161.

2. C. Norwod. *Advice for Life: A Woman's Guide to AIDS Risks and Prevention.* (New York: Pantheon Books, 1987) pp. 45-51.

Anchor Two: Support

We Deserve Help

1. J. Bradshaw. *Bradshaw on Family: A Revolutionary Way of Self-Discovery.* (Deerfield Beach, FL.: John Bradshaw Health Communications, Inc.: 1988). Bradshaw's work on family systems, parenting and basic person needs can be a useful tool for single parents as they re-examine their own childhoods.

2. T. L. Cermak, M.D. *A Time to Heal.* (Los Angeles: Jeremy P. Tarcher, Inc., 1988).

This book provides valuable information about stressed as well as normal families and can help parents develop a parenting philosophy which meets children's needs, even if their own needs were unmet as children. Cermak also offers workshops at his center in California.

3. J. Mastrich and B. Birnes. *Strong Enough for Two*. (New York: Collier Books, 1990). This book can help parents discover the roots of "having to do it all" tapes.

4. M. McKay, et al. *Thoughts and Feelings: The Art of Cognitive Stress Intervention*. (Richmond, CA: New Harbinger Publications, 1981.)

Hitting the Wall

1. K. Keyes. *Handbook to Higher Consciousness*. (Previously cited.)

Selecting Child Care or Infant Care

1. *Developmentally Appropriate Practice in Early Childhood Programs Serving Children from Birth Through Age 8—Expanded Edition* (Washington, DC: National Association for the Education of Young Children, 1987).

2. A. Dombro and P. Bryson. *Sharing the Caring: How to Find the Right Child Care and Make it Work for You and Your Child*. (New York: Simon and Schuster, 1991).

3. D. Phillips. *Quality in Child Care: What Does Research Tell Us?* (Washington, DC: National Association for the Education of Young Children, 1987).

4. S. Greenspan and N.T. Greenspan. *First Feelings: Milestones in the Emotional Development of Your Baby and Child*. (New York: Viking Press, 1985).

5. A. S. Honig. "High Quality Infant/Toddler Care," *Young Children Vol. 41*(1), pp. 40-46.

6. T. B. Brazelton, M.D. *Working and Caring*. (Reading, MA: Addison-Wesley, 1983).

Dating

1. S. S. Janus, Ph.D., and C. L. Janus, M.D. *The Janus Report on Sexual Behavior*. (New York: John Wiley and Sons, 1992.) p 169.

   Although reports may vary, the rates of extramarital affairs by men range from 58 through 73 percent, and by women from 35 through 48 percent. According to *The Janus Report on Sexuality*, which is the first broad-scale national sex survey since Kinsey, one-third of the men and one fourth of the women admitted to having at least one extra-marital sexual experience.

Discipline

1. L. Canter and M. Canter. *Assertive Discipline for Parents*. (New York, Harper & Row, 1988).

2. T. Gordon. *Parent Effectiveness Training*. (New York, Bantam Books, 1976).

Protecting Our Children

1. "Teenagers Themselves: Teenagers Speak Out About Sex, Drugs, Parents, Prejudice, Religion, School, Fun and Other Things," *Glenbard East Echo* (New York: Adama Books, 1984).

2. Dryfoos, *Adolescents at Risk: Prevalence and Prevention* (New York: Oxford University Press, 1990).

3. *Beyond Rhetoric: A New American Agenda for Children and Families: Final Report of the National Commission on Children* (Washington, DC: U.S. Government Printing Office, p 228.)

Anchor Three: Solvency
Blood Out of a Turnip

1. J. Frank Laurer. *The Power of Affirmations*. (Houston, TX: Frank Laurer, 1980).

2. P. Laut. *Money is My Friend*. (Cincinnati, OH: Vivation Publishing Company, 1989).

3. N. Hill. *Think and Grow Rich*. (Hollywood, CA: Wilshire Book Company, 1937).

The Big Four

1. U. S. Congress, Congressional Budget Office. *Trends in Family Income*. (Washington, DC: Government Printing Office, 1988.)

2. J. Espenchade. *Investing in Children: New Estimates of Parental Expenditures*. (Washington, DC: The Urban Institute Press, 1984.)

3. N. Alexander. "School Age Child Care: Concerns and Challenges," *Young Children*, (43(1), 1986.) pp. 3-10.

Our Time is Worth More Than Money

1. S. Wilson. *Getting Organized*. (New York: Warner Books, 1978.)

2. The Gallup Organization, Inc. *A Study of the Parental Experiences of American Parents*. (Chicago: The Family Resource Coalition, 1988.)

Education & Solvency

1. F. Clark and C. Clark. *Hassle Free Home Work: A Six Week Plan for Parents and Children to Take the Pain Out of Homework*. (New York: Doubleday, 1989).

This book takes an unorthodox approach to learning and is based on research from the authors' Human Development Clinic, in which they "help raise children's intelligence by changing the pictures in their minds." I highly recommend this book for single parents.

2. J. Kozol. *Savage Inequalities: Children in America's Schools*. (New York: Acorn Publishers, Inc., 1991).

By examining the blatant differences in educational resources that exist for children in impoverished neighborhoods, Kozol's book reinforces the urgency for single parents to become advocates for their children's educational processes.

Child Support

1. D. L. Chambers. *Making Fathers Pay: The Enforcement of Child Support*. (Chicago: University of Chicago Press, 1979.)

2. K. McCoy. *Solo Parenting: Your Essential Guide*. (New York: New American Library, 1987.) pp. 153-156.

Silk Purses

1. G. Christopher, *The WSEPtional Woman's Guide to Self Employment* (Chicago: The Women's Self Employment Project, 1989)

   This women's economic development program has helped many single parents improve their economic status through micro-enterprise efforts. Many have used self employment as an alternative to AFDC.

Anchor Four: Strength

Boundaries

1. *The Holy Bible: King James Version* (U.S.: World Bible Publishers, Inc., 1989).

   All biblical quotes are from this edition.

2. M. M'Biti, *African Religions and Philosophy* (Portsmouth, NH: Heinemann Educational Books, Inc., 1969). p 117.

3. Mitchell. *The Gospel According to Jesus: A New Translation and Guide to His Essential Teachings for Believers and Unbelievers*. (New York: Harper and Row, 1991) pp 2-5.

Mind Over Matters

1. J. Kennedy. *Touch of Silence: A Healing for the Heart*. (San Diego, CA: Cosmoenergetics Publications, 1989). pp. 17 and 18.

2. C. Tebbets. *Self Hypnosis*. (Rocklin, CO: Prima Publishing and Communications, 1988).

3. J. Murphy. *The Power of the Subconscious Mind*. (Englewood Cliffs, NJ: Prentice-Hall, Inc., 1963).

Images

1. S. Gawain. *Creative Visualization*. (New York: Bantam Books, 1978).

2. S. King. *Imagineering for Health: Self Healing Through the Use of the Mind*. (Wheaton, IL: Theosophical Publishing House, 1981).

3. H. F. Waters. "Watch What Kids Watch," *Newsweek*, (8 Jan., 1990) pp. 50-52.

4. American Academy of Pediatrics Task Force on Children and Television. "Children, Adolescents and Television," *American Academy of Pediatrics News*, (April, 1984).

Part III: Conclusion

Single Parents and the Whole Society

1. L. Sagen. *The Health of Nations: Five Causes of Sickness and Well-Being*. (New York: Basic Books, 1987), p 85.

   Sagen introduced his chapter on family health with a quote from Dr. Martin Luther King, Jr., which was delivered at the Abbott House in Westchester County, New York, in October, 1965.

2. F. Furstenberg. "Good Dads - Bad Dads: Two Faces of Fatherhood" *The Changing American Family and Public Policy*, ed. A. J. Cherlin (Washington, DC: The Urban Institute Press, 1988), p. 193-216.

3. E. Pleck. *Domestic Tyranny: The Making of American Social Policy Against Family Violence from Colonial Times to the Present*. (New York: Oxford University Press, 1987), pp. 182-250.

Resources

The Innocent

The Family Resource Coalition
200 South Michigan Avenue
Chicago, Illinois 60603
312/341-0900

Family Service America
44 East 23rd Street
New York, NY 10010
212/674-6100

Parents Without Partners
7910 Woodmount Avenue
Suite 1000
Bethesda, MD 20814

New Beginnings, Inc.
612 Hennaber Avenue
Takoma Park, MD 20912
301/587-9233

National Center for Family Studies
Catholic University of America
626 Michigan Avenue, N.E.
Washington, DC 20064
202/635-5996/5431

Fatherhood Project
c/o Bank Street College of Education
610 West 12th Street
New York, NY 10025
212/222-6700

Mothers Matter
171 Wood Street
Rutherford, NJ 07070
201/933-8191

Single Parents Resource Center
1165 Broadway, Room 504
New York, NY 10001
212/213-0047

The Sisterhood of Black Single Mothers, Inc.
1360 Fulton Street, Room 413
Brooklyn, NY 11216
718/638-0413

Healthy Mothers/Healthy Babies Coalition (HMHB)
409 - 12th Street, S.W.
Washington, DC 20024-2118
202/863-2458
800/533-8811

Anchors:
Self Esteem

National Self-Help Clearinghouse
33 West 42nd Street
New York, NY 10036
212/840-1259

National Association for Children of Alcoholics
Clearinghouse
31582 Const. Highway, Suite B.
South Laguna, CA 92677

Association for Infant Massage
c/o Leslie Day
79th Street Boat Basin, Box 9
New York, NY 10024
212/877-1268

Center for Energetic Studies
2045 Francisco Street
Berkeley, CA 94709

Bailey Fit or Fat Center
P. O. Box 230877
Tigard, OR 97223

Holistic Health Organizing Committee
4169 Park Blvd.
Oakland, CA 94601

Nutrition for Optimal Health Association (NOHA)
P. O. Box 380
Winnetka, IL 60093
708/835-5030

Support

Parents Resources, Inc.
P. O. Box 107
Planetarium Station
New York, NY 10024
212/873-0609

Effectiveness Training, Inc.
531 Stevens Avenue
Solono Beach, CA 92015-2093

Parents Anonymous National Office
2230 Hawthorne Blvd.
Suite 208
Torrance, CA 9505

800/421-0353
800/352-0386 (CA)

Ken Keyes College
790 Commercial Avenue
Coos Bay, OR 97420
503/267-6412

Child Care Action Campaign
99 Hudson Street, Room 1233
New York, NY 10013
212/334-9595

National Association for Child Care Resource and
Referral Agency (NACCRRA)
2116 Campus Drive, S.E.
Rochester, MN 55904
507/287-2220

National Institute for Latchkey Children
P. O. Box 652
Glen Echo, MD 20812
301/229-6126

National Federation of Parents for Drug Free Youth
1423 North Jefferson
Springfield, MO 65802
417/836-3709

Center for Child Protection & Family Support
714 G. Street, S.E.
Washington, DC 20003
202/544-3144

National AIDS Information Clearinghouse
P. O. Box 6003
Rockville, MD 20850
301/762-5111
800/458-5231

Safe Kids Are No Accident
111 Michigan Avenue, N.W.
Washington, DC 20010
202/338-7227

Solvency

Money Management Institute
2700 Sanders Road
Prospect Heights, IL 60070
708/564-6291

Barbara Bush Foundation for Family Literacy
1002 Wisconsin Avenue, N.W.
Washington, DC 20007
202/338-2006

Federal Association for Men and Women Resuming
Their Educational Training
Consumer Information Center
Department 508
Pueblo, CO 81009

U. S. Department of Housing and Urban Development
Fair Housing Office
451 Seventh Street, S.W.
Washington, DC 20410
202/708-2213

Committee on Boarding Schools (CBS)
75 Federal Street
Boston, MA 02110
617/723-6900

Council for American Private Education (CAPE)
1265 I Street, N.W., Suite 412
Washington, DC 20006
202/659-0016

National Child Support Advocacy Coalition (NCSAC)
P. O. Box 4629
Alexandria, VA 23308
703/799-5659

National Child Support Enforcement Reference Center
Department of Health and Human Services
6110 Executive Road, Room 820
Rockville, MD 20952
301/443-5106

National Shared Housing Resource Center
6344 Greene Street
Philadelphia, PA 19144

United Student Aid (USA) Funds
8115 Kane Road
P. O. Box 50437
Indianapolis, IN 46250
317/849-6570

Advisory Council on Camps (ACC)
174 Sylvan Avenue
Leonia, NJ 07605
201/592-6667

National Foundation for Consumer Credit, Inc.
8701 Georgia Avenue
Silver Spring, MD 20910

Money is My Friend
Vivation Publishing
P.O. Box 8269
Cincinnati, OH 45208

Strength

Self-Help Center
1600 Dodge Avenue, Room S-122
Evanston, IL 60201
708/328-0470

American Association for Counseling and
Development (AACD)
5999 Stevenson Avenue
Alexandria, VA 22304
703/823-9800

Families Anonymous
818/989-7841

Grief Recovery Institute
8306 Wilshire Blvd.
Los Angeles, CA 90211
213/650-1234
800/445-4808

Positive Pregnancy & Parenting
Fitness B. Healthy, Inc.
51 Saltrock Road
Baltic, CT 06330
203/822-8573
800/822-8573

Ministry of Prayer
3251 West Sixth Street
Los Angeles, CA 90020
213/385-0209

A Course in Miracles
Published by: The Foundation for Inner Peace
P. O. Box 635
Tiburon, CA 94920

About the Author

Gail C. Christopher

Gail C. Christopher, D.N., pioneer in both the self-care and family support movements, has co-founded and directed several nationally acclaimed programs that benefit children and families. A renowned speaker and social change activist, Dr. Christopher is a popular guest on national television programs. Credits include "Good Morning America" and "The Oprah Winfrey Show." She was the featured expert on two nationally televised specials: The PBS documentary, "Crisis on Federal Street" and the CBS prime-time special, "Back to School '92." Dr. Christopher is the President of a Chicago based human resource company and the successful single parent of three children.

Index